ALSO BY ROBERT NEUWIRTH

Shadow Cities

STEALTH OF NATIONS

STEALTH OF NATIONS

The Global Rise of the Informal Economy

ROBERT NEUWIRTH

Pantheon Books   New York

Pantheon Books and colophon are registered trademarks of Random House, Inc.

Library of Congress Cataloging-in-Publication Data
Neuwirth, Robert.
Stealth of nations : the global rise of the informal economy / Robert Neuwirth.
p. cm.
Includes bibliographical references and index.
ISBN 978-0-375-42489-2
1. Informal sector (Economics) 2. Entrepreneurship. I. Title.
HD2341.n4185 2011 330—dc22 2011005961

www.pantheonbooks.com

Jacket design by Emily Mahon

Printed in the United States of America
First Edition
2 4 6 8 9 7 5 3 1

And I shall sell you sell you
sell you of course, my dear, and you'll sell me.

—Elizabeth Bishop

Contents

The Global Rummage Sale   3

Grade A, Plan B, Middle C, System D, Vitamin E   17

DIY City   29

The Global Back Channel   67

The Culture of the Copy   86

Can Anybody Tell Me How to Get to the Bridge?   113

The Upside of Down the Trade   130

Once Upon a Time in the West   145

Against Efficiency   169

The Honest Con Men   186

Why Not Formalize the Informal?   203

Freedom to Trade   213

My Stealth Family   261

Stealth Sources   265

Index   275

STEALTH OF NATIONS

The Global Rummage Sale

It is the great multiplication of the productions of all the different arts, in consequence of the division of labour, which occasions, in a well-governed society, that universal opulence which extends itself to the lowest ranks of the people. . . . Observe the accommodation of the most common artificer or day-labourer in a civilized and thriving country, and you will perceive that the number of people of whose industry a part, though but a small part, has been employed in procuring him this accommodation, exceeds all computation.

—*The Wealth of Nations*

These are the products of some people's lives. Biscuits, balloons, and battery-powered lint removers. Rag dolls, DVDs, and cut-price datebooks. Individual packets of laundry detergent, roach killer, rat poison, face cream. Fresh fruit and finger puppets. Sunglasses and magnifying glasses. The Un-Bra (a pair of gravity-defying, self-adhesive, strapless silicone push-up cups.) Counterfeit Calvin Klein cologne cling-wrapped in Styrofoam clamshells.

A vendor selling slide whistles blasts a mocking trill—several times a minute, seven hours a day. Across the street, a husky man standing in front of a huge heap of clothes hollers, "*Cuecas baratas! Cuecas baratas!*"—"Cheap underpants! Cheap underpants!"—in an increasingly hoarse tenor. Next to him, a hawker with a tray full of pirated evangelical mix tapes blasts a stereo powered by a car battery. Two women

3

toss tiny toys in the air—twin pinecone-shaped pieces of metal lashed together with elastic. These *novas brincadeiras*— new jokes—clack together like raucous rattlesnakes, creating a din destined to drive mothers and schoolteachers bonkers. Around the corner, two vendors with plastic windup launchers shoot small helicopters high above them (they drift back down, rotors a-frenzy) while another stands, back to the breeze, and silently releases child-size soap bubbles from a scoop that looks like a giant Ping-Pong paddle. The bubbles squirm after being born, their edges hesitant. They wobble on the weak current and burst an instant before they touch anything.

In her office six floors above the everyday economic carnival, Claudia Urias, general secretary of Univinco, a nonprofit dedicated to promoting and improving the market, took in the tumult rising from the street. She shook her head. "*É uma confusão total*," she declared. "It's total confusion."

Despite her up-close knowledge of the street, however, Claudia is wrong. Rua Vinte e Cinco de Março (the street of March 25) in the center of São Paulo, Brazil, only seems like absolute anarchy. The street market here—the largest in the city, where retailers from other markets come to buy, because many of the items you can get on this street are either unavailable or far more expensive elsewhere, even from wholesalers—has unwritten rules and an unofficial schedule, almost as if all its merchants were punching a clock. The chaos here is meticulously organized.

Each market day starts well before dawn. At three thirty a.m., four men converge on a short commercial alley just the other side of the Tamanduateí River. Thin sheaths of onion skins crunch under their feet, perfusing the air with their scent. The men, however, seem immune to the acrid atmosphere. They enter a run-down warehouse and emerge with several dozen battered wooden crates and splintered and stained plywood sheets. They rope this haphazard cargo on top of dollies and roll them along Avenida Mercúrio and across the river to Rua 25 de Março. There, they pile the boards on top of the crates to make two rows of makeshift tables along a pedestrian alley that leads from Rua 25 de Março to Rua Comendador Abdo Schahin.

This is the opening ritual of a site-specific street performance, the construction of the stage set for São Paulo's wholesale market for pirated CDs and DVDs. Within a few minutes, several dozen dealers arrive. Some roll up in compact vans and sell their contraband right from the vehicles. Others arrive on foot, carrying duffel bags. They plop the bags on the tables, unzip, and—*É isso ai!*—as if a starter's gun has fired, the market has begun. First-run movies are often available a day or two after they open in theaters.

By four a.m., Édison Ramos Dattora is on the case. Édison is a *camelô*—an unlicensed retail street vendor. He came to the big city almost two decades ago and spent fifteen years selling chocolates, clothing, and small gift items on the trains at Estação Júlio Prestes, one of the city's commuter rail stations. For the past three years, he has moved into the more lucrative trade selling pirated movies and CDs on the city's streets. Business is so good that his wife, who used to work a sales job in the legal economy, has joined him in the illicit trade. Édison hits the wholesale market for both of them, so his wife can stay home with their young son. They buy movies for fifty centavos each—or thirty cents—and resell them for at least twice as much. Most often they work separately, to maximize the amount of the city they can cover, but when the streets are particularly busy—before a big holiday, for instance—they join forces to handle the demand.

Being unlicensed dealers in illegal copies of well-known films may put them at odds with the movie companies and the cops, but Édison is proud of his profession and insists

5

that it is no different from the work his wife used to do in the aboveground economy. "It's the same as any job, with the same goals, only done differently," he said. Street peddling has given his family a life that has transcended the dreams he had growing up in Brazil's agricultural midlands. He now has an apartment in the center of the country's biggest city, a house in the suburbs (rented out, to bring in extra income), and a bank account and credit card. Édison earns enough money that, a few years back, he traveled to Europe to try his hand at street vending there (though he enjoyed his journey, sales were better in Brazil, he told me.) As he spoke, three members of the Guarda Municipal—the local police force— sauntered by on the Viaduto Santa Ifigênia, one of the long pedestrian bridges that span the low-lying downtown park/ plaza called the Anhangabaú. Édison fell silent. His wares were safely zipped inside a pink schoolgirl's satchel at his feet, but he stared after the cops and waited until they were at the far end of the viaduct before he picked up the thread of the conversation.

It takes about an hour for Édison and his fellow *camelôs* to finish their purchasing. That's when Jandira pulls up in her small pickup, as she has six days a week for the past ten years. She parks in the same spot every day—a corner next to the pirate market—and does her business right from the back of her truck. Her trade is *bolo* and *pão*. Each day she bakes eighteen cakes—usually chocolate, chocolate/vanilla swirl, and orange—and twenty-five loaves of bread, and makes *cafezinho* (black or with milk, but always heavily dosed with *adoçante*— artificial sweetener). She sells these items to the street market workers and their customers. At one real per slice and fifty centavos for a coffee, her average sale totals less than a dollar, but her low prices have yielded good profits. "With this clandestine job," she said as she proffered a slice of orange cake, "I have bought two cars, a house in Minas Gerais [a province about five hundred kilometers north of São Paulo], and sent my kids to private school."

The pirate market ends at sunrise. The haulers, who had disappeared while the market was in full stride, return. There's some haggling and shouting until the wholesalers hand over the daily "vig," the extra cash the haulers demand to do their job. Once the dealers ante up and vacate their posts, the haulers toss the crates and boards in piles on the sidewalk. They load up their dollies and roll the crude infrastructure back across the river to the onion broker's place. A few wholesalers huddle in darkened doorways, making quick transactions with *camelôs* who were late to the fair. The rest move briskly off. By five thirty, there's no sign of the presence of the pirates except a thick scattering of plastic DVD wrappers in the gutter.

It's still early. A few *catadores*—self-employed recyclers who prowl the streets looking for cardboard, plastic, and metal that they can sell to scrap dealers—catch some shut-eye in front of the gated storefronts of the Centro, their half-filled handcarts tilted back so they won't roll away. Downtown is still dormant, but Rua 25 de Março is already welcoming the next wave of street sellers.

Merchants from China dominate this second line of sales. They arrive a little before six a.m., pulling small folding carts on which they have packed their inventory and the spindly accordion-style folding tables that function as their mobile stalls. Each has a different specialty: one bracelets, another backpacks, a third sunglasses. Most cater to the latest fads: New York Yankees caps in camouflage, orange and green plaids, and other unofficial patterns, pirated *futebol* jerseys for local clubs like Corinthians, Palmeiras, and Santos—some of them indistinguishable from the real McCoy, others with the dripping ink and blurry logos that are the mark of bad knock-offs the world over. They sell their products to street sellers and small-scale retailers who cannot afford to buy in large quantities or don't have the warehouse space to store excess goods. Street vendors who sell sunglasses, for instance, could buy their wares at one of the wholesale outlets two blocks away on Avenida Senador Queirós, which offer the lowest prices. But these stores don't open until nine a.m. and you have to purchase at least twenty pairs of each style if you want to shop there. Here on the street, the Chinese will sell you three pairs for five reais—at 1.7 reais to the dollar, that's about $1 a pair. Roving street retailers resell each pair for three reais, or about $1.75, thus garnering a 75 percent profit over the price they pay the Chinese vendors. Because of the middlemen on Rua 25 de Março, camelôs who can't afford or don't have the space to store scores of sunglasses can buy a small quantity of different styles at a price that will still guarantee a strong profit when they resell them in their neighborhoods.

The Chinese turn on Rua 25 de Março lasts about an hour. By seven o'clock, the merchants have started repacking their wares and moving off. And by seven thirty, only a few stragglers are left, steering their overstuffed carts toward the bland commercial buildings downhill from the Praça da Sé, where many of them store their goods.

The street readies itself for another shift. First the legal camelôs start rolling in. Eighty handicapped people have been approved by the city to do business on the streets around Rua 25 de Março, but few of the original licensees remain. Most of the disabled vendors have clandestinely sold or leased their street hawking right to other, able-bodied people, who now run the carts. They, in turn, employ haulers who roll their sturdy steel carts from the nearby parking garages, where they park the carts overnight, to their official positions on the street. The haulers unwrap the blue tarpaulins that swaddle these carts during their off-street hours and protect them from the elements when they're on the street. At eight, the largest legal store on the street—Armarinhos Fernando, which sells school supplies, stationery, appliances, and a wide variety of household goods—also opens for business. (This store, which controls almost a full block in the middle of Rua 25 de Março, has an unwritten but highly effective policy prohibiting *camelôs* from setting up any table, no matter how makeshift, on the sidewalk; the store can't keep them out of the street, however, and many set up impromptu booths just off the curb.)

At almost the same time, a dozen men and women in orange jumpsuits swarm by. These are the foot soldiers of the city's sanitation department. They stride down the street with stiff-bristled brooms and long-handled shovels, toting plastic bins in their wake. They sweep up the cardboard and plastic sleeves that are the residue of the pirate DVD fair and the corn husks, papaya skins, coconut shells, and splintered boxes left over from the nearby wholesale fruit and vegetable market.

By eight thirty, the unlicensed hawkers who give the street its chaotic daytime appeal have arrived. There's Paulo Roberto, who spends seven hours a day tossing tiny plastic Spider-Men against the marble facade of a small office building at number 821. Each four-inch-long blue man with gummy red feet and hands sticks for a few seconds, then begins to teeter. Tentatively at first, then picking up speed, the little man rappels down, flipping at the waist. As one Spider-Man descends, Paulo Roberto flips another on high. And then another and another and another, until he has ten on the wall. All of them, pulled by gravity, make the slow, staggered journey down. Paulo Roberto doesn't have to shout. The pivoting men are his sales pitch. They are made in China, imported to Paraguay, smuggled across the border into Brazil, and trucked down to São Paulo. He tells me he buys them for eighty centavos—or about fifty cents—each, and sells them at R$2.50 each, three for R$5. If he sells them one by one, he generates a profit of 200 percent. But there are several other merchants on the street who sell the same toys, and the competition has made sales slow. Paulo Roberto wouldn't divulge his income. "I survive," was all he said.

Around the corner, always on the same spot on Rua Comendador Afonso Kherlakian, there's an old man who sells two practical joke items: extremely realistic plastic patties of dog shit, and noisemakers that sound like a chicken when you pull a cord. His time on the street is spent standing above his plastic piles pulling that cord over and over, hundreds, perhaps thousands of times a day. When it rains, many of the merchants leave the street. But not this fellow. He simply crooks his head, rests an umbrella against his neck, stares down at his artificial poop, and keeps on pulling.

And there's Márcio, a thin man with an apologetic smile and a graying Caesar curl of hair. He patrols the block just outside the Armarinhos Fernando discount store, holding up a rack of pens (since he's got no table, he's exempt from the store's unofficial ban on camelôs on the sidewalk). He's been doing this business on Rua 25 de Março every day for the past ten years. Márcio buys his pens and markers for fifty centavos each from a nearby wholesaler. He sells his pens for one real (perhaps seventy-five cents), a bit less than they charge inside the legal store. On a good day he will sell forty pens, so his profit is twenty reais, or about $12—meaning that his paltry street sales give him an income that is approximately equal to Brazil's minimum wage (and, since he doesn't report his income or pay taxes, his take-home haul may well be higher than that bare-bones minimum).

It's 9:08. For the early morning street sellers, it's already late. The daytime vendors are in place. The legal stores on the street are rolling up their steel gates. This is the time Jandira leaves. She must pack up quickly, in case the Guarda Municipal decides on a show of force. Some mornings, the cops muster early, in an effort to prevent Jandira and the Chinese middlemen and the *camelôs* from doing business. On those days, the vendors fan out down the street, no one selling anything, simply waiting for the police to disappear. On other days, the police attempt to fake out the hawkers, letting their enterprises get started, and then marauding down the street, overturning tables and dumping the merchandise of any vendor who's not quick enough to pack up and flee. Jandira unrolls a plastic sheet that covers the back of her pickup and, with a lilting, "*Para amanhã, queridos*" ("Till tomorrow, my dears") to the people still munching her cake and sipping her coffee, heads back home. Her work isn't finished, however. Once at her house, she will clean her plastic cake carriers, scald her thermoses, and prepare a new batch of cakes and breads. Then she will sleep for a few hours, and wake well before the sun rises to pack up her goodies and make the coffee, so it will be fresh when she reclaims her post.

As Jandira pulls off, a crowd bursts through the doors to Galeria Pagé, the market's oldest indoor mall. Almost ever since it opened, in 1962, Galeria Pagé has been a magnet for merchants trying to get a leg up on their competition by buying at below-wholesale prices. Today, the Galeria has six floors stuffed with dealers in mobile phones, electronics, toys, and knickknacks. Several hundred businesses operate here, and more than fifty thousand customers visit every day. Many of the area's unlicensed vendors buy from wholesalers in Galeria Pagé (for instance, Márcio buys his pens from a stall in the mall). Before any rainstorm, a cavalcade of *camelôs* and legal merchants queue in front of wholesalers on the ground floor to buy packs of a dozen umbrellas for $1 apiece. Street vendors will resell them for five reais ($3) while stores will retail the same umbrellas for around eight reais, or approximately $4.50.

The *camelôs*, Jandira, Paulo Roberto, and their ilk are all unregistered. They pay no taxes or fees in their cash-only businesses. By contrast, most of the businesses in indoor malls like Galeria Pagé are licensed, and many are incorporated as legal trading entities. But that doesn't mean that they are legit. Reginaldo Gonçalves, the building manager of Shopping Mundo Oriental, a shiny mall on Rua Barão de Duprat that has carved out a niche as the place for customers seeking somewhat higher-end products than are sold in Galeria Pagé, requires each prospective tenant to prove that his or her company is registered with the government before he will offer a lease. But, he admits, this means almost nothing. "I'm not saying they are all totally legal," he explained. "They have certificates. They are filed with the government. But we have a saying here in Brazil: 'If you work one hundred percent legally, you cannot survive.'" He shrugged and mimed the universal "see no evil, hear no evil, speak no evil" hand gestures. "They do what they do. They do their business and I'm not responsible."

Reginaldo may not be liable, but his comment makes an important point about the street market: all the businesses of the area, legal and illegal, are intertwined. Landlords think there's nothing unusual in collecting rent from tenants who are doing some kind of illegitimate business. Legal stores willingly supply the illegal market. Hardware stores in the area, for example, stock an inordinate number of different models of hand trucks and wheeled carts, which are popular with illegal street vendors. Discount stores offer an unusually large array of folding tables and lightweight metal and plastic racks that are highly prized by the folks who deal in pirated DVDs (you can clip DVD sleeves to the rack to create an enticing display, and even if the police do manage to yank it away from you as you flee, you've lost none of your inventory—because the sleeves are all empty). Other merchants provide the thick plastic tarps that peddlers use to cover their wares for overnight storage and to protect their goods from a sudden downpour. Legitimate fruit merchants from the nearby wholesale market sell papayas, pineapples, and mangoes to unlicensed hawkers who bring them by wheelbarrow to Rua 25 de Março and sell them by the slice. Licensed beverage distributors sell cases of soda and beer to unlicensed *camelôs*, who, in turn, vend the drinks to thirsty shoppers. Local parking garages and commercial buildings rent off-hour storage space to the *camelôs*. Vendors can pay by the hour to stash their bags on the roof of nearby shoeshine pavilions and newsstands. There's even one enterprising local merchant who has cornered the market in cardboard boxes, which are popular with the *camelôs* because you can rig them up as impromptu tables and balance lightweight products on top—and if the police muscle by, you can grab your display and hustle away, leaving only the cardboard behind, and limiting your loss to fifty centavos—or about thirty cents.

The pace of sales on Rua 25 de Março crescendos through the day, with hordes of new hawkers arriving as others move off to sell in different locations around the city. By late afternoon, however, the market changes once again. The old man packs his poop patties and noisemakers in a plastic sack and trundles off, and vendors like Márcio and Paulo Roberto follow suit. But the crowds only increase. This is when Édison and his fellow pirate vendors return to the street. The afternoon rush is not particularly good for the guys selling small toys and stationery, but it's great for the DVD sellers, because shoppers who have been at work in downtown offices are generally looking for something fun to bring home. Alongside Édison, other itinerant dealers are pushing battery-powered plastic toys, games for PlayStation and Xbox, discount computer operating systems, stuffed animals, and pirated name-brand backpacks.

As the sun drops, the market thins out. As soon as night falls, it's gone. The streets around Rua 25 de Março remain curiously sedate until the haulers start things up again at three thirty in the morning, and Édison and Jandira and Paulo Roberto and Márcio and all the others reclaim their places at their specific nonassigned times.

Roving vendors have been part of the DNA of downtown São Paulo for better than three centuries. In the 1700s, hawkers sold produce and household goods on the narrow lanes of the central city, and farmers set up impromptu vegetable stands on the bridges in and out of town. As downtown developed into an office zone, the real estate industry decided that the flea market environment was unbecoming for high-end commerce, and hired guards to push the street trade away. For many, the easiest place to migrate was down one of the steep hills toward the Tamanduateí River, where immigrants from the Middle East had established stores. The market here was reminiscent of the ancient souks of Beirut, where there has always been street selling, so the new arrivals fit right in. In an accidental irony, the illegal market emerged on a street whose name commemorates March 25, 1824, the date Emperor Dom Pedro I approved Brazil's first constitution. So this strip of asphalt that honors the inauguration of the rule of law is the domain of a market that exists, for the most part, outside it. More than a hundred years on, there's still no statute that says the street market can exist, and most of the merchants here do business without licenses, without being registered or incorporated, and without paying taxes.

According to the *camelôs* I spoke with, the market still runs on these old-fashioned rules: Vendors pay no rent to occupy the curbside, and there's no protection money, taxes, or other fees. Édison described how the process works: "You simply ask, 'Can I set up next to you?' and if it's okay, you do it." (If it's no, and you set up anyway, you will surely have a fight.) Márcio, too, reported that he didn't have to pay for the right to stand outside Armarinhos Fernando and undersell the bigger store. For her part, Jandira told me that she started selling on the street a few blocks away and took her current corner when the person who had occupied it gave it up. She holds it by custom and she will continue to operate there until she chooses to leave the business. The only people on the street who pay for the right to be there, Édison told me, are the handicapped merchants, who pay the city for their licenses, and the pirate wholesalers, who must throw some money to the haulers who shuttle their impromptu stalls on and off the street, and pay rent to the onion broker who beds down their crude infrastructure each day.

The trade on Rua 25 de Março draws four hundred thousand people on the average weekday—and many more on Saturdays. On important holidays, the market attracts a million shoppers a day. "They don't come to pass through; they come to buy," said Claudia Urias of Univinco, the non-profit dedicated to promoting the street. On this she's undeniably correct: the eight thousand merchants in the market (according to a recent census, sixty-five hundred of them—or 80 percent—are either unlicensed or evading registration requirements in some way) do more than R$17 billion of business a year—or almost $10 billion. Brazil is a massive country with a population of perhaps 190 million and a strong industrial base, but, if it were incorporated as a single business, this one street market in one city would qualify as one of the five largest Brazilian-owned firms operating in the nation.

As the end-of-the-day crowd churns along, a vendor releases another soap bubble from her Ping-Pong-paddle scoop. A giant egg, it makes its embryonic journey down the street, then loses its form and merges with the air. That shaky and elusive oval, those *novas brincadeiras* that clack together so hideously, the fake designer sunglasses displayed in Styrofoam like butterflies pinned in a collector's portfolio, those boxes full of *futebol* jerseys and baseball caps, those Santa Claus sacks of pirated movies, those midget action figures that journey halfway around the world before being flung on the side of a building so they can be sold on the street for cheap, all the vendors and customers and haulers and, yes, even the cops who harass the market: they join together to create something significant. It takes a massive number of transactions and tasks performed by people all over the world to bring all these things together in this place. The lives and labor of dozens, hundreds, thousands—millions, if you include every street market in every city, village, and town in every country on the planet—stand behind each product.

There is another economy out there. Like those floating soap bubbles, its edges are diffuse and it disappears the moment you try to catch it. It stands beyond the law, yet is deeply entwined with the legally recognized business world. It is based on small sales and tiny increments of profit, yet it produces, cumulatively, a huge amount of wealth. It is massive yet disparaged, open yet feared, microscopic yet global. It is how much of the world survives, and how many people thrive, yet it is ignored and sometimes disparaged by most economists, business leaders, and politicians.

You can call it System D.

Grade A, Plan B, Middle C, System D, Vitamin E

Merchants engaged in the hazardous projects of trade, all tremble at the thoughts of being obliged, at all times, to expose the real state of their circumstances. The ruin of their credit, and the miscarriage of their projects, they foresee, would too often be the consequence.

—*The Wealth of Nations*

You probably have never heard of System D. Neither had I until I started visiting street markets and unlicensed bazaars around the globe.

System D is a slang phrase pirated from French-speaking Africa and the Caribbean. The French have a word that they often use to describe particularly effective and motivated people. They call them *débrouillards*. To say a man (or woman) is a *débrouillard(e)* is to tell people how resourceful and ingenious he or she is. The former French colonies have sculpted this word to their own social and economic reality. They say that inventive, self-starting, entrepreneurial merchants who are doing business on their own, without registering or being regulated by the bureaucracy and, for the most part, without paying taxes, are part of "*l'economie de la débrouillardise.*" Or, sweetened for street use, "*Systeme D.*" This essentially translates as the ingenuity economy, the economy of improvisation and self-reliance, the do-it-yourself, or DIY, economy. A number of well-known chefs have also appropriated the term to describe the skill and sheer joy necessary to improvise a gourmet meal using only the mismatched ingredients that happen to be at hand in a kitchen.

I like the phrase. It has a carefree lilt and some friendly resonances. At the same time, it asserts an important truth: what happens on Rua 25 de Março and in all the unregistered markets and roadside kiosks of the world is not simply haphazard. It is a product of intelligence, resilience, self-organization, and group solidarity, and it follows a number of well-worn though unwritten rules. It is, in that sense, a system.

It used to be that System D was small—a handful of market women selling a handful of shriveled carrots to earn a handful of pennies. It was the economy of desperation. But as trade has expanded and globalized, System D has scaled up too. Today, System D is the economy of aspiration. It is where the jobs are. In 2009, the Organisation for Economic Co-operation and Development (OECD), a think tank sponsored by the governments of thirty of the most powerful capitalist countries and dedicated to promoting free-market institutions, concluded that half the workers of the world— close to 1.8 billion people—were working in System D: off the books, in jobs that were neither registered nor regulated, getting paid in cash, and, most often, avoiding income taxes. In many countries—particularly in the developing world— System D is growing faster than any other part of the economy, and it is an increasing force in world trade. What's more, after the financial crisis of 2008/2009, System D was revealed to be an important financial coping mechanism. A 2009 study by Deutsche Bank, the huge German commercial lender, suggested that people in the European countries with the largest portions of their economies that were unlicensed and unregulated—in other words, citizens of the countries with the most robust System D—fared better in the economic meltdown of 2008 than folks living in centrally planned and tightly regulated nations. Studies of countries throughout Latin America have shown that desperate people turned to System D to survive during the most recent financial crisis.

This spontaneous system, ruled by the spirit of organized improvisation, will be crucial for the development of cities in the twenty-first century. The twentieth-century norm—the factory worker who nests at the same firm for his or her entire productive life—has become an endangered species. Even in China, where massive factories offer a better financial future than farming, they give no guarantee of job security. So what kind of jobs will predominate? Part-time work, a variety of self-employment schemes, consulting, moonlighting, income patching. By 2020, the OECD projects, two-thirds of the workers of the world will be employed in System D. There's no multinational, no Daddy Warbucks or Bill Gates, no government that can rival that level of job creation. Given its size, it makes no sense to talk of development, growth, sustainability, or globalization without reckoning with System D.

Adam Smith understood this intuitively back in 1776, when he published *The Wealth of Nations*. As Smith wrote, "The whole consumption of the inferior ranks of people, or of those below the middling rank, it must be observed, is in every country much greater, not only in quantity, but in value, than that of the middling and of those above the middling rank." Despite this, most economists don't recognize System D as a part of the legitimate financial order. (Economics is, as Arjo Klamer, professor of the economics of art and culture at Erasmus University in Rotterdam, put it in a recent book, "the study of choice and allocation of scarce resources"—which means it involves how people really live, a subject far too important to be left to the economists.) Instead, most of the world's economic gurus add System D into a gray-market category that was introduced a generation ago by British anthropologist Keith Hart: "the informal economy."

When Hart coined the phrase in the early 1970s, he thought he had minted a nonjudgmental term to describe the hyperkinetic open-air economy he found in Accra, Ghana, where peddlers, hawkers, vendors, and others with no fixed location, and without registering with or being regulated by the government, did a massive amount of business on the side of the road. His goal was to recognize rather than stigmatize this homegrown economic sphere.

Under the umbrella of the informal, though, Hart unwittingly aligned roadside vendors with another part of the business world that is also informal—the criminal underground. Kids who hawk oranges at highway intersections without reporting their income are operating outside the law. But so are the clandestine cartels that traffic in human organs. Paulo Roberto, who sells those gummy, plastic fantastic Spider-Man action figures on Rua 25 de Março, is unlicensed. But so are the rogue networks that run guns all over the world. All of these people evade government regulations and fail to pay taxes. The way they do this and the stakes involved are completely different, but that doesn't matter: the kids and the camelôs are just as informal as the crooks. This unfortunate linkage has infected academic studies and the popular press. One recent study of migration and street economies in southern Europe concluded that there was a "connection between working in the underground economy and deviant behavior," though it provided no hard evidence that this link actually exists. In a similar fashion, a December 27, 2010, wire service dispatch in the Turkish newspaper *Hürriyet* began with a classic yellow-journalism lead—"Unregistered economic activity is causing serious problems across the world"—but the rest of the article simply compared the estimated size of the informal economy in Turkey with that in other countries and offered absolutely no evidence of any problems this had actually created. Still, simply asserting that there's a huge problem makes readers think it's true. More and more, people identify the business practices of street markets as shadowy and underhanded. A woman selling carrots is no threat to anyone. Indeed, we might describe her as a self-starter, an estimable entrepreneur, a hardworking mother providing for herself and her family. But once she gets linked to the economic underground, her labor becomes a bit more questionable. Where did she get her produce? How can she afford to sell at such a low price? Are her carrots cheap because they were irrigated with contaminated water? Or did she soak old, devitalized carrots that had been tossed in the trash by merchants at the wholesale market so they would perk up? Perhaps she stole these root vegetables. Is her scale giving false weight? To be informal adds layers of doubt to her activities. The late Nigerian writer and social activist Ken Saro-Wiwa captured the spirit of this linguistic destabilization (though in a different context—he was talking about how political discourse changes during the buildup to war) in his novel *Sozaboy*: "Before before, the grammar was not plenty and everybody was happy. But now grammar begin to plenty and people were not happy. As grammar plenty, na so trouble plenty."

Perhaps the only people who had the good sense to ignore the term "informal" were the very ones whose lives it purported to describe. Few of the merchants who operate on the roadsides or in the chaotic marketplaces of the developing world have any idea what the informal economy is.

I found this out the hard way. My first foray into the world of unlicensed trade was a trip to Lagos, Nigeria. I spent my first few days in the African megacity walking up to merchants in the city's street markets, introducing myself, and telling them I was writing a book on the informal economy. Without exception, they gawked at me and refused to talk. My words seemed to fill them with terror. Na so trouble plenty.

Fortunately, I was working with two locals who were helping me navigate the chaotic and cramped markets of the city. Olayemi Adesanya and his younger brother Taye simply translated my words into English the people in the market would understand. Here's what Taye told one merchant: "He's writing a book about businesses that exist solely on individual effort, with no help from the government."

In this impromptu interpretation, Taye conjured something crucial about the modern economic system. There's nothing natural about the free market. It's a fiction, an artificial construct created and held together with the connivance of government. This point was made with great force and insight decades back by two innovative economic thinkers. Antonio Gramsci, the Italian Marxist, analyzed the state of the world while serving time in jail in the early 1930s and argued that the free market was a political creation. "*Laissez-faire* too is a form of state 'regulation,' introduced and maintained by legislative and coercive means," he wrote in his famous essay "The Modern Prince." "It is a deliberate policy, conscious of its own ends, and not the spontaneous, automatic expression of economic facts." For Gramsci, selling the masses on the desirability and inevitability of the free market enabled the ruling class to maintain and extend its hegemony. A decade later, economic historian Karl Polanyi came to a similar conclusion from a different point of view. Polanyi believed in the importance of markets but, in his most famous work, *The Great Transformation*, critiqued the impact of conceiving "the free market" as the natural way of the world. If society is devoted to the principle of profit as the root of life, he wrote, "the idea of freedom thus degenerates into a mere advocacy of free enterprise—which is today reduced to a fiction by the hard reality of giant trusts and princely monopolies." (Polanyi's contemporary, the economist Joseph Schumpeter, compressed this thought into a more striking image: "The stock exchange is a poor substitute for the Holy Grail.") Polanyi saw the free market as a political construct and argued that the pursuit of profit alone would not liberate people from slavery or guarantee that we could not poison the planet. He called for moral and ethical principles to ride herd over financial success, and argued that our economic actions needed to be embedded within a larger sense of shared social values. "The end of the market society means in no way the absence of markets," he explained. "These continue, in various fashions, to ensure the freedom of the consumer, to indicate the shifting of demand, to influence producers' income, and to serve as an instrument of accountancy, while ceasing altogether to be an organ of economic self-regulation."

Whatever the theoretical backstory, Taye's words had an immediate impact. The trader—Charles Ezeagu, sales representative for Astron, a firm that imports its own brand of kitchen appliances from China to Nigeria—smiled and nodded and invited me to sit down and have a chat. The word "informal" didn't express his worldview. To him, Astron wasn't surreptitious or suspect or in any way informal: instead, he and his firm were engaging in an open, independent, admirable exercise in self-reliance.

The same thing happened in Guangzhou, China. I was eating lunch with Ethan Zhang, who ran an unlicensed handbag design firm out of his apartment in a gated community in the Sanyuanli neighborhood. He wasn't sure what I wanted and had agreed to meet me only because I had studied Chinese with a close friend of his. When I told him I was writing a book on the informal economy, he paused, chopsticks in midair, and began to get that look. "What is this informal?" he asked in alarm. That's when I spoke the words I had learned from Olayemi and Taye. The syllables worked their magic, even across cultures and languages: Ethan popped the bitter greens in his mouth and raised his hands in the air as if he were at a revival meeting. "That's me," he said as he chewed. "I'm not incorporated, I don't have a license, and I don't pay taxes."

Alex Wei, who runs Icompy, a computer firm in Ciudad del Este, Paraguay, that does tens and perhaps hundreds of millions of dollars in business every year, is one of the few System D merchants I encountered who was well versed in the terminology. But he had no patience for the academic nomenclature. "What is informality?" Alex asked. "The government knows about it. The customs officials know about it. The customer knows. Informality doesn't mean that people don't know. Everybody knows." It's true: everybody does know the informal economy, even if they don't know what the term means. Everybody knows that people smuggle things across borders, that they sell things on the street without a license, that they report less income to the government than they actually make. (Nobel Prize–winning economist Joseph Stiglitz told me that this was standard operating procedure for most mom-and-pop businesses in the United States until the spread of credit cards ensured that the majority of purchases were no longer cash transactions and thus had to be reported on the books. "We shouldn't feel that much moral superiority over Nigeria," Stiglitz said. "Our small businesses did it too.")

In fact, as Henry Mayhew, a journalist who chronicled the costermongers (pushcart peddlers) in the street markets of London in the 1850s, recognized, the informal economy existed long before the formal economy. "If ancient custom be referred to," Mayhew wrote, "it will be found that the

Shopkeepers are the real intruders, they having succeeded the Hawkers, who were, in truth, the original distributors of the produce of the country."

Even Keith Hart has come to recognize the shortcomings of the phrase he coined. "The label 'informal' may be popular because it is negative," he wrote in a paper delivered at a conference in 2004. "It says what people are not doing—not wearing conventional dress, not being regulated by the state—but it does not point to any active principles they may have for doing it. It is a passive and conservative concept that acknowledges a world outside the bureaucracy, but endows it with no positive identity."

That's why I propose to jettison the phrase "informal economy" and to adopt, instead, the moniker "System D." Of course, changing the name is cosmetic surgery. But language does encapsulate some of the deeper values inherent in a society. Rebranding the informal economy as System D provides an opportunity to strip away layers of preconceptions and judgments, to reduce the association with criminality, and to give this economic arena a chance to prove the naysayers wrong.

The growth of System D presents a series of challenges to the norms of economics, business, and governance—for it has traditionally existed outside the framework of trade agreements, labor laws, copyright protections, product safety regulations, antipollution legislation, and a host of other political, social, and environmental policies. Yet there's plenty that's positive, too. In Africa, many cities—Lagos, Nigeria, is a good example—have been propelled into the modern era through System D, because legal businesses don't find enough profit in bringing cutting-edge products to the third world. China has, in part, become the world's manufacturing and trading center because it has been willing to engage System D trade. Paraguay, small, landlocked, and long dominated by larger and more prosperous neighbors, has engineered a decent balance of trade through judicious System D smuggling. The world over, System D is synonymous with entrepreneurialism and employment. The global economy may be contracting, but System D is providing jobs. The digital divide may be a concern, but System D is spreading technology around the world at prices even poor people can afford. Squatter communities may be growing, but System D is bringing commerce and opportunity to these neighborhoods that are off the governmental grid. System D is distributing products more equitably and cheaply than any big company can. And, even as governments around the world are looking to privatize agencies and get out of the business of providing for people, System D is running public services—trash pickup, recycling, transportation, and even utilities.

Friedrich Schneider, chair of the economics department at Johannes Kepler University in Linz, Austria, has spent decades calculating the dollar value of what he calls the shadow economies of the world. He admits his projections are imprecise, in part because, like privately held businesses everywhere, businesspeople who engage in trade off the books don't want to open their books (most successful System D merchants are obsessive about profit and loss and keep detailed accounts of their revenues and expenses in old-fashioned ledger books) to anyone who will write anything in a book. And there's a definitional problem as well, because the border between the shadow and the legal economies is blurry. Does buying some of your supplies from an unlicensed dealer put you in the shadows, even if you report your profit and pay your taxes? How about hiding just one dollar in income from the government, though the rest of your business is on the up-and-up? And how about selling through System D even if your business is in every other way in compliance with the law? Finding a firm dividing line is not easy, as Keith Hart warned me in a recent conversation: "It's very difficult to separate the nice African ladies selling oranges on the street and jiggling their babies on their backs from the Indian gangsters who control the fruit trade and who they have to pay rent to."

Schneider suggests, however, that, in making his estimates, he has this covered. He screens out all money made through "illegal actions that fit the characteristics of classical crimes like burglary, robbery, drug dealing, etc." This means that the big-time criminals are likely out of his statistics, though those gangsters who control the fruit market are likely in, as long as they're not involved in anything more nefarious than running a price-fixing cartel. Also, he says, his statistics do not count "the informal household economy." This means that if you're putting buckles on belts in your home for a bit of extra cash from a company owned by your cousin, you're in, but if you're babysitting your cousin's kids while she's off putting buckles on belts at her factory, you're out.

Schneider presents his numbers as a percentage of the total market value of goods and services made in each country that same year—each nation's gross domestic product. His data show that System D is on the rise. In the developing world, it's been increasing every year since the 1990s, and in many countries it's growing faster than the officially recognized GDP. If you apply his percentages (Schneider's most recent report, published in 2006, uses economic data from 2003) to the World Bank's GDP estimates, it's possible to make a back-of-the-envelope calculation of the approximate value of the billions of underground transactions around the world. And it comes to this: the total value of System D as a global phenomenon is close to $10 trillion.

Which makes for another astonishing revelation. If System D were an independent nation, united in a single political structure—call it the United Street Sellers Republic (USSR) or, perhaps, Bazaaristan—it would be an economic superpower, the second-largest economy in the world (the United States, with a GDP of $14 trillion, is numero uno). The gap is narrowing, though, and if the United States doesn't snap out of its current funk, the USSR/Bazaaristan could conceivably catch us sometime this century.

But, of course, System D is not a country, not unified, not a political entity. It is deeply rooted in the existing power arrangements—indeed, it seems to specialize in exploiting the economic and political fault lines of the globe—but it is fractured and haphazard and, for the most part, silent. System D is a massive in-between space, strikingly independent, yet deeply enmeshed in the legal world. It involves small-scale entrepreneurs but links them to global trading circuits. It is the economic way of the global majority, guided not by corporations or politicians or economists, but by ordinary citizens.

DIY City

Private people who want to make a fortune, never think of
retiring to the remote and poor provinces of the country,
but resort either to the capital, or to some of the great commercial towns. They know, that, where little wealth circu-
lates, there is little to be got, but that where a great deal is in
motion, some shares of it may fall to them.

—*The Wealth of Nations*

The garbage trucks were the Pied Piper. Andrew Saboru followed their dripping loads around the city. "The dump at
Ajegunle got filled, so we followed them to Isolo," he said.
"The dump at Isolo got filled, so we came here." This dump—
Olusosun—is a burning scar of trash alongside the road that
runs from the middle-class commercial and residential neighborhood of Ojota to the Lagos state government secretariat
in Alausa. It is the largest garbage dump in Nigeria, Andrew
noted with pride, but he harbored no illusions that it would
be the final stop of his journey: "When this is filled we will
follow the trucks to the next place."

Behind him, a dozen scavengers pulled items out of the
pile. Flames licked the surface of the trash a few yards farther
on. Far across the dump, hardly visible in the smoke and dust,
a line of trucks waited to deposit a portion of today's detri-
tus, and scores of people flocked after them, ready to pick
through the haul.

Andrew was sixteen when he started his life in the dump. He grew up in Ajegunle, a neighborhood feared by almost everyone in Lagos even if they've never set foot there (indeed, if there's one place that people in Lagos are less likely to visit than the dump, it's probably Ajegunle). To most Lagos residents, Ajegunle is the toughest place to grow up, the community with the least evidence of public services, a neighborhood devoid of any connection to the rule of law, a place where crime and decay rule.

Ajegunle is a poor neighborhood—but, for the most part, it's a community of workers and strivers, not thugs and criminals, and not as bad as the bluster has it. Essentially, it's a System D neighborhood, built by the strength of local people. Most of the community's streets, for instance, started life homemade—as parallel muddy fingers leading into Lagos Lagoon. Over time, they were reclaimed from the tidal inlet, filled in with soil, sand, clay, and garbage. Today, the streets are paved, but at their far reaches, they spill into the marsh, petering out in a sodden mess of reeds, plastic bags, trash, and muck. Here, a spidery network of wooden pedestrian bridges skims the marshy flats, allowing people to move around the community without hiking out to the main road and back in again. These bridges are public conveniences, but they are not public works. In a customary relationship that carries no force of law, they are "owned" by the families who built them—and these families still run them as personal tollbooths, collecting five naira—or about three cents—each time a person crosses over or back. These private boardwalks seem proof of the city's crackpot nature: can there be a neighborhood in any other comparably sized city in the world where you have to pay to use the sidewalks?

To many, Lagos is the urban nadir, the vilest, most squalid and criminal place on the planet. Basil Davidson, the British-born historian of Africa whose love for the continent is palpable in all his works, recalled his emotions when he first touched down in what was then the Nigerian capital back in the 1940s, when the city had a population of about two hundred thousand: "Lagos already seemed to me, as it still does, a perfectly horrible place to be, and anywhere else would be better." Lagos is, so the narrative goes, the most dangerous city that isn't in a war zone, a metropolis of schemers, a dark, desperate, and duplicitous place where every encounter is a potential threat. It's a story told over and over—and often parroted with perverse pride by Lagosians themselves.

Today the city is home to between nine million and seventeen million people, depending on where you draw the lines and who's doing the counting. Lagos is one of the fastest-growing cities on the planet, with an estimated three thousand people arriving every day. Yet the infrastructure has not kept pace. This makes everything here seem supersized—the traffic jams worse than anywhere else, the pollution thicker, the poverty more appalling.

Decades of military dictatorship took their toll too, fostering the creation of a tough, self-dealing shell, as the brutalized people struggled to survive in a corrupt and inefficient system. Dash, or bribery, became the way of the city. A traffic cop stops you? Dash him. A street thug accosts you? Dash him. A government official balks at doing his job? Dash him. The pay-to-play economy was replicated almost everywhere, from the highest government projects down to the most insignificant street encounters—and this made everyday life here seem to ooze menace. A dozen years of civilian rule— the generals gave up power in 1998, though even then, the popularly elected president of Nigeria, Olusegun Obasanjo, was a former military strongman—have removed some of the most obvious threats, but the city still doesn't make it easy for outsiders. The buses have no route signs, the taxis have no meters (you have to negotiate strenuously if you don't want to be cheated), and, if there's a tie-up, people might simply pull onto the wrong side of the road—flashing their lights or honking their horns—and blast the wrong way down the highway. On bad days, Lagos has a Victorian pall, and it seems impossible—and potentially dangerous—to breathe too deeply.

At first glance—even at second or third—Lagos doesn't appear to make sense. The angry-looking red-eyed guy in flip-flops, cutoff shorts, a tank top, and a Rasta cap hanging out on the corner might be an unemployed miscreant, or he might be your bus conductor. The woman selling embroidered jeans from an eight-foot-by-eight-foot wooden stall might be eking out a survival wage, or she might be a transnational merchant who just returned from a purchasing foray in the Far East. The kids running after a car on the highway might be thugs out for a payoff, or merchants seeking to sell you something. To a newcomer trying to take it all in, Lagos seems a vast and menacing swirl of humanity struggling for a buck.

But when you've stayed put long enough, your view of Lagos changes. What had been an undifferentiated mess suddenly becomes sensible—or, perhaps more accurately, comprehensible. The traffic jams remain intolerable, but at least they're understandable in a city that has outgrown its colonial infrastructure. The feeling of threat remains because, with electricity seldom available, the nighttime landscape is a series of black holes set between feeble flares of light from the kerosene burners used by the few small-scale merchants who stay open late, but the tales of crime fall away—a part of history, but not current reality. If Max Weber was right that "the 'city' is a market place," then Lagos is the absolute apotheosis of a city. This is a self-made place, where barefoot guys working out of mud-and-stick kiosks may be leaders of networks that have already found the next big thing. Lagos is the world's largest street market, and everything here—from buying something to drinking a soda on the street to simply talking with your neighbor—is an exchange.

That's not to say poverty isn't a problem. Vast portions of the city are shantytowns. But it's a mistake to read too much into the look of the place. People migrate to Lagos because of the lure of its irrepressible commerce, and they stay put because the nonstop turmoil of trade gives them a chance to thrive. Transactions—verbal, monetary, or otherwise—are all around you. A woman sells French lace from a table in a popular restaurant. A man stands on a crowded rush-hour bus and begins spouting in biblical tones. But it soon turns out that he's a peddler, not a preacher. He pulls copies of *Think and Grow Rich* and *Rich Dad, Poor Dad* from his backpack and passes them to the passengers. By the time his stop has come, he has sold more than a dozen volumes. At two thousand naira per copy—or about $15—that's $180 in sales in a single journey. At a traffic tie-up near the Sheraton hotel, vendors parade by hawking steering wheels, candy, cookbooks, tires, newspapers, toilet seats. A friend who wanted to buy a car didn't hit a local dealer. Instead, he took a forty-five-minute bus ride to Cotonou in the Republic of Benin. There, just across the border, he bought an SUV that originally came from New York (amazingly, the seller provided the original title), paid a System D fixer to smuggle it across the border, paid another System D specialist to get it registered, and negotiated System D to get it fully checked out and repaired—parts purchased from a street market, spark plugs changed by an unlicensed roadside mechanic whose garage was a grease stain in the weeds, dents and scrapes eradicated by an informal panel beater (a.k.a. an auto body man) who had hacked a clearing in the bush, new tires and rims courtesy of a vulcanizer whose workshop was a corner of a public parking lot, wash and wax courtesy of some roustabouts who hung out on the corner not far from his house. At each stage, there was haggling, joking, storytelling, and, ultimately, a deal.

System D was present at my arrival (an unlicensed taxi driver waiting outside Murtala Muhammed Airport cheerfully asked for five euros after allowing me to use his mobile phone to make a local call), and it was there when I left town (a fellow had taken over one of the stalls in the airport bathroom and was retailing a rack of Italian suits). There are dozens—hundreds, thousands—of these exchanges going on around you all the time. It's bewildering, exhilarating, exhausting, and sometimes horrifying. In a world of unrelenting deal making, you have to be aware of ebbs and swells in the crowd, alert to the hands grabbing at you to pull you off to this or that kiosk, attuned to the voices greeting you from far and near—"*Onye öcha! Oyibo!*" (Igbo and Yoruba for "white man") "Mr. Yellow! Mr. Peter! Mr Richard. Orange man!" (this last, which always made me laugh, was a line from a television commercial for a popular orange drink)— and attentive to the local mores of kibitzing. Trade may make Lagos seem frenzied and disorganized, it may sometimes appear aggressive and threatening, but trade built the city and continues to define its culture. Spend enough time there and you come to realize that it is exactly this—the irrepressible hubbub, the hyperentrepreneurial give-and-take, the ceaseless frenzy of talk and exchange—that holds the city together. Lagos is the first megacity in sub-Saharan Africa, and it may well be the first city in the world to be designed, in large part, by System D.

According to local officials, 80 percent of the working people in Lagos are in System D. Nationwide, their economic efforts account for a mass of trade and exchange that is worth as much as 70 percent of Nigeria's gross domestic product—or approximately $145 billion.

In itself, this is nothing new. System D has defined the

fabric of many major cities throughout history. The back-streets of ancient Rome, for instance, were every bit as crazed and contentious as anything in modern-day Lagos. Here's how historian Jérôme Carcopino described his image of the imperial city:

> The *tabernae* were crowded as soon as they opened and spread their displays into the street. Here barbers shaved their customers in the middle of the fairway. There the hawkers from Transtiberina passed along, bartering their packets of sulphur matches for glass trinkets. Elsewhere, the owner of a cook-shop, hoarse with calling to deaf ears, displayed his sausages piping hot in their saucepan. Schoolmasters and their pupils shouted themselves hoarse in the open air. On the one hand, a money-changer rang his coins with the image of Nero on a dirty table, on another a beater of gold dust pounded with his shining mallet on his well-worn stone. At the cross-roads a circle of idlers gaped round a viper tamer; everywhere tinkers' hammers resounded and the quavering voices of beggars invoked the name of Bellona or rehearsed their adventures and misfortunes to touch the hearts of the passers-by. The flow of pedestrians was unceasing and the obstacles to their progress did not prevent the stream soon becoming a torrent. In sun or shade a whole world of people came and went, shouted, squeezed, and thrust through narrow lanes unworthy of a country village.

London, too, was a System D city. In the 1300s, thousands of workshops and businesses found their homes in unlicensed back-alley sheds called selds, and the informal stalls of just one neighborhood—Cheapside—employed 8 percent of the city's population. Five hundred years later, when London was the seat of the world's strongest empire and the de facto capital of the global economy, its streets were still dominated by System D. Henry Mayhew, a crusading journalist of the mid-nineteenth century, painted a portrait of London street life that joined the frolic of the carnival with the desperation of begging and the energy of a flea market:

Here is a stall glittering with new tin saucepans; there another, bright with its blue and yellow crockery, and sparkling with white glass. Now you come to a row of old shoes arranged along the pavement; now to a stand of gaudy tea-trays; then to a shop with red handkerchiefs and blue checked shirts, fluttering backwards and forwards, and a counter built up outside on the kerb, behind which are boys beseeching custom. At the door of a tea-shop, with its hundreds of white globes of light, stands a man delivering bills, thanking the public for past favors, and "defying competition." Here, alongside the road, are some half-dozen headless tailor's dummies, dressed in Chesterfields and fustian jackets, each labeled, "Look at the prices," or "Observe the quality." After this is a butcher's shop, crimson and white with meat piled up to the first-floor, in front of which the butcher himself, in his blue coat, walks up and down, sharpening his knife on the steel that hangs to his waist. A little further on stands the clean family, begging: the father with his head down as if in shame, and a box of lucifers held forth in his hand—the boys in newly washed pinafores, and the tidily got-up mother with a child at her breast. This stall is green and white with bunches of turnips—that red with apples, the next yellow with onions, and another purple with pickling cabbages. One minute you pass a man with an umbrella turned inside up and full of prints; the next you hear one with a peepshow of Mazeppa, and Paul Jones the pirate, describing the pictures to the boys looking in at the little round windows. Then is heard the sharp snap of the percussion-cap from the crowd of lads firing at the white target for nuts; and the moment afterwards, you see either a black man half-clad in white, and shivering in the cold with tracts in his hand, or else you heard the sounds of music from "Fraizer's Circus" on the other side of the road, and the man outside the door of the penny concert beseeching you to "Be in time—be in time!" as Mr. Somebody is about to sing his favorite song of the "Knife Grinder." Such indeed is the riot, the struggle, and the scramble for a living, that the confusion and uproar of the New-cut on Saturday night have a bewildering and saddening effect upon the thoughtful mind.

Mayhew reported that there were perhaps forty thousand street merchants in London, and estimated their combined turnover at between £1,250,000 and £1,500,000 sterling—or, depending on whether you use comparable retail prices or average incomes to compute the purchasing power of the currency, somewhere between £100 million and £1 billion ($160 million to $1.6 billion in U.S. currency) today. Even at the lower estimate, this was, as Mayhew wrote, "a sum so enormous as almost to make us believe that the tales of individual want are matters of pure fiction."

All over Europe, System D was enmeshed in everyday life. "With or without permission," historian Fernand Braudel wrote, "the pedlars found their way everywhere, under the arcades of St. Mark's in Venice, or onto the Pont Neuf in Paris. The bridge of Åbo in Finland was covered with shops: so the pedlars simply occupied both ends of the bridge." As in Åbo and Paris and Venice, so in modern-day Lagos: the Eko and Carter bridges, which connect the mainland to the city's historic downtown on Lagos Island, have long had commerce on them, under them, and along the approaches to them.

In medieval Europe and modern Lagos, the garbage heaps were the lowest rung in the street-level economy—offering long hours, difficult work, but a way out of poverty. Andrew chased the dump trucks twelve hours a day for sixteen years. There were hundreds of scavengers like him, but there was no solidarity. "Each one works for his pocket," he told me, meaning that he and his colleagues worked alone, as independent laborers, competing with one another, determining their own hours and negotiating their own prices. Andrew, however, was determined that he would not remain a scavenger forever. And, in 2003, he took his first step away from the trash-filled trucks. He graduated from scavenging and became a contract scaler, trekking around the dump weighing the material his fellow scavengers gathered, paying them by the kilo and getting paid for his services by a recycling dealer. In 2007, he made the next leap. With a nest egg of a hundred thousand naira (or about $800) from his work as a scaler, he set himself up as a dealer in recycled materials. Andrew gestured at a mass of stuff behind him from which chair legs and springs stuck out like cockeyed metal palm fronds. This was one of his scrap piles. Finally, he had skipped the middleman. He sells plastic to the Chinese, rubber to the Muslims, scrap iron to whoever will give him the best price. When he was a scavenger, he was at the dump all day. Now, his hours are more rational—from seven to ten in the morning and from three to seven in the afternoons (the p.m. hours are "the big hours," he said, because most scavengers are desperate to sell their entire day's takings). Each month, he invests a hundred thousand naira, and each month he earns a hundred and twenty thousand, for a 20 percent profit margin. From his work buying reusable refuse in the dirty city's most disgusting place, Andrew makes almost three times the governmentally mandated minimum wage. (In 2010, Nigeria more than doubled its minimum salary, but Andrew's income remains higher than the new baseline.)

Of course, most people who collect trash earn less than that—which is why it took Andrew sixteen years to save enough to make his move up the career ladder. But as I picked my way out of the dump, I came upon a group of scavengers who gather metal from the city's streets. They were lolling in the shade of a kiosk, waiting for the scrap dealers to arrive with their scales, and passing a cigarette of what the Nigerians call Indian hemp—or marijuana—between them. Segun "Satin" Peters, who has been pushing his cart around the city streets for thirteen years, told me that he averages two to four thousand naira per week. And, in certain really good weeks, he said, he can earn seven thousand naira—the entire old monthly minimum, in just seven days.

There are approximately two thousand scavengers who work the dump. Some people live here. You can see their shacks—tightly bound with plastic to prevent the dust from penetrating—at the far reaches of the pile, where the dump trucks don't go and the fire is unlikely to reach. Those who work the dump suggest that these shanties belong to seasonal migrants from the north of Nigeria—members of the predominantly Muslim Hausa tribe who come down to sell their animals at the local abattoir and work the dump for extra cash (for his part, Andrew insisted that the Muslims didn't live at the dump, and that they simply used the huts for storage). There's a church and a mosque in the dump as well, and even some roving restaurants, as women from the surrounding community who have sensed a market opportunity serve the hungry scavengers. They bring in freshly cooked food in pails covered with wet cloths to keep the grit from contaminating what they sell. The scavengers know the approximate time the women pass through and congregate at various lean-tos within the dump to buy their meals.

Andrew does not live in the dump. He has a tidy one-room apartment ten minutes away, across busy Ikorodu Road and down the hill into Ojota, on a quiet cul-de-sac called Unity Close. The room, which he shares with his younger brother, who works with him in the dump, has many comforts: a ceiling fan, a stereo and CD player, a flat-screen TV.

Legally, Olusosun is the property of the Lagos Waste Management Authority—LAWMA—a state agency. But the scavengers, scalers, and others are its true ground-level operators. They report that they pay no rent or fees or even bribes for the right to earn their living from the trash. Andrew pointed to a truck as it rumbled by. Several dozen scavengers gathered around it, almost greedy in their zeal. "How can you ask for money for something like that?" he asked. "In the dump site, nobody's paying for anything. It's free."

Deep within the trash pile, Fatai Kunrunmi, who heads the Scavenger's Association, watched approvingly as figures moved through the dark brown swirl. "This is the season of smoke," he said, explaining that the harmattan—the wind that originates in the Sahara and swoops through West Africa from November through March—fans the flames that are slowly consuming the trash, and produces a thick drift of soot and ash. His T-shirt offered a bright counterpoint to the dirt-dimmed air: "Vicks Lemon," it said. "For the healthy way, take four a day."

It was almost time for Andrew to take up his work for the afternoon shift. He handed over a business card. It showed nothing about the garbage, nothing about the dump, nothing about recycling. His business's name is Right Time Investments, and Andrew is currently looking for a way to increase the capital with which he can buy materials from the scavengers. "If you invest half a million," he said in a semi–sales pitch, "you will get six hundred thousand back. In one month. There's a good future in this business. All we need is the capital." To this end, he has opened an account at Intercontinental Bank, which has a branch on Ikorodu Road, halfway between the dump and his home. But he knows that, no matter how much money he saves, Intercontinental Bank will never loan him any money. His business is not big enough and is not registered. And even if it were, the bank might balk at his bookkeeping, or the lack of signed contracts with the scavengers who sell him stuff ("Whose property is it anyway?" one of the bank's lawyers might grumble. "We don't want any exposure to lawsuits"), or the high risk of loaning money without collateral. And even if he could jump those hurdles, the interest the bank would charge on the loan—most likely greater than 20 percent—would make the infusion of cash far too expensive. At the same time, microcredit, which many in the West point to as a solution for the needs of small-scale merchants throughout the world, won't help either. A subsistence microloan from a local bank, or through a Web-based entity like Kiva, which allows people in the West to support small-scale entrepreneurialism, is a valuable approach for the lowest tier of businesspeople (sadly, though, the combination of fees and interest charged on microloans are often higher than what is normally charged by banks). But Right Time Investments needs a bigger boost than the largest microcredit outfits can offer. Essentially, Andrew's business is too micro for macrocredit and too macro for microcredit.

Despite the impediments, Andrew refuses to be despondent. He believes Lagos will open itself to those who are committed and diligent. "Lagos is a city for hustling," he told me. "If you have an idea and you are serious and willing to work, you can make money here. I believe the future is bright." Then he marched off into the ashen air, ready to invest his energy once again in the trash-to-cash future.

You might say that Patrick Anari is a human faucet in a thirsty city that doesn't have a water system. Patrick works the busy Lagos highway interchange known as Mile 2. He chases after every bus that pulls up, proffering half-liter plastic bags of what is called "Pure Water."

Lagos has no municipal water pipes. Unless the local government suddenly gets a lot more foresighted and interested in investing in infrastructure, it never will. Instead, those who can afford it—and the majority of people can't—drill deep wells (locals call them boreholes), and pump water up. They filter it, test it, and, if it tests as good, drink it. For those who don't have the money, System D invented Pure Water.

The name is a creative misnomer. It may be called "pure" but most of the time it didn't start out that way. The firms that produce Pure Water dig their own boreholes, pump the water up, and, after filtering and testing (and, if the tests indicate problems, adding chemicals to make it drinkable), package it for sale. It is available at the bus stops and roadsides and comes with your meal in many restaurants.

Chinee Water, a tiny firm in Festac Town, a community on the east side of Lagos, pumps out sixty thousand bags of water a day during the dry season, and thirty thousand a day during rainy months. As a small operator, Chinee's water is relatively costly—it charges 2.5 naira (a bit less than two cents) per half-liter bag, 1.75 naira if you buy more than two thousand bags at a time. Even if all its bags are sold at that wholesale discount price, Chinee still takes in better than a hundred thousand naira—or $800—a day. Bigger companies sell their water for a significantly lower price. Still, said Uche Ike, the company's managing director, business was good enough to cover all salaries and still pay off the cost of machinery in one year.

The production of Pure Water was undeniably an innovation that brought safe water to the masses. But it has an underside that is a growing ecological disaster. The people who buy Pure Water simply bite one edge off the bag, squeeze the water out into their mouths, and toss the crumpled nylon on the ground. In Lagos, plastic bags are clogging rivers, sewers, and waterways. Even if they were carefully collected, recycling would be hard, because the moisture the water leaves in the bags would corrupt the recycling process. Better Life Water, another small outfit in Festac, reported that it sells a hundred and twenty thousand small bags of water each day during the dry season. Even if, between Chinee and Better Life, a third of the bags are recycled or properly disposed of—and that's highly unlikely, given that neither the firms nor sellers like Patrick Anari have any control over where people put the bags when their drinking is done—this would still mean that these two small firms are responsible for almost a hundred and twenty thousand individual pieces of nonbiodegradable and nonrecyclable litter every day.

Despite the downsides, Pure Water is the cheapest way for people in Lagos to get drinking water. The demand is strong, and Patrick puts in long hours—from seven thirty a.m. to six thirty p.m., six days a week. In an average day he sells two hundred bags of the stuff. He buys his water from a large distributor who sells more than Chinee and Better Life put together and thus can afford to maintain extremely low prices. Patrick pays just 1.5 naira per bag but resells them for five naira. That's a profit of 3.5 naira per bag—or seven hundred naira a day on two hundred bags of pure water, minus the twenty naira Patrick pays for blocks of ice to chill the water. In a month, Patrick earns more than sixteen thousand naira, double the country's officially designated minimum wage.

It is one more way that System D meets a need and provides an income in a situation where government seems unable to provide a public service.

Yusuf Musa never thought public transportation would be the key to his success in private business. He came to Lagos in 1997 from Bauchi, in the north of Nigeria, seeking opportunity. He spent one year without a job, living with a friend in the central neighborhood of Surulere, and sizing up the city. Then he began working as a vendor at the side of the road. There, he noticed another System D business that seemed immune from boom-and-bust cycles and the variations in demand that plague street selling. So, after another year, he took his savings and rented one of the Chinese-made motorcycles that have become the short-distance public transport system of the city.

Authorities estimate that there may be as many as a million motorcycle taxis—*okada*, in local patois—in Lagos. Yusuf owns four of them. He drives one himself—a Jincheng that cost him fifty-seven thousand naira, or about $440 (this Chinese brand was long the most common motorcycle in Nigeria, but its hold on the market has recently been eroded after a price war led by the importers of the Indian-made Bajaj)—and leases the others to three steady drivers.

Like all *okada* drivers, Yusuf and the people he rents to have none of the licenses or registrations they are supposed to carry. They have no driver's licenses, no license plates, no business licenses, no registrations, and no insurance. But despite this, *okada* are immensely popular. People in Lagos take *okada* to go shopping or go get a bite to eat. Businessmen take *okada* to get from one appointment to another. Workers take *okada* to get from the main bus stops, which are on the outskirts of many communities, to their homes or offices, which may be on backstreets. They haul goods on them—large-screen TVs, ten-foot-long strands of rebar, massive sacks of onions. Whole families take *okada*—three people on the back or well-dressed couples with their young children sandwiched between them (to bolster bike safety, the government recently banned *okada* from carrying more than one passenger and required that drivers and passengers both wear helmets).

Yusuf operates in Festac Town, a solid middle-class community on the eastern edge of the city along the Badagry Express Road between the highway interchange at Mile 2 and the turnoff for Alaba International Market. There are no set prices. Like most street exchanges in Lagos, the fare is subject to give and take. "No price is stable," one driver told me, adding that he would naturally expect me to pay three times as much as a local person. In Festac, a trip from deep within the community to either First Gate or Alakija, the junctions where local roads feed out onto the Badagry Express Road, costs approximately forty naira—or perhaps thirty cents. These small fares add up: at a minimum, Yusuf told me, an *okada* driver takes in a thousand naira, or about $7, in a day. On busy weekends, the take easily doubles. Sundays in particular are good—because Nigeria is a devout country. You will often see a smartly dressed couple—the man in a colorful suit, the woman wearing a luxurious wax-print dress with matching headgear, seeming gift-wrapped for worship—on the back of an *okada*.

Yusuf drives Monday through Thursday, takes Friday off—it is the start of the Muslim Sabbath and he hits the mosque by two p.m.—and drives Saturday and Sunday. He says he still drives because he has to keep track of the trade to make sure the guys who rent from him are honest. "Because I'm driving, I know what's going on," he said. "The people who rent from me can't tell me a story; they can't pretend that the market is bad." He grosses more than eight thousand naira a week from his own driving and takes in five hundred naira a day each from the three bikes he rents—for a total of nine thousand a week. That's sixty-eight thousand naira a month (or better than $450)—almost four times the government's newly increased minimum wage.

Yusuf is a member of Festac United Okada Riders, a semi-official union, to which he pays forty naira every day. He and the people he rents to also pay twenty naira each—or about fifteen cents—to the local government for what is called a ticket and essentially serves as an under-the-table permit that allows them to pick up passengers on the streets of Festac that day. If any of the four of them are caught without a ticket, they can be fined and even thrown in jail.

Yusuf and his drivers are lucky the local government does not charge more. Governments throughout history have recognized that peddlers, hawkers, and others who need to do business on public thoroughfares will often pay more than other businesspeople for the permission to operate on the street. For instance, in Los Angeles in 1883, a banker whose business was worth more than $50,000 paid $35 a year for a city license, while a peddler with a horse-drawn cart paid $40.

Despite the semi-official permission, and despite their presence all over the city, riding an *okada* can be risky. In a city where traffic jams are the norm, where the roads are rutted and, during the rainy season, severely flooded, and where no one pays attention to lanes (and, at times, to the direction cars are supposed to go), a fraction of an inch can be the difference between a thrilling ride and a serious injury. Stuck in a particularly horrendous traffic jam on the way to a meeting in the central Lagos neighborhood of Ijora, I decided to hop off the bus in the middle of the highway and flag down a passing *okada*. I made my deal, straddled the back of the bike, and we zoomed off. The driver careened between cars and trucks, bounced in and out of potholes, and, honking at other *okada* and at people who were trudging through the jam on foot, twisted his way through the snarl. As we snaked around, I felt the heat of chrome and steel against my knees. This wasn't the exhaust manifold of the bike. It was the heat generated by my pants rubbing against car bumpers and truck bodies. It was only a five-minute ride and I made it unharmed, but it was clear that, with an unlucky jolt, or if a massive tanker truck lurched forward at the wrong time, I could have lost my kneecaps. Indeed, several friends in Lagos have been severely injured in *okada* accidents.

The bikes in Lagos generally have inefficient two-stroke engines and have become a leading cause of pollution in the city. Massed at an intersection, the drivers shift into neutral and twist their throttles, and the exhaust blows gray and gritty. A million motorcycles mean more pollution in the already oppressively polluted city.

Despite the risks and the clear environmental consequences, *okada* remain popular. And Yusuf insists that *okada* drivers provide a needed public service. "If you stop *okada* in Nigeria today, people will suffer," he said. "With this business we are helping people."

Buses are the other common form of mass transit in Lagos, and, as with *okada*, this huge enterprise, with tens of thousands of vehicles, is a System D creation. Once upon a time decades ago, this was a public system. The government owned the *molue*—large buses that fit thirty or forty people—and *danfo*—smaller jitneys that fit between a dozen and twenty, depending on how the seating is installed. But the authorities walked away from public transportation. In desperation, the bus system was kept alive by the National

Union of Road Transport Workers (NURTW)—but in the most haphazard manner you can imagine. The union essentially bought the city's fleet of seventy-five thousand buses. "The source of funds was people who are big and successful in government and business," explained Alhaji Rasaq Olusola Ahmed, the assistant secretary of one of the union's branches in the Lagos neighborhood of Mushin. "We pay them back incrementally." In other words, the politicians sold the system to themselves and other rich people, and each yellow van is some well-connected person's cash cow.

That means there's a great incentive to keep each bus rolling every day but little incentive to invest in major repairs. The owners don't want to spend because they want the money for their pockets, and the drivers and conductors have no incentive to repair the vehicles because they get less money if the van is off the road while being fixed. The VW, Dodge, Chevy, and Nissan vans that ply the streets, most of them painted school-bus yellow and tricked out with home-welded bench seats, are so banged-up and rusted—or, as they say in Nigeria in a puff of honest doublespeak, "fairly used"—that it seems doubtful that they could go anywhere, particularly on the crowded, cratered roads of the sub-Saharan megacity. The passenger compartments of some of the older *danfo* and *molue* are connected to the chassis only with baling wire. What repairs they do get are just enough to push them forward for another day of life. It's not unusual for a bus to literally come apart—the universal joint breaking, wheel bearings dropping out, the exhaust system flopping to the roadbed in a cloud of black soot, a hose springing loose and spraying strange messages in steam—while passengers are still inside. At those moments, the conductor will refund part of your fare, and will often try to flag down passing buses to get you where you're going.

Rasaq, the local labor leader, who has dubbed himself with

the name Decency on his business card, pointed out that the NURTW is meticulously organized. Incorporated in 1978, it has approximately 1.5 million members—two hundred and seventy members in each unit, fourteen units in each branch, and four hundred branches across Nigeria. The drivers are union members. So are the conductors. And so are the guys whom Decency called checkers and whom most of the rest of the city call, with obvious disgust, *agberos* (according to Nigerian newspapers and dictionaries, the word *agbero* originally had no negative connotation and is simply Yoruba for "conveyor of passengers" or "laborer who carries heavy loads").

The *agberos* hang out at major bus stops and chase after the conductors to take twenty or thirty naira from them every time they pass. If the conductors refuse to pay—and they try this all the time, pulling up the windows and locking all the doors so the checkers can't get a handhold—the *agberos* spring into action. I've seen them try to tear the wad of cash out of a conductor's hand. I've seen them grab the spare tire out of the back and hold it hostage until they get their thirty naira. I've even shoving matches that go on so long the passengers threaten to call the cops (who will seek an even bigger payment to look the other way) if someone doesn't back down.

Decency insisted that this strange system, in which union members extort money from other union members, was actually an important part of the union's organization. He said the checkers collected twenty naira from each bus once a day—and that the money went to pay the local government for a ticket, so that the police can't arrest the drivers for operating illegally.

But Omotola Eleshin, an *agbero*/checker at Mile 2, told a different story. "I take money from the transport," he said when asked what he did for his job. He reported that his haul was thirty naira per vehicle and amounted to as much as ten thousand naira a day (this meant that he earned in a day more than what the government suggests people should earn in a month). And when asked what he gave back to the bus drivers and conductors, he laughed. "I give them nothing," he said. "They just give it to me; they pay it as tax."

Omotola said he pocketed all the money and put it in his personal account at Spring Bank. This, according to Decency, was a bit of bravado. Most of this cash goes to pay the owners of the buses, to pay off government officials, and to fund the union officers. Essentially, through the *agberos*, the union collects unofficial dues from union members to pay off the buses and to finance the union bosses and to keep the union and the bus system in business another day.

It's insane. It's completely improbable. But it works. The conductors and drivers don't unilaterally raise the fares. The buses go where they say they're going (though you have to get used to the idea that the scruffy-looking kid with a creased and sweaty wad of currency who is hanging off the side of the bus calling out the incomprehensible destination—which is most often different from the destination printed on the side of the van—will take your money and remember what change you are due and will even give you directions where to go if you have to transfer). The buses don't necessarily halt at every stop: if you're not at a major intersection, you have to flag them down, and when you need to get off, you have to get the conductor's or driver's attention by shouting, "*O wa o*"— Yoruba for "It has come" or "It is here."

Omotola offered some final thoughts as he prepared to fight for his informal payment from the next batch of buses that pulled up at Mile 2. "We are not thieves," he said. "We are not fighting anybody here. This is our right." On their banged-up, home-welded, taped-together bodies and their balding, ready-to-burst tires, the *danfo* and *molue* move the city. And Lagos inches forward, courtesy of System D.

Fourteen people packed into the *danfo* to go from Ikeja to Oshodi. It was supposed to be a short trip—just a few minutes, at a cost of forty naira (approximately twenty-five cents).

First, the bus ran out of gas. It bounced off the road and into a dusty dirt lot. The driver said nothing. He simply brought the van to a stop and fished in his pocket for a wad of cash. He peeled off a few sweaty hundred-naira notes and handed them to the conductor, who grabbed a yellow plastic jug from the floor in the front of the van and, after asking the fellow who fixed flats at the edge of the road which was the nearest filling station that actually had gas, trotted off on his quest.

A few riders hailed passing *okada*, negotiated their deals, and sped off. The rest—whether because of the heat or because no one was in a hurry or because no one had the extra cash for a motorcycle ride—waited in silence under a severely stunted tree.

The driver raised the hood and whirled the wing nut off the top of the carburetor, and removed the lid and the air filter. He flicked at the throat of the carburetor to make sure it wasn't sticky. Then he leaned against the scarred bumper and became immobile in the heat, like everyone else.

When the conductor huffed back up with the sloshing bucket, the driver regained mobility. He pulled the rag that was serving as the van's gas cap out of the spout, rolled up a dirty piece of paper to act as a funnel, and sluiced most of the contents into the tank. Before it was empty, he took a mouthful of what remained in the plastic jug, walked to the front of the van, and spit the gas directly into the open carburetor.

The driver jumped into the cab, the conductor shoved from behind, and, with a jerk, the engine came to life. It gasped and popped at first. The driver shifted into neutral and floored it. The engine hiccuped and belched flame. Then the idle steadied. He jumped out, jammed the air filter in and the lid back on, and smashed the hood down. Then he and the conductor and the rest of us climbed back in and the bus roared back onto the roadway.

But the crude fill-up hardly mattered. A few minutes later, we were mired in what seemed like an eternal traffic jam. The tie-up—or "go-slow," as locals call it (a great understatement, since the go-slows are often no-goes, and traffic can remain snarled for hours)—was the first indication that I had entered the space-time singularity that is Oshodi. Oshodi is a major junction, where the Apapa-Oworonshoki Expressway crosses the Agege Motor Road. Tie-ups are normal—the result of the confluence of dozens of bus lines and the entrepreneurial zeal of merchants whose kiosks and booths creep out into the roadways to get closer to the action. Markets thrive on congestion, and Oshodi, particularly at rush hour, offers congestion magnified.

In maybe twenty minutes, the bus nudged forward a couple of inches. Most of the passengers figured they could move forward faster on foot, so they dropped down and joined the moving throng. A welcome relief, because, even with the harsh sun, it was cooler off the bus than on it.

Being in Oshodi involved accepting the rhythm of the market. You moved at Oshodi's speed; it didn't move at yours. Hundreds of people slipped in and out of the clogged lanes of the roadway, maneuvering around tables and in and out of traffic alongside roving merchants who carried poles festooned with anything that could be balanced and moved without too much effort: pants, shirts, wallets, belts, bras, scouring pads. Every so often, an *okada* bore down from behind, the driver sneaking up on some pedestrians and then, with a blast from a custom horn that sounded like it should be attached to an earthmover instead of a two-stroke bike, making them jump for their lives.

The commerce stretched for miles. Kiosks sold fabric, household goods, used shoes, vegetables. It was late afternoon, and the itinerant meat dealers were out, trying to make sales as people headed home. They displayed unfamiliar chunks of dead red on sheets of cardboard—cow tails with tufts of hair still visible at the ends, sawed-off haunches and legs, viscous landscapes of honeycombed white innards, curving slants of skin—and honed their knives on small rocks or on the edge of the railroad track that paralleled the road. The blood ran down the brown displays and dripped onto their sandals. When the commuter train came through, they lifted their wares with practiced ease and stepped out of the way of the slow-moving locomotive, then took their places again when the train had eased by. Merchants had encroached on one lane of the street, and buses eager for passengers had stymied the other lanes. Threading in between them and deftly dodging around delivery trucks, the crowd crossed from one side of the market to the other.

Close to the junction, it became apparent that the only thing holding up traffic here was the commerce itself. There were certainly more vehicles converging than the road could carry. But that wasn't really the problem. The Apapa Oworonshoki Expressway actually vaults over the Agege Motor Road. There's no direct junction. The problem here was the sheer volume of commerce. Too much of the road had been occupied by merchants and, given the sprawl of kiosks, buses didn't bother to pull over, but simply stopped wherever they could to allow people to disembark and troll for new passengers to jump aboard, thus adding to the mess. And the cops contributed in their own way, trying to get the buses to move by whacking their bumpers with short pieces of rebar that they wielded like clubs. This provoked fights, as the drivers shouted at the cops, who, of course, were incapable of doing much more than shouting back. Alongside the cops, the *agberos*, dressed in the dirty green-and-white jackets of the National Union of Road Transport Workers, chased the buses, wads of creased notes between their fingers, seeking their regular payoffs.

There was a pedestrian bridge nearby, but it looked abandoned. That was because a crew of area boys—kids who strong-arm passersby for money—had commandeered the bridge, and it was deserted except for a few people sleeping on the barricaded stairs.

From the top of the flyover, Oshodi had its own sound track—a propulsive combination of amplified music, car horns, and the massed murmurings of thousands of people talking at once: the hawkers shouting out their wares and the conductors shouting their destinations—"Ketu," "Ojota," and "New Garage" on one side of the road, "Cele" and "Mile 2" on the other—and the people making their deals. In the view from that bridge, Oshodi seemed overwhelming and threatening. Yet there was something deeply human about it, too. We are all constituent parts of an increasingly angry and insane and difficult-to-comprehend world of trade. Oshodi made this global reality manifest—and being there, being a small part of it, was as thrilling as it was disquieting.

Just below the overpass, a sprawl of kiosks marked the Owonifari Electronics Market—one of twenty submarkets that made up Oshodi. Here, Prince Chidi Onyeyirim sold electronics and served as vice president of the merchants' association. Sheltered from the sun by the overlapping corrugated tin roofs, he had slipped his shoes off and was lolling on a stool getting a primitive pedicure in the midst of the turmoil. "In this country, we believe in self-development," he said as the nail cutter snipped and filed. "With self-development, we develop the market."

The market's self-development has meant that the merchants have created a self-governing association, which engages in negotiations with the political structure and keeps peace and security. Fatai Agbalaya, the market chairman, sat in his small stall around the corner from Prince Chidi's outpost surrounded by Panasonic, Sanyo, and Samsung boxes. "This is the first market the government established, in 1979," he reported. "The government owns the market, but we set up our businesses on our own capacity."

But, he told me, the merchants here were small. They bought their goods from other, bigger markets—Alaba International and Ikeja Computer Village—whose merchants did the importing. So I knew where I had to go.

Alaba is at the fringe of the city. I had a vague contact there—Jude C. Anyika, proprietor of Father Electronics, from whom a friend had recently bought a TV. So I looked him up. He was eating draw soup in his small office just off the main drag when I walked in and started my spiel. A ceiling fan whisked above his head and the slippery green okra-based chowder dripped off a chunk of yellow *garri* (a dense cassava sponge that is served in thin slabs; you break off a bit, knead it with your hands, and dip it into the soup) as he motioned for me to sit down.

"What have you brought for me?" he asked after a few seconds. He plopped the *garri* in his mouth and molded another bunch between his fingers, rolling the doughy mass around a bit before slopping it into the soup, eating it, and licking the dark green droplets that remained on his skin. "When you come to see me, it is customary to bring something. It is customary that I should not do work for you unless there is something to benefit me. For instance, you can see what size I am. You can bring something fashionable from New York in my size."

I told him that I hadn't brought anything for him because,

in my business, that's not allowed. Paying for a story is a kind of bribe, and if I engaged in this, how could I criticize a politician who also asked for cash in return for providing information for a story? Another chunk of *garri* paused on the way to his mouth as he considered this. But, I continued, what I wrote could get the word out about the market. My writing could bring news of Alaba to the wider world. He continued his meal in silence. After a long and uncomfortable wait, he slapped the last dripping morsel into his mouth and rinsed his hands in a bowl of cold water. Then we bargained. I had promised myself that I would not give him anything. But I quickly broke that promise. Before he would introduce me to the market leaders, he said he needed credit for his phone, and I bought him a thousand-naira recharge card (total value about $7.).

This was, you might say, a bribe, albeit a small one. But no one in Alaba—or, indeed, in all of Nigeria—would understand it that way. Mr. Anyika—known as "Father" to many of the younger traders in the market—isn't Alaba's press agent. He sells electronics and makes money only when he makes a sale, not when he talks with a reporter. In Nigeria, when someone goes beyond the necessities of their job to help you out, some kind of recognition, and not a simple thank-you and a handshake, is appropriate. Indeed, it's expected. Nigerian traders call this "showing appreciation." Most Lagos traders even classify certain forms of traditional bribery as showing appreciation—for instance, when they offer a bit of money to a customs official to work with them to reduce import tariffs at the port.

On the surface, Father doesn't appear to be a big shot. His shop is humble, with just enough room for a desk and chair for him, a small sofa for customers, and an impressive stack of empty cardboard boxes—GoldStar, LG, Panasonic, Samsung, and a host of other brands I had never heard of—

running from the floor to the ceiling. But Father has been in the market for a long time, and his contacts are deep. After he loaded the credit into his phone, Father made a brief call—it probably cost only pennies—and the action began. As deliberate as his movements had been while eating, he was now the opposite, nimble and wired. He grabbed my wrist in one of his large soft hands and yanked me along behind him. We jumped a sewage ditch filled with bubbly snot-green goo and charged across dusty Alaba Ojo Road. Porters carrying stacks of stereos on their heads shared the pavement with overloaded wagons full of loudspeakers, sixteen-wheelers carrying containers, and buses honking to attract passengers. Alongside the traffic, touts tugged at passersby, shouting, "What are you here to buy?" In the old market parlance of New York's Lower East Side, these guys are hookers, because they are paid to get the customers interested—to hook them—and then to reel them into shops and arcades that aren't on the main drag. In Alaba, the touts take this task literally, hooking people's arms and attempting to drag them toward the kiosks in the inner recesses of the market. Though this may feel threatening, the touts don't really want to steal. They want you to visit the kiosks that employ them, and you can always yank your arm away.

We hopped the divider in the center of the road and plunged into a thicket of kiosks on other side of the market. Here, in addition to people selling electronics, young boys packed VCDs (video CDs—the standard format for movies in most of Nigeria) into plastic slips and added lurid color-Xeroxed covers. I expected these to be pirated Hollywood productions, but as we flashed past, I caught sight of the titles. These flicks were from Nollywood, the Nigerian film industry, which distributes direct to disk. So these were not pirated copies. This was legitimate production.

We made several turns and stopped at a building in a

barren courtyard surrounded by barbed wire. After a brief conversation with two burly security guards, we went inside. This was the headquarters of the secretariat of the International Market Association. All major markets in Lagos, no matter how haphazard they seem, have self-organized leadership groups, whose business is to make market matters flow without impediment. They must ensure that the merchants and the customers are happy, that the market is conducive to trade, and that the market is safe. (You almost never find the cops patrolling the streets or inside the markets, unless they're looking to harass people and extort payoffs; instead, you see them riding shotgun on trucks full of cash that move around on the city's highways, or pulling people over at certain crowded intersections in the hopes of extracting a bit of appreciation from drivers desperate to avoid a ticket.)

Inside the quiet and almost vacant structure, I sat with Sunday Eze, Alaba's general secretary, and Remi Onyibo, the market's second vice president. They extolled Alaba's virtues. It was the largest electronics market in all of Africa. Every day, they said, the five thousand merchants in Alaba do $10 million worth of business. Multiply this out and over the course of a year, and the exchanges that take place in this single System D street market amount to $3.1 billion.

Like Alaba, Ikeja Computer Village grew from modest roots to become a global powerhouse. Two decades ago, when a store called Correct Technologies opened on a quiet residential block not far from Toyin Street in Ikeja, a middle-class Lagos neighborhood, it must have seemed a foolhardy venture. At the time, the market for computers was tiny; even in the United States, more than two-thirds of the families didn't have a computer in their homes. Lagos, with its sprawl of tin roofs and its haphazard power grid, seemed inalterably stuck in the digital dark ages. Despite its dumbed-down infrastructure, however, Lagos is not a low-tech city. Here, what you see is not necessarily what you get. That mud-and-stick kiosk over there has a dusty photocopier powered by a small diesel generator. The setup may look incongruous, but it is a functioning copy shop. All over the city, even in the most disreputable neighborhoods, cyber cafés are flourishing. The machines they have are often unnamed brands, with innards assembled from various sources, the USB ports may not work or may be infected with a virus, there may be no CD/DVD player, the image on the monitor may flicker between garish oversaturated tones and dusty gray scale that matches the sky outside, but you can browse, chat, update your Facebook page, or check on your favorite star's latest tweet. In one of the Internet centers I frequented, many of my fellow browsers were carefully copying and pasting the same letter into hundreds of e-mails: they were the foot soldiers of Nigeria's famous 419 Advance Fee Fraud (the name refers to section 419 of the Nigerian penal code, which deals with financial malfeasance), firing off e-mail scam letters that promise a huge block of money from a frozen foreign bank account if you forward your personal and financial info to a complete stranger. If I didn't remember to dump the cache and reset the memory protocols of the machine every time I browsed, these savvy Nigerian netizens could ensure that I started receiving new spam messages almost immediately after I left the café.

That there's a profusion of proficient gearheads in a city that seems to lack the infrastructure necessary for high technology is a direct result of the System D marketplace that has grown to be known as Ikeja Computer Village. In version 1.0 of the market, Correct Technologies and the few other stores that started bringing in computers sold decade-old dual-floppy-disk MS-DOS machines and, for the most advanced, desktop units with the faster 486 chip. Ikeja Computer Village version 2.0—today's market—boasts three thousand vendors and is a hub for buyers from all over Africa seeking the most up-to-date equipment. Hawkers hit you up as soon as you enter. They proffer questionably cheap copies of Windows 7 and palm four-gigabyte flash drives at you as if they're contraband. They pull packs of SIM cards from their pockets and fan them like skilled Vegas croupiers. Other itinerant vendors have rigged up mobile displays—coatracks on which they hang plastic mobile phone cases (sprucing up your old mobile with a new plastic housing is big business in Lagos) or homemade wooden wheelbarrows containing blister-packed portable hard drives. Outdoor merchants operate from small desks on the sidewalk, the innards of mobile phones and computers spread around them. These people can troubleshoot your phone, or flash it (unlock the phone so you can use any GSM service provider, another big business in Lagos), or add memory to your computer, or open up your laptop to replace a faulty drive.

Most of the stores have little room for storage, so the equipment they sell—desktop models, flat-panel monitors, copiers smeared with old toner—line the sidewalks. The retailing space of Slot Systems Limited, one of the most successful mobile phone retailers in Computer Village, is nothing more than a small concrete bunker with a price list taped to the wall, an iron-gated window where you hand over your cash and they give you your item, and a security guard sitting at a desk with an electrical outlet, who flips open the box and plugs the device in, thus proving that it works, before directing you out of the store. Upstairs in many of the buildings are wholesalers and importers, whose tiny commercial outposts have just room enough for a desk, a chair, and a display case. They often supply the hawkers with their wares.

Finally, at the top of the Computer Village food chain, there are several firms that no longer have anything to do with street sales. They have been so successful that they have turned themselves into brands known throughout the country and often have whole buildings to themselves. BRIAN Integrated Systems (also called Balogtech in honor of its CEO, Tunji Balogun) builds its own computers at an assembly plant in the inland city of Ilorin, and is an official partner with Microsoft. Gafunk Nigeria Limited, which also has its own building, imports name-brand computers and components from all over the world—think HP, Dell, Acer, Epson, Canon, and Lexmark.

"This is the highest concentration of information technology products in all of Africa," said John Oboro, who heads the Computer and Allied Products Dealers Association of Nigeria, the group that manages the market, with a satisfied grin. "The turnover here is billions of naira." A billion naira would be $7 million, but the dollar value of trade in the market is likely far more than Oboro admitted. A recent report in Lagos's *Business Day* newspaper asserted that for every computer sold legally (formal channels in Nigeria account for two hundred and fifty thousand to three hundred thousand computers per year), fifteen are sold via System D. "That would put informal market figures at about 3.7 million," *Business Day* concluded. Computer Village, industry analysts suggest, is responsible for half that amount, or about 1.8 million computers. If the average computer costs $400, then Computer Village generates $720 million in sales in a year.

Without this hyperactive System D marketplace, all of West Africa would be digitally deprived. Merchants in Alaba would not be able to e-mail or text their suppliers, dump pickers would not be able to afford a mobile phone, and merchants from across the continent would not be able to get low-priced laptops. Ikeja Computer Village, in short, is bridging the digital divide one sale at a time.

· · ·

The streets were a mixture of earth, trash, and motor oil pounded to a fine finish by thousands of footfalls. Barefoot men, bent almost double, tugged at hand trucks and grasped at the jagged nubs of snapped motor mounts to urge car engines over the greasy hummocks. One massive motor slipped on its dolly and pincered a man's right hand. He shouted and his colleagues halted their toil. They shifted the hunk of dirty metal and he wordlessly wrapped the tail of his sweat-stained shirt around his crushed and bloodied fingers. Then it was back to work with his one good hand helping to heave the grimy hunk of metal along its obsidian track. The journey ended in the half-light of a dusty warehouse. There, the manager of an engine resale company waded out into the thicket of blackened steel that had come to the market from countries in Asia and Europe. He licked his finger and swiped at the engine block. "See," he said. Each motor had a mark etched into it, denoting whom in the warehouse it belonged to.

Out on the street, throngs of *okada* maneuvered in and out of the pedestrian flow. Most of the passengers were purchasers. They made their deals and hefted their goods on their shoulders or on their heads—a tailpipe swinging like a bantamweight crane, a pack of wheel wells roped together and clacking against one another like low-frequency cowbells, a stack of old stereos tied up bondage-style with see-through cling wrap, balanced like a headdress on a tribal deity. The bikes whizzed past kids selling tiny bags of peanuts, women carrying buckets of soda bottles on their heads, kiosks selling tools, hawkers selling mobile phone recharge cards, roadside stalls offering fried Indomie (a brand of spiced instant noodles that is a common cheap meal in Nigeria). Trucks dropped off containers straight from the port, disgorging banged-up car bodies, piles of coiled springs, used copper bushings, mounds of dusty hubcaps. Panel trucks delivered photocopiers, computers, TVs, gaming consoles, troves of mobile phones freezer-packed in Styrofoam cartons. The guts of global production splayed out in a series of chaotic stalls.

This is Ladipo Market, in the centrally located Mushin section of Lagos. In a dirt-floored warehouse, so silent it seemed like you could hear the dust motes collide, Sunday Aniekwu stood amid stacks of Kyocera Mita, Ricoh, Sharp, Canon, and Minolta printers, copiers, and fax machines. He buys these used machines locally, but they originate in far-flung places: the United States, Hong Kong, Malaysia. He brings in fifty machines every week and, as long as they are known brands, will dispose of them all before the next order arrives.

There was a pile of car transmissions adjacent to the photocopiers. And peeking out from beyond them, Ugochukwu Eleazars presided over an impressive array of long curved shapes swaddled in paper and tape. These latter-day mummies were car windshields, manufactured by the Chinese firm XYG (a.k.a. Xinyi Glass) and imported into Nigeria by the firm he manages, Tonel Franklyn Limited. "It's a good business," he reported. "But the problem is the cash. You get one container, you wait until your customers purchase the goods, and then you go for another container. We can't buy with credit, but we have to give credit to our customers."

Eleazars would like XYG to open a factory in Nigeria, which his firm would manage. With the vast labor pool and low wages of Lagos, he is sure it would be a winner. "It would be cheaper to make it in Nigeria," he said, tapping one of his well-wrapped windscreens. But, he noted, a factory requires a reliable and predictable source of energy, and Nigeria is a country with a power grid but no power. So, at least for now, manufacturing locally is simply a pipe dream. He must continue to import.

Down a slick and narrow alley behind one of the ware-

63

houses, Emanuel Uche, a machine dealer, showed off his products: used pumps, hydraulic lifts, generators, lawn mowers, arc welders, Weedwackers, and other machines culled from all over North America, Europe, and Asia. Along another passageway, a car mechanic sat amid a sprawl of oily parts, wiping a spark plug on a dirty piece of paper to clean the points. Around the corner and down another slippery road, in a crude hut with a sliding glass door (amazingly, in the midst of this seemingly downtrodden market, it's air conditioned inside), was the office of a travel agent and her husband, who deals in mobile phones that he imports from China.

The oily alleys of Ladipo are the last place you'd expect to find global traders. Part chop shop, part semiauthorized auto repair and spare parts center, part haven for cheap high tech, this market seems to define "haphazard." Yet here, on the second floor of seemingly vacant warehouse, you step into a space with no light except for gleaming screens. Peacemaker Temple, one of the merchants standing in the greenish glow, seized the chance to talk with one of the rare foreigners visiting the market. He shouted over the storm of twenty-first-century e-noise. In this damp warehouse, amid the cumulative reverberation of dozens of TV sets, volumes cranked to the max, he wanted it known: "This business is global," he said. The future lies in trade with China. And he wants to be part of it.

Halfway across town in the waterside squatter community of Makoko, Ogun Dairo put a match to a pile of wood chips she had carried in from the nearby sawmills in Ebute-Metta. The chips were soggy and didn't burn. Instead, they smoldered—and that was the essence of her tiny piece of global exchange.

Ogun Dairo has three large grills under a thatched-roof pavilion. And it is here, without a license, on land that until recently didn't exist (the squatters are slowly filling in the lagoon with laterite and compressed garbage) and that she still doesn't own (though, as the current occupant of land created by squatters, she has as much of a legitimate ownership claim as anyone else), that she smokes fish. She doesn't catch the fish herself. She buys it from a cold-storage facility near her home. And she doesn't sell the fish herself. She simply tucks the tail into the mouth, creating a compact, ring-shaped item that doesn't have to be flipped as it is smoked, exposes it to the smoldering chips for a few hours, and then packs it in boxes. Those boxes—she normally fills between five and seven a day—go to a distributor who in turn sells them to women (for some reason, the street sellers of fish are always women) who retail the fish all over the city. "The profit margin is not all that much," she said. "The profit is made by the turnover." It's a classic business model: the more fish she can buy and smoke, the more she can sell and the more money she makes. And it has supported her family of five for thirty years.

I asked where the fish came from. I figured she'd say that the lagoon, so polluted near the city, was cleaner upstream or farther out to sea. Perhaps her neighbors rowed out in their boats and brought back the catch. Or perhaps the fish came from elsewhere in Africa—even distant Lake Victoria. But I wasn't prepared for her answer.

"Europe," she said. The fish was caught far to the north, frozen, and shipped to Lagos, where it was transported from the port to one of the city's most notorious shantytowns to be smoked, and then sold for a few naira of profit on the roadsides of the West African megacity.

Contrary to popular impression, there is economic development in Africa. It's all over the place, hidden in plain sight in places like Oshodi, Alaba, Computer Village, Ladipo, and Makoko. It evades our gaze because our notions of growth and development are conditioned by a set of rules we have internalized in the West. We expect economic development to be highly organized and subject to bureaucratic regulation, monitoring, and measurement. We expect local, state, and national governments to be involved. We expect major corporations to be the anchors of development. Yet the great economic engine of Lagos—and, indeed, of most of Africa—is unstructured, unofficial, and, to many, unfathomable, a result of the self-development of System D. On their own, formal businesses don't provide enough jobs or generate enough money for the continent to grow. Though most economists dismiss System D, arguing that unregistered, underground businesses are condemned to be subsistence efforts and are too small to grow, the entrepreneurial energy and laboring zeal of the mass of people in Africa can be realized only on the street. For the majority of the population, it is System D that offers the hope of a better future.

The Global Back Channel

To buy in one market, in order to sell, with profit, in another, when there are many competitors in both; to watch over, not only the occasional variations in the demand, but the much greater and more frequent variations in the competition, or in the supply which that demand is likely to get from other people, and to suit with dexterity and judgment both the quantity and quality of each assortment of goods to all these circumstances, is a species of warfare of which the operations are continually changing, and which can scarce ever be conducted successfully. . . .

—*The Wealth of Nations*

With only a mobile phone and a promise of money from his uncle, David Obi did something the Nigerian government has been trying to do for decades: he figured out how to bring electricity to the masses in Africa's most populous country.

It wasn't a matter of technology. David is not an inventor or an engineer, and his insights into his country's electrical problems had nothing to do with fancy photovoltaics or turbines to harness the harmattan or any other alternative sources of energy. Instead, seven thousand miles from home, using a language he could hardly speak, he did what traders have always done: he made a deal. He contracted with a Chinese firm to produce small diesel-powered generators under his uncle's brand name, Aakoo, and shipped them home to Nigeria.

David never intended to become a player in the power sector. He came to Guangzhou, China, in 2005 with a tourist visa that entitled him to stay thirty days. But he didn't come as a tourist. He came with ten crisp hundred-dollar bills, and a dream of being a trader.

It was a difficult initiation. He knew no one and he didn't speak the language. He got a room in a cheap hotel in the city's Sanyuanli neighborhood, just north of the central train station, and barely went outside, except to get food at a nearby restaurant. Four months into his trading adventure, in his first major attempt at global trade, he blew his entire stake on an ill-advised deal for laptop computers,

So he did something desperate. He had noticed that many African merchants visited two local malls that specialized in selling discount clothing. He went to those malls—the Cannan and Tianen export markets are across the street from each other, so it's easy to move back and forth—and offered his services to various African entrepreneurs who were there. If they paid for some food and offered him a couple of *kwai* ("a few bucks," in Chinese slang) on the side, he would help them organize their trading forays.

David had started in trade in the auto parts market in Nnewi, a city in the east of Nigeria. He knew nothing about clothes. But selling is selling and buying is buying, and he knew from experience that his profit would come from the increment between the two. Over time, he learned that, with a tiny bit of creative accounting, he could work in a little extra profit for himself on every deal. "If the factory gives you something for eight naira, you tell the person who hired you that it is nine," he said, and you pocket the addition. At approximately a hundred and fifty naira to the dollar, this amounts to less than a penny on each item. Then, over time, he discovered that he could expect to earn an equal increment from the other side of the equation. Once he attracted enough African buyers, some of the Chinese clothing whole-salers suggested a new kind of arrangement: whenever his Nigerian clients bought at one of their stalls, that merchant would pay him a commission. So David started making money on both sides of every transaction, in addition to the cash he squeezed for himself from every transaction.

Gradually, his position stabilized and he was able to get back to the business he knew best—buying and selling auto parts and machinery. Now, David's deals are bigger—sometimes $150,000 at a time. He regularly ships full containers back to Nigeria, and, instead of a penny, he gets 2 percent off the top thrown his way by Chinese manufacturers (on a deal worth $150,000, that would be $3,000) and at least an equal amount from his Nigerian clients. With his success, David has moved out of the Sanyuanli hotel he used to occupy. Today he lives in an upwardly mobile neighborhood not far from the Garden Hotel, the city's premier destination for foreign businesspeople. By Guangzhou standards, he is positively middle-class.

Still, David knows that, by comparison with many Nigerian dealers, his operation is extremely small. He's amazed that anyone would find the business he did in generators to be noteworthy. "There was an opportunity, that's all," he said as he sipped a draft beer in the dark and quiet coffee bar/restaurant across the street from the apartment complex where he lives. "If you want something, my business is to get it produced and get it down to Nigeria."

Despite his modesty, there's something extraordinary about the deals he makes. We tend to think of globalization as a process led by the West, in which major multinationals outsource jobs to low-wage countries and create new markets for their products throughout the developing world. The companies and their defenders insist that globalization improves conditions for everyone, building a new middle class and introducing better labor conditions and standardized, safe products to regions that never had these things before. Critics say it is economic colonialism, allowing outside interests to lay waste to downtrodden nations while company coffers in the West go *ka-ching*.

But David Obi and thousands of others like him represent something different. Without documentation or approval or any assistance from their governments, they have created a bootstrap circuit of global trade unrecognized by governments and uncelebrated by economists.

It has always been this way. Peddlers, packmen, and other unlicensed System D traders were among the earliest globalizers. A thousand years ago, they followed the ragged armies of the Crusades—these massive and ill-equipped platoons amounted to what one historian called "walking cities"—to keep the soldiers supplied with food, clothing, and armaments, because national governments couldn't handle the logistics. System D knew no particular religion or politics, and the same dealers often traded with both sides. Later, networks of peddlers exploited mountain passes through the Pyrenees and Alps to move goods from North Africa and the Middle East to Europe and Scandinavia and back again, often finding routes around border outposts and customs agents. Even when cities seemed impregnable—ringed with walls and battlements as in Renaissance Italy—the area around the city gate served as a kind of free trade zone where the deals happened out of the earshot of the governing authorities. As Fernand Braudel, the historian of the development of modern capitalism, put it, "Rich or poor, pedlars stimulated and maintained trade, and spread it over some distance." The allure of unreported profit through unlicensed trade attracted an unlikely and diverse bunch. The French poet Arthur Rimbaud, for instance, gave up literature in the 1890s and dedicated the rest of his life to System D. Rimbaud, then twenty-six years old, migrated across the Mediterranean to North Africa and set himself up as a trader in the region he once called "the inopportune south," moving guns, spices, fabric, coffee, and other goods in camel caravans in and out of Aden (then a British colony and today a major port of Yemen) and Harar, Ethiopia. The great poet was unfortunately mostly a failure as a global deal maker.

In today's world, the distances traders travel have become greater than the short hop across the Mediterranean and down the Red Sea. James Ezeifeoma, whose Jinifa Allied Limited is one of the oldest firms in Lagos's Alaba International Market, still remembers the time it took to make his first trip. In 1987, he and a friend pooled their money—a total of $4,000—and headed to Singapore to buy fans and air conditioners. "You had to go to Singapore through Italy, and sleep at the airport for two days to get your connecting flight to Bombay or New Delhi," he recalled. "Then you had to fly to Thailand and later to Malaysia, to finally get a flight to Singapore." Total travel time: three or four days.

These days, things are much easier. The target for traders is China, and bargain-conscious merchants have a choice. They can fly Ethiopian Airlines, which has service from many African cities to Addis Ababa, and from Addis to Dubai and on to Beijing and Guangzhou. They can travel China Southern Airlines, which is based in Guangzhou, and also offers service to Africa, with stopovers in Dubai and Beijing. And people who want to travel in style can take Emirates, which flies direct from a number of African cities to Dubai and from Dubai to China.

James offers a great perspective on how important the global back channel of System D has been to his market and to the Nigerian economy. When he started in Alaba— working as an apprentice for someone else—the merchants were still hacking away at the teak forest to make the market.

James lived in his master's stall, sleeping on a mattress made from flattened cardboard boxes. The jungle—full of monkeys, snakes, and reptiles—was his toilet. Alaba Ojo Road, which runs through the center of the market, was a dirt track, and, during the rainy months, he and his colleagues had to lay wood planks along it so the massive trucks coming to make deliveries wouldn't bog down in the mud. Today, his firm has an air-conditioned, marble-tiled showroom, and his massive desk is filled with trophies from global brands—Sony, Panasonic, Zenith—attesting to his retailing ability. "Maybe because our market is haphazard and informal, people think we are criminal," James said. "But we play a very big role in the global economy."

Perhaps the clearest indication of the importance of this System D back channel to Africa can be found on the streets of Guangzhou, the south China trading city formerly known as Canton, where I met David Obi. *Southern Metropolis Daily*, one of the city's most highly regarded newspapers, has reported that there are a hundred thousand Africans living full-time in Guangzhou. Though the official Guangzhou statistical agency puts the number at thirty thousand, other observers have suggested that there could be as many as three hundred thousand Africans living in the city. Sanyuanli, the district to the north of Guangzhou's central train station, is home to so many Africans that taxi drivers have given it an unofficial new name: Chocolate City. While the cabbies most likely weren't referencing the 1975 P-Funk classic about Washington, D.C., the phrase does express a reality of Guangzhou: at rush hour, Sanyuanli seems more African than Chinese. (It's not only Africans who come to China to trade—when I was in Guangzhou I met Arabs, Argentines, Filipinos, Turks, and Americans who had all come to take advantage of System D—but the Africans seem to be the only ones who have established themselves as a permanent presence in the People's Republic.)

"Without Nigerians, this Sanyuanli would be nothing," David said of the neighborhood where he used to live. "The money we're bringing into China is substantial. I don't think the Chinese government is aware of how much cash is involved. If Africans stopped coming to China today, believe me, China would truly hurt." The Africans are almost all in the country illegally (like David, most have overstayed their three-month tourist visas) and doing business without a license or any registration. But they are all pursuing the same goal—world trade.

There are few solid statistics on the size of this underground global back channel—because most of the merchants, both African and Chinese, camouflage the extent of their trade. And it's impossible to estimate the number of containers that come from China into Africa—because many merchants smuggle their wares out of China and into their home countries in order to avoid restrictive trade laws and huge import duties. (One Chinese dealer told me that shipping costs and customs duties sometimes cost more than the value of the goods that are being shipped; for instance, a container containing items worth $9,000 could cost more than $10,000 to get out of China and into Africa.) The only sure statistics are these: the Chinese government estimated that bilateral trade with Africa would surpass $100 billion in 2009, with exports accounting for more than $40 billion, up 40 percent from 2007. The growth in bottom-up globalization, though, is likely not included in these statistics, because most of it occurs off the books.

On the street, however, the impact is undeniable. Guangzhou hosts an array of cottage industries designed to cater to the African traders: hotels, restaurants that serve African food (one of them is called, perhaps in deliberately bad taste, Darkie Kitchen), money changers, shipping agencies, translators, and fixers—Chinese who set themselves up to do business like David used to, offering to link traders with manufacturers and showrooms. There are coffee bars where traders hang out (these are particularly popular with merchants from the French-speaking African countries and Arab North Africa). In addition, thousands of Africans can be found on Saturdays worshiping at a mosque near Yuexiu Park, and on Sunday afternoons at the English-language mass at Sacred Heart Cathedral on Yide Lu in Guangzhou's old downtown.

David Ibekwe, a merchant whose shop is in ASPAMDA, the Auto Spare Parts and Machinery Dealers Association market in Lagos, first traveled to Guangzhou from Lagos eight years ago with a very specific goal: to find cheap auto parts that he could import back home. Now he goes back and forth several times a year—so much so that he rents a pied-à-terre apartment in the city instead of paying high hotel bills, and says he actually prefers living in China to living in Nigeria.

David got his start at ASPAMDA the old-fashioned way, through the Igbo tribe's apprenticeship system. Forced to quit his education after just one year of high school, David became an apprentice to an uncle who sold auto parts. In Igbo tradition, an apprentice spends as many as seven years serving a master. As is the norm for most apprentices, he has to do what his boss asks—wash the car, cook the food, serve as a security guard, haul trash, babysit the kids, whatever. In the process, he also learns the fundamentals, nuances, and tricks of the trade. Then, when the apprenticeship is over, the Igbo tradition adds something innovative and valuable. At the end of an apprenticeship, if the worker has done a good job, his boss has to "settle" him in business. Here's how David describes the process: "Normally if you bring in a young guy to serve as apprentice, they serve for five or six or seven years. So if he does well and there's no problem, his master will now settle him. You bring out a very big amount of money and you are using this money to help him start his life." That means renting him a shop and providing him start-up capital so he can enter the trade as a competitor. It is totally expected that the newly settled apprentice will take some clients away from the master.

To be an apprentice in the Igbo tradition may seem like the definition of exploited labor. But, through the concept of "settling," the system serves as a behind-the-scenes financing mechanism, giving young entrepreneurs an infusion of cash with which to build networks around the globe. As Abiola Akiyode-Afolabi, a human rights advocate and executive director of the Lagos-based NGO WARD C—the Women Advocates Research and Documentation Centre—put it, "The best system for transferring knowledge informally is the Igbo apprenticeship system."

When David's uncle settled him, David decided to become an importer. At the time, China was not yet very open to foreigners. "We preferred Taiwan and India," he said, because those countries were easier with visas. But, as China began to promote itself as a manufacturing center, he recalled, "they were begging us to come to come to their place and see what they can do." So he decided to attend the Canton Fair, the twice-yearly exposition of Chinese manufacturing prowess that has been held in Guangzhou since 1957. The fair is big business for China: 2007's fair drew more than two hundred thousand buyers and yielded almost $74 billion in sales, according to official statistics.

Like all outfits that import things into Nigeria, David's company is registered with the Nigeria Corporate Affairs Commission (all firms that import items to Nigeria must be registered). But that doesn't mean he's totally legit. His firm exists with one toe in the legal world and the other nine in System D. For instance, David's firm imports an average of one container a month of auto parts. He handed me an invoice for a shipment that would be arriving soon at Apapa, the main Lagos port. The value of the goods, on paper, was $51,000. At that price, he said, it would cost more than $20,000 to clear the goods from the port. This would, of course, add almost 50 percent to the price he would have to charge for those auto parts. So, he explained, he will work with customs officials to cut the stated value of goods in a container. This will greatly reduce the customs duty he must pay on his imports—and he will show his appreciation by sharing the savings with the customs inspectors.

Speaking in general terms, I described this to Dera Nnadi, the public relations officer for Apapa port. "Nigeria didn't invent corruption," he said. "It exists everywhere." Then he tugged at his full dress uniform—he even had his shoes shined for the interview, because it was being videotaped—and noted that operations at the port had recently been privatized, which had made loading and unloading more professional and less subject to bribery and corruption. When I reported back to David, he just laughed.

David held up a folded piece of rubber. It was a new product. He was negotiating with a Chinese company to manufacture inner tubes for motorcycles, which he thought could be a big seller. Given the state of the roads—rutted and ruined—and the fact that the *okada* speed down highways that are littered with rusting objects and stray pieces of debris, blowouts are frequent. He hoped an inexpensive inner tube could be a big seller. (When I saw him a year later, David told me that the inner-tube venture had been a bust, and that he had lost money on the deal. But he wasn't unduly concerned: "All investment comes with some risk," he said, sounding like a latter-day Adam Smith.)

Over the past eight years, David has turned many high-value deals with China, and there are a number of Chinese traders who owe their success in business to his purchases. Linda Chen is one of them. Six years ago, Linda was about to graduate from a Chinese university with a degree in chemistry. She dreamed of a job in the global economy mixing fragrances for U.S. consumer giant Procter & Gamble. She even applied for a job with the U.S. firm, but the competition was intense—thousands of applicants for a couple of openings—and she wasn't one of the chosen two. Today, at age twenty-seven, she has gone in a different direction. She owns her own auto parts business—and its success, with sales of ten million yuan, or $1.4 million, annually, is a result of the Nigerian influx into Guangzhou: 95 percent of the goods Linda sells go to Lagos. David was her first customer.

"Water pumps," she said. "Even now I can remember the first item he bought." Though they no longer do much business together (David's orders are large and he wants tight controls on the quality of what he buys, so he goes directly to the factories to produce his auto parts), Linda and David have remained friends. He regularly recommends that fellow Lagos auto parts dealers start importing from her, because he knows that they can trust her, that the goods she sends will be the right quality at the right price.

Like David and her other African customers, Linda operates in the space between System D and the legal economy. Linda started in business without being incorporated. In order to avoid being caught by the authorities, she made a deal with a large manufacturer to tell the government that she was working as an agent for his firm. It wasn't true, but the lie saved her the heavy cost of licensing and registration. Though she recently went legit and registered with the government, she admits that she still massages the financial information she reports to the government in order to reduce her tax bill. And, like her Nigerian counterparts, she sometimes provides fake receipts, so she can report lower earnings and pay lower fees at the port. "If you're selling a box cutter for three dollars, you might say it costs a dollar twenty," she reports. "If you fill a container with forty thousand dollars in goods, you might say it's just three thousand dollars."

Linda interrupted our conversation to take a phone call from Nigeria. "How fa?" she asked, sliding from awkward standard English into flawless Nigerian pidgin. "How are things?" She exchanged pleasantries for a few seconds, then pushed forward with what she really wanted: to collect a bill. She told the man she would not send his auto parts to Nigeria until he came up with the cash. When she hung up, she shook her head. "At first, I could not understand Nigerians. Now, I speak African English and I can't understand American or British English."

When she started in business, Linda dealt with most of her smaller customers by phone or e-mail. But starting in 2008, she began traveling to Lagos once a year to keep current with the market and meet Nigerian buyers who can't afford a trip to Guangzhou or can't get a visa.

David Ibekwe went to Guangzhou again in the summer of 2008. He was convinced that he would once more find it a perfect place to strike good deals, buy lots of auto parts, and make a serious profit. "It was a very good trip," he said when he got back to Lagos. "I enjoyed myself. But for business it was worthless."

David's trading fell victim to one of the pitfalls of the cash-based economy of System D: fluctuations in global exchange rates. The economic underground depends on the formal system of national currencies, and the dollar is the universal translator of System D. To buy things in China, David had to covert his naira into dollars in Nigeria and then, once in China, convert his stash of dollars into Chinese yuan. But the naira had fallen substantially against the dollar. In early 2007, the official exchange rate was a hundred and twenty-eight naira to the dollar (and you could do a bit better than that on the black market), but by midway through 2008, the rate had ballooned to almost a hundred and fifty. At the same time, the dollar had dropped against the yuan. Where one dollar was worth 7.7 yuan in early 2007, it was worth only 6.8 yuan in 2008. The twin currency transactions that enabled David to buy in China in 2007 had, one year later, conspired to reduce his purchasing power by more than 30 percent. One yuan that cost David 16.6 naira in 2007 cost him 22 naira a year later—and that increase killed his plans.

Linda Chen was feeling the pinch, too. She cradled a car headlight in her palm. Back in 2006, when the dollar was worth almost eight yuan, she could buy that headlamp from the factory for 8.8 yuan ($1.10, or 137 naira) and sell it for 9.6 yuan ($1.20, or 150 naira), which yielded close to a 10 percent profit. Even if she didn't raise her prices, in today's currency, she would have to charge her Nigerian customers $1.40, or 210 naira per headlight—and she knew that her clients in Lagos could not pay that much. So she was attempting to sell the headlamp for $1.30, which meant her profit margin had fallen to less than 2 percent. But it was proving difficult to find takers, because even that price was steep: 195 naira, 30 percent more than what she had charged in 2006. Linda would have to sell far more headlights than she ever had to make this low-profit transaction work, and she has begun to worry about the ultimate viability of her company. "The cost of material in China is continuing to go up and the dollar is continuing to go down," she said, sounding more like a traditional capitalist than a denizen of the shadow economy. "I have to consider what to do."

Ethan Zhang, the Guangzhou handbag designer, faced a different issue—one that revolved around price as a cultural question. He wanted to get into global exchange, and particularly into designing bags for the U.S. market, but found that the different price points expected in China and the United States made life difficult for his business.

"Why do Americans expect to get nice handbags so cheap?" he asked. A Chinese girl who earned perhaps two thousand yuan a month, he explained, would not have a problem buying a bag for two hundred yuan, or about $30. Indeed, she might do this every month, if she found styles she really liked that matched an outfit she planned to wear. She would do this even if the expense ate up 10 percent of her monthly salary. By contrast, most Americans balked at paying that much for a bag, and Ethan found that U.S. wholesalers wanted to pay far, far less. (Though the Chinese still typically save a larger percentage of their income than Americans do, the growing number of upwardly mobile Chinese teens and young adults are far more consumerist and willing to spend on certain items than their American counterparts.)

Ethan keeps his costs superlow. He has no permits. His firm is not registered. He pays no taxes. Indeed, he doesn't even have the *houkou*, or residency permit, required to live in Guangzhou. He runs his design studio and pattern-making shop out of two connected ground-floor apartments in a gated community in Sanyuanli. He sleeps in one room and runs the business in the other rooms, providing lunch and dinner every day for the ten people who work for him.

"If I want to get a license, then I will need a bank account and an office in an office building," Ethan said. "Ten or twenty thousand [or between $1,500 and $3,000] can get me a license. Not having a license may be a problem in several years. But now I don't think it's a problem. In China, there are many richer people and most of them don't pay taxes." He paused, then added a short complaint that you hear as much in China as anywhere else: "And where do the taxes go? When you go to the hospital and you don't have money there is no care." (This is one of the surprises of life in contemporary China: despite the rhetoric of social solidarity, the government essentially ended the public health system years ago.)

Ethan echoed Linda in suggesting that most merchants did not report all of their sales to the government, and that they would work with customers to mislead authorities. "In China, in the private economy, most of the people in these little companies, they don't offer invoices," he said. "When you need an invoice, they will offer you an invoice from another firm, in whatever amount you want." This, essentially, hides their business from the Beijing government and at the same time enables buyers to lie to their governments about the value of what they are importing. Indeed, he said, many of these companies were little more than a guy with a cell phone and a friend in a factory.

Like Linda, Ethan is a young entrepreneur. He graduated college in June 2005—his degree is in information technology from the Beijing University of Posts and Telecommunications—and arrived in Guangzhou the following month. But he found that he wasn't truly interested in IT. He wanted to be in business. In his first entrepreneurial experiment, he made a beginner's mistake. He invested all his cash in memory cards for cameras and mobile phones and tried to crack the market as a wholesaler. But he hadn't scoped out the market enough to understand that the business was intensely competitive, and that prices were falling. The result: he lost everything. To increase his knowledge of the business world, he decided to get a job. First, he worked as a clerk, typing, cleaning, and repairing computers. He lasted four months before deciding that the computer business was not for him. After that, he took a job on an assembly line in a thousand-person factory, making handbags. "After a month," he told me, "I understood how a factory is run, so I quit again."

He saw that the markup from manufacturing to retail was high enough in the handbag biz that it could make him a good income. So he decided to become a designer. He spent several months wandering the leather mall and cruising online shopping sites, looking at handbags. "I was just like a thief, but just with my eyes," he said. Soon, he was sketching his own designs and, with a stake of ¥1 million (about $150,000) from his family, who had owned a coal mine and a gold mine in the northern province of Xianxi, he began his work.

But Ethan's concern about the price he could command for his handbags seemed a bit disingenuous. On the same day he complained so bitterly about how cheap U.S. consumers were, Ethan invited me to join him for dinner. It wasn't a social encounter. As is the practice with many Guangzhou merchants, it was a business meeting—in this case with the owner of the factory that was doing his handbag production.

Wen, the factory owner (he asked that I use only his first name) had spent ten years as a worker on a production line before he had saved enough money—¥300,000, or about $44,000—to open his factory. His business isn't registered or licensed, and he pays only a small portion of what the government could legally charge him in taxes. He maintains his factory on the outskirts of Guangzhou, he told me, because he feared that if he were more centrally located, the government would seek him out and force him to register and pay his back taxes. He employs thirty workers when things are slow and expands to sixty workers during busy times. He doesn't run his factory as an assembly line. Instead, he organizes work groups—generally three people—who do all the tasks necessary to produce one bag at a time. For Ethan's most recent order, this worked well, because the bags were high-concept, and required lots of hand stitching. But it was exactly that complexity that had necessitated their meeting.

Ethan and Wen negotiated between mouthfuls. At one point, after we had made our way through a dozen different dishes and half a dozen pots of tea, Ethan headed to the bathroom and my translator took advantage of the moment to give me a hasty summary. Ethan was paying just ¥20—or about $3—for each bag Wen's factory workers produced. Wen wanted Ethan to bring the price up. But Ethan had refused. A deal, he said, was a deal. And, of course, the workers—who were receiving only a small slice of that twenty yuan—had no seat at the table. This wasn't a discussion about wages.

Earlier in the day, Ethan had told me how much he was selling the bags for: ¥70 per purse. So, even though he was selling the bags locally, Ethan's wholesale price would be more than triple what he was paying Wen to produce the bags. Despite his pursuit of high-end quality, Ethan was still paying a rock-bottom price for his handbags.

The problem is, there's a potential downside for traders who try to get the lowest possible prices. David Mwangi, who hails from Nairobi, Kenya, came to Guangzhou in 2006 to guide goods from Asia to East Africa. In one of his first deals, he ordered a huge shipment of flash drives and drove a hard bargain. He was sure to make a profit. But, to his chagrin, when he got the goods to Nairobi, he discovered that "ninety percent were useless." His next deal, he decided to test the items out in China. He bought eight hundred thousand CD-Rs—rewritable CDs—and went through all of them. "The total order was garbage," he said. David was so outraged that he actually called the cops and reported these companies as thieves. But that, of course, went nowhere. In System D, there's not a lot of protection from shoddy workmanship.

When I met him in 2007, David was already thinking

what had previously been unthinkable. We were drinking lukewarm Zhu Jiang beer outside a grocery store just off Xiao Bei Lu (another predominantly African area of the city—this neighborhood caters mostly to East Africans and traders from the former French colonies of West Africa). David leaned back on his stool and spoke with great resignation. "It's impossible to make money in China," he said. His Chinese suppliers were operating with too skimpy a profit margin and were increasing their profit by decreasing the quality of the goods. Vietnam, he had heard, might be the next frontier—a country with lower costs and higher-quality production. Thus, David was following a principle set out by Adam Smith himself: "The capital of a wholesale merchant, on the contrary, seems to have no fixed or necessary residence anywhere, but may wander about from place to place, according as it can either buy cheap or sell dear."

Back in Nigeria, David Ibekwe was also mulling the idea of wandering into a new market. He is facing a new element of competition in his auto parts importing business. With costs in China rising and the naira falling, Chinese merchants have started venturing to Nigeria on their own, looking to skip the middleman—namely David—and to get their own hooks into the local market. These entrepreneurs are not manufacturing in Africa, but they are seeking to sell products for cheaper than their African counterparts. To compete with these Chinese traders, David will have to buy cheaper, lower-quality products. There will be more defective parts per order and all the parts will be less durable. But, he said, this represented the only chance he had to beat the Chinese at their own game.

Or he could move in a new direction altogether. He quizzed me on a possible start-up venture: importing used cars from the United States into Nigeria. This is another vast System D operation that would involve bringing them into the open port at Cotonou and paying to move them across the border and down into Lagos. (Dealers smuggle used cars into Nigeria in order to avoid high customs fees and because the federal government prohibits importers from bringing in cars that are more than seven years old.) It would be a costly endeavor—in part because it would put him in competition with scores of other Nigerians who have years of experience in the same business. But David knew one thing that he thought made it viable: it wasn't a market the Chinese were likely to corner.

The Culture of the Copy

The prudent man is always sincere, and feels horror at the very thought of exposing himself to the disgrace which attends upon the detection of falsehood. But though always sincere, he is not always frank and open; and though he never tells any thing but the truth, he does not always think himself bound, when not properly called upon, to tell the whole truth.

—*The Theory of Moral Sentiments*

Chief Arthur Okafor never admitted that the products he sold were knockoffs. He did not agree that they were fakes. And he was outraged if anyone ever said they were counterfeits. He put his hand over his heart, as if he were taking an oath. "These are real copies," he declared.

He lounged against a glass display case in front of one of the kiosks in the Guangzhou Dashatou Second Hand Trade Center. The evidence of the deal he had just made was spread in a three-hundred-and-sixty-degree pattern around him: precisely folded cardboard boxes, geometrically shaped shards of Styrofoam, dozens of small plastic bags, rolls of packing tape, and a series of large Styrofoam coolers—they might have been carrying wild salmon—embalmed in freezer tape.

It was Friday afternoon. He was due to head back to Lagos in less than twenty-four hours. "Do you know how much money I came here with?" he asked. "Forty thousand dollars." He paused. "And do you know how much I am going home with?" He smiled, raised his arms, and fluttered his fingers in the air as if he were releasing fairy dust.

In his unwavering refusal to acknowledge the obvious, Chief Arthur was expressing an old mercantile truth: piracy has been a normal business practice for a very long time. This was pointed out more than a century ago by the philosopher Friedrich Nietzsche. "The brigand and the man of power who promises to defend a community against the brigand are probably at bottom very similar beings," Nietzsche wrote in 1880, "except that the latter obtains what he wants in a different way from the former: namely through regular tributes paid to him by the community and not by imposts levied by force. (It is the same relationship as that between merchant and pirate, who are for a long time one and the same person, where one function does not seem to him advisable he practices the other. Even now, indeed, merchant's morality is really a *more prudent* form of pirate's morality: to buy as cheap as possible—where possible for no more than the operational costs—to sell as dear as possible.)"

There's a long history to back this up. Sir Francis Drake, who circumnavigated the globe from 1577 to 1580 and helped lead the British navy when it defeated the vastly superior Spanish Armada in 1588, made three major voyages across the Atlantic. On each of them, his purposes were largely the same—to pilfer cargo from Spanish traders and to pillage the port cities Spain had established to handle its trade. And on each journey, the sailors who staffed his vessels were the same type of men—sometimes, indeed, the same men. Yet only one of his voyages to the New World was a legal trading mission. The other two times Drake sailed across the Atlantic, he was a pirate. What was the difference between his pirate ventures and his official voyage? A piece of paper signed by the queen. In his rakish lexicon *The Devil's Dictionary*, the cynical American writer Ambrose Bierce caught the absurdity of this when he defined piracy as "commerce without its folly-swaddles, just as God made it."

To be sure, Chief Arthur didn't attempt to pillage the market where he made his purchases or to seize his mobile phones by force. But that thin sliver of difference between legal trade and illegal marked everything Chief Arthur did. He didn't have any official paperwork permitting him to buy things in the market. He had traveled to Guangzhou on a tourist visa. He was buying unlicensed copies of legal phones, and was planning to sneak them back to Lagos. Though he didn't engage in the violence Drake used to achieve his goals, Chief Arthur was definitely a pirate. But in every other way, he was doing the same thing all merchants do—making a deal.

You wouldn't find the Guangzhou Dashatou Second Hand Trade Center if you weren't looking for it. It's not in historic old Canton centered at a bend in the Pearl River. It's a world away from quiet and quaint Shamian Island, where foreign couples seeking to adopt Chinese babies pose for photos in front of the waterfall in the overdone lobby of the White Swan Hotel. It's not in Tianhe, the shiny, high-end section of town. And it's doubtful that any of the businesses in this market have ever attempted to attend the Canton Fair, the trade show that has been the city's commercial calling card to global businesses for better than five decades.

In fact, you might not even find this market if you walked right past it. The Second Hand Trade Center hides itself well. It's up an escalator from a well-stocked but deserted ground-floor market on a busy but unremarkable commercial street. A few blocks away, in a park sheltered by the Haiyin Bridge, a dozen retirees take lessons in ballroom dancing. A gaggle of System D bicycle repairmen smoke cigarettes around a fountain at the base of the bridge, ready to fix flats for a few extra coins. This is a second job for most of them, a bid to make a bit of extra cash. While they waited for customers, the repairmen kept a nervous eye out for agents from the municipal agency they knew as City Control, who, they said, could confiscate their tools and pocket their money.

The Guangzhou Dashatou market is essentially a series of stalls rented out as independent booths. But this modest place is at the center of one of the amazing untold stories of globalization. The merchants here are Chinese. But most of the customers, like Chief Arthur, are from Africa. The trade is generally brisk—on Fridays it can be overwhelming—and it's accompanied by what seems like a permanent sound track: the rasp of unspooling packing tape and the whir of currency counters. Each box that leaves the market is heavily sheathed in plastic tape—to ensure a secure seal and to make it hard to tamper with. And the economy here, as in almost all haphazard markets around the world, is cash-only. All payments are made in yuan, and, as the largest denomination in Chinese currency is one hundred yuan—worth about $14—people making big deals carry massive bundles of cash. Chief Arthur, for instance, who was carrying a wad of four hundred hundred-dollar bills, had to convert them into almost three thousand hundred-yuan notes—a stack of bills large enough that he needed a briefcase or duffel bag to carry it around. Any merchants he bought from knew that if they counted this much money by hand, they would likely make mistakes. That's why almost every kiosk in the Guangzhou Dashatou market is armed with a battery-powered currency counter, and they use them to count and recount the stacks of bills that change hands. Each kiosk also has several safes, to store all the cash they take in.

There's essentially one product sold in this place, and it's the reason the market exists: mobile phones. A few kiosks sell batteries and chargers. But the bulk of the market is the handsets themselves. Mobile phones are big business in China. According to government figures, China exported six hundred million mobile phones in 2008. And that's only the official number. The phones sold here are unofficial. That's because, despite the name of this shopping center, the phones in the Guangzhou Dashatou Second Hand Trade Center are not secondhand at all. Some are what the Chinese call *shan zhai*, pronounced "shan" (rhymes with "con") "jai" (rhymes with "high"); in literal translation, the name refers to the mountain hideouts used by medieval gangsters. They are displayed in glass cases, each one individually wrapped in plastic like single slices of American cheese. There's "Sansung," "Motorloa," and "Sany Erickson." *Shan zhai* products are a staple of Chinese industry, and they exist in almost every line of business. In Guangzhou's garment and leather markets, you can find stores named Hogoo Boss and Zhoumani and Verscc and S. Guuuci, and, my favorite, a store that sells key chains and wallets under the brand name Alicia Keys.

In truth, though, the products with these often hilarious names are not the primary business of the Guangzhou Dashatou Second Hand Trade Center. The real business here is piracy. This humdrum collection of kiosks is perhaps the city's leading mall dedicated to counterfeit brand-name phones. These phones look like the originals and even have the brand logo—though they are pirated versions of the popular models.

In the Guangzhou Dashatou Second Hand Trade Center, you can buy dozens of varieties of Nokia phones that appear identical in almost every respect to the actual models. For instance, a genuine Nokia N73, much coveted when Chief Arthur was there in 2007, retailed for around twenty-nine hundred yuan (or about $400). A reconditioned model was available for a thousand yuan ($140.). The pirated N73 at the Guangzhou Dashatou market was beautiful—a seemingly perfect replica of the original. The display was as sharp as the official model. The features all seemed to work (though, of course, this is hard to gauge without using the phone for a long time). And the price? Six hundred yuan—or $85, one-fifth of what it would cost to get a real N73. Of course, there's a discount if you buy in bulk. Even if the phone was a high-design, low-functioning copy, many people in the mall were lusting after it.

Cheap prices on name brands means big profits for people like Chief Arthur, even if they are dealing in lower-end models. Take the Nokia 1110. It had four characteristics that made it perfect for the hard-core traveler. First, it was unexciting and low-tech. A monochrome display, no camera, and no Internet capability meant that it would never be a target for thieves. It was long-lived—one charge kept it running for five days, even if you talked a lot—a boon in countries like Nigeria, where electricity is not readily available most of the time. It had great reception. And it was durable. At Slot, in Ikeja Computer Village, I bought an 1110 for five thousand naira, or about $40. I priced the same phone in the Guangzhou Dashatou Second Hand Trade Center, and, without even bargaining, was offered one for $10—and that would likely drop to $8 if I bought in bulk. So do the math: a thousand phones for $8,000. Throw in $1,000 for an air ticket and another $1,000 for incidental expenses. And even if you allocate $10,000 to ship those phones to Nigeria—most likely a vast overstatement—the profit is still extraordinary. For a total outlay of $20,000, you could earn $40,000. The bottom line: 100 percent return on the initial investment. It was the promise of this kind of profit that drew Chief Arthur back to Guangzhou nine times in the course of two years. To him, buying and selling pirated mobile phones seemed as close to a sure thing as any investment could be.

And it's not difficult to get pirated merchandise into

Nigeria, as David Ibekwe, the auto parts dealer, explained: he imports containers full of what he calls CB—contraband— through the port at Cotonou, in the neighboring Republic of Benin. Cotonou is what David calls an "open port," with minimal customs controls and few restrictions on pirate merchandise. Cotonou is a favorite destination of System D importers, because getting the goods off the boat is incredibly efficient. A load can languish for weeks, or even months, at Apapa, the Lagos port, Jean-Paul Azam, a French economist who has studied trade in West Africa, has noted, while, if at Cotonou, it could be whisked away from the wharf and en route to its destination in just twenty-four hours. Azam estimates that less than 10 percent of what comes into Cotonou's port is declared to the customs agents of the Republic of Benin. Once his goods have cleared the port in Cotonou, David told me, he hires smugglers to bring his wares across the border into Nigeria.

"You see this brand?" David asked, stabbing his finger at a blue box. "The original is from Taiwan, but this one is manufactured in China." He directed me toward another stack of boxes with the name SASIC in yellow against a blue background. "This brand is from France, but it's manufactured in China." In other words, these were fakes, made to look like the original and emblazoned with the same brand name, but not made by the company or with its consent. (When I sat down with David's friend Linda Chen in Guangzhou, the shelves in her three-room suite of offices in a drab commercial building in Sanyuanli were lined with dusty boxes of Chinese-made knockoffs of brands such as Meyle, Bosch, and Glacier Vandervell. Linda told me that the firms that make the highest quality counterfeits actually offer guarantees similar to the ones offered by the real producers themselves, and customers can return damaged or defective parts. Cheaper fakes, of course, offer no such protection for the buyers.)

The genuine items, David continued, would sell for "more than double the price" of the fakes. He thought for a moment and revised his estimate upward. "More than triple the price, believe me. More than that." The genuine items, in other words, would be too expensive to sell in Lagos.

Not long after Chief Arthur sprinkled his fairy dust in the Guangzhou Dashatou Second Hand Trade Center, I sat on the top floor of China Plaza, one of the fanciest malls in Guangzhou, listening to someone talk about piracy from the inside. Feiyang (the name he requested to be known by) took a sip of a heavily sweetened iced coffee drink and pointed down at the Puma store far below him. "Even there," he said. "Most legitimate stores sell fakes. Otherwise they would make no money."

Puma, Feiyang said, was the most commonly pirated brand of clothing in China, and many of the highest-quality fakes—"triple A," he called them—were so good that even the people who designed them probably couldn't tell the difference. Indeed, he noted, they're often produced by the same factories that have contracts with the brands: they produce genuine items on the day shift, and counterfeits on nights and weekends.

Feiyang knows the business well. He spent several years working for a company that dealt in pirated versions of name-brand men's sportswear. He did the books, worked in the store, visited the factory. About the only thing he didn't do was sell the counterfeit items—which meant that although he worked in a highly profitable business, he didn't get rich. Salespeople, Feiyang reported, were paid on commission—and the commissions were huge, often amounting to five or ten thousand yuan a month ($750 to $1,500), as much as five times more than a salesperson at a legal store would earn.

The Chinese government, Feiyang said, took a relatively hands-off approach to pirate manufacturers—except at times when Western brands were pressing it to crack down. For instance, in the run-up to and immediately after the Beijing Olympics in 2008, the government, anxious for worldwide approval, inaugurated a harder line on piracy. Even so, it was relatively easy to avoid being detected by the authorities. For instance, he said, at the factory and in the showroom, it was common to work on holidays. Why? Because public officials were generally not working at that time. "Government rests on vacations and weekends, so that's when we did business," he said. And Feiyang's boss seemed to have an arrangement with the cops. He would normally close the store just before the police raided. And, even if a raid caught them off guard, the owner was never around when the authorities arrived, as if he had been tipped off about the police action. The raids didn't really deter their business either. If the authorities shut a location and confiscated its merchandise, Feiyang said, that same firm would be up and running with a new name at a new location in just a few days.

Interestingly, most of the companies that produce pirated goods pay some taxes, Feiyang said, because they do a certain amount of legal business in addition to their pirate activities. But, he said, like everyone else, they report only a small fraction of their income to the government. "Normally, the tax they pay is fake, because nobody will check how many goods you sell. Everyone knows they are making money, but they will not bother to check the revenue."

As he stared out over China Plaza—this luxurious mall is a symbol of the success of the government's economic policies, as there's a growing middle class with money to burn on shopping—Feiyang said he doubted that the authorities would ever seriously challenge the pirate manufacturers. "The government will not intervene. Everyone knows the people who are manufacturing fake products. But if you put a big tax on it, no one can make a living, and to this extent the country will be worse off. Even if they are doing fake products, they are employing people, so the government will not crack down."

Michael Jeremiah, a Nigerian merchant who created his own brand—Vectro—and contracted to have it manufactured in China, found this out in one of his dealings with a Chinese manufacturer. He registered his brand name in Nigeria (though, he admitted, he still manipulated shipping manifests and didn't pay his full taxes), and found it had good sales. So he went back to China to order more and discovered that his Chinese manufacturer was dealing identical products, with the same Vectro name, to India and Pakistan. He was outraged. "I told them it was a breach of contract," he said. He complained to the cops—to no avail. "They can copy your goods and you don't even have the right to defend your trademark," he said, seeming unaware of the irony that a merchant from Nigeria, a friendly market for pirated brands, was now the one complaining about piracy.

About the only thing that could kill the pirating industry, Feiyang continued, was its own success. As more people were making fakes, profit margins were shrinking. "There are so many competitors in the market, the only way out is to create your own brands," he said. Linda Chen agreed. With her profit margins falling, she believes that the way forward is to produce products under her own brand name that are as good as the fakes she is currently selling.

Handbag designer Ethan Zhang sees the growth of fakes as an example of exactly what is wrong with the dominant business model in China. "For years, consumers were asking mainly for the cheap things. But now, the RMB [the Chinese currency] is appreciating. All materials are appreciating. Labor costs are appreciating. The cost is higher and higher. If we keep making cheap things, the customer doesn't offer enough profit, so I cannot offer enough to my employees. If we keep making cheap products, I think industry may disappear one day." It was a dire prediction—made all the more bold because he made it in 2007, before the economic meltdown that crashed U.S. and European economies, forcing an estimated hundred thousand Chinese factories to close in 2008 alone.

Ethan advanced a new idea—new for China, at least—that he believed would remedy the situation. Twenty percent of the customers, Ethan said, produce 80 percent of the profits, yet most Chinese businesses were honed in on the 80 percent of the customers who produce only 20 percent of the profits. This, Ethan continued, had exposed most Chinese businesses to an endless course of rising costs and falling profits. (Having never studied economics in school, Ethan probably didn't know that the 80/20 conundrum was one of the famous observations of Vilfredo Pareto, an influential conservative economist from the early twentieth century.)

"Our way out is to focus on the other twenty percent"— the people who produce the real profits, Ethan said. "The problem is making enterprises change their strategies from low price to high service. I think this is a very important development stage for Chinese companies." Ethan argued that Chinese manufacturers will ultimately have to tilt away from piracy and toward starting their own high-end brands. (Two years after Ethan told me this, *The New York Times* reported that Chinese firms were beginning to adopt Ethan's standpoint, and that companies that had been manufacturing cheaply for resale under Western brand names were starting to produce their own lines of products, to see if they could capture the high-end market locally and abroad.)

Still, most people who monitor piracy don't think it's going to drop off—at least in the short term. For instance, the International AntiCounterfeiting Coalition, a Western nonprofit sponsored by major corporations and brands, has issued several reports indicating their belief that, with hundreds of thousands of industrial workers facing unemployment and dislocation after the global recession cut production contracts in 2008 and early 2009, China will opt to allow more piracy in order to prop up employment and avoid potential civil unrest.

In its position on piracy, China is following an economic philosophy that reaches back long before Chairman Mao and even before Karl Marx. It's a theory that was popularized by Bernard Mandeville, an eighteenth-century philosopher, satirist, political theorist, pamphleteer, and economist. In a series of nursery school–style rhymes called *The Grumbling Hive*, published in 1705, Mandeville argued that illegal and immoral deals—everything from cheating to overcharging to piracy to not paying taxes—were actually the norm in the business world and were good for society. "All trades and places knew some cheat, no calling was without deceit," Mandeville wrote. "Every part was full of vice, yet the whole mass a paradise."

Mandeville's doggerel chant was a big seller—in part because of one of those cheats and deceits. *The Grumbling Hive*, he explained when he had the opportunity to reissue the poem in expanded form in a 1714 book he called *The Fable of the Bees*, had been "printed above eight Years ago in a Six Penny Pamphlet," but was "soon after Pirated, cry'd about the Streets in a Half-Penny Sheet." These unauthorized cheapskate reprints gave him no money but helped make his pamphlet famous and helped give him the opportunity to publish a new edition. One contemporary publisher described the process in a letter to readers that ran as an introduction to a 1706 edition of the collected writings of the popular satirist Ned Ward: "there are so many Piratizing Printers, who lye upon the Catch, that no Saleable Poem or Pamphlet, of Twelve-pence, or Six-pence Price, can be started into the World, but the next Day you shall have it Bastardiz'd [and] . . . Bawl'd about for a Penny or Two-pence, nay, sometimes for a Half-penny, in every Gossipping Alley, amongst Porters Wives and Basket-Women."

Mandeville's new and expanded edition introduced some philosophical and pragmatic musings into his poetic text. He suggested that all forms of trade—including quite respectable, legal ones—were deceptive. "Where trade is considerable, fraud will intrude," he wrote. As an example, he asserted that there were "innumerable Artifices, by which Buyers and Sellers out-wit one another, that are daily allowed of and practised among the fairest of *Dealers.* Shew me the *Tradesman* that has always discover'd the Defects of his Goods to those that cheapen'd them; nay, where will you find one that has not at one time or other industriously conceal'd them, to the detriment of the *Buyer?* Where is the Merchant that has never against his Conscience extoll'd his Wares beyond their Worth, to make them go off the better?"

To be fair, Mandeville was not the first to notice this predisposition for cheating in commerce. As far back as the ancient Greeks, thinkers have considered making money through buying and selling a suspicious activity. Aristotle, for instance, differentiated economics—which he defined as the skills involved in managing a household—from creating wealth through trading. "There is no bound to the riches which spring from this art of wealth-getting," he wrote. To Aristotle, this potential of unlimited financial gain was a problem because it could turn people from the more important goal of living a good life to the kind of conniving that went along with the pursuit of profit. In fact, he reported approvingly, the city-state of Thebes barred merchants from holding public office unless they had been out of the trading life for a decade. In the fifth century of the modern era, Pope Leo IV expressed the dominant view of trade and exchange when he opined, "It is difficult for buyers and sellers not to fall into sin." And, in the 1400s, the great Muslim philosopher/historian Ibn Khaldun noted the link between trickery and trade: "Cunning, willingness to enter into disputes, cleverness, constant quarrelling, and great persistence. These are things that belong to commerce," he wrote. "Commerce is a natural way of making profits. However, most of its practices and methods are tricky and designed to obtain the (profit) margin between purchase prices and sale prices. The surplus makes it possible to earn a profit. Therefore, the law permits cunning in commerce, since (commerce) contains an element of gambling."

As trade grew and became more of a normal activity in society, the dishonesty that Ibn Khaldun noted came to be accepted and, in Mandeville's case, celebrated. Mandeville's prescription for society could be read as a tribute to the power of business in all its forms. "The great art then to make a nation happy and what we call flourishing consists in giving everybody an opportunity of being employed, which to compass, let a government's first care be to promote as great a variety of manufactures, arts, and handicrafts, as human wit can invent. . . . It is from this policy, and not the trifling regulations of lavishness and frugality, (which will ever take their own course, according to the circumstances of the people) that the greatness and felicity of nations must be expected." Mandeville's concern was growth and employment, and it's likely he would have argued that successful brands and successful counterfeits both have their place in the market because they increase employment and increase consumption. This doesn't sound far from China's current domestic economic policy.

Almost from the day he published his singsong poem, Mandeville has been caricatured as extolling what might be called frat-house capitalism—no rules and all risk. But the truth is far more complex. For instance, Mandeville scandalized contemporary audiences when he argued that the government should open its own licensed brothels and should pass laws to put private whorehouses out of existence. He argued that these royally chartered houses of prostitution—"publick stews," he called them—would be honest, law abiding, healthy for clients and sex workers, and would cut down on extramarital affairs among the aristocracy. It may have sounded lunatic to his contemporaries, but Mandeville's argument amounts to a plea for government intervention and regulation (you might call him a closet Keynesian) of an industry gone awry. Even the simple rhymes of *The Grumbling Hive* show that Mandeville favored some government intervention in the market: "Vice is beneficial found / when it's by justice lopp'd and bound."

Adam Smith, too, acknowledged that merchants could be expected to manipulate trade for their own gain. "The interest of the dealers, however, in any particular branch of trade or manufacture, is always in some respects different from, and even opposite to, that of the public," he wrote in *The Wealth of Nations*, adding that "the proposal of any new law or regulation of commerce which comes from this order, ought always to be listened to with great precaution, and ought never to be adopted till after having been long and carefully examined, not only with the scrupulous, but with the most suspicious attention. It comes from an order of men, whose interest is never exactly the same with that of the public, who have generally an interest to deceive and even to oppress the public, and who accordingly have, upon many occasions, both deceived and oppressed it." Though he disagreed with Mandeville's endorsement of unbridled spending and consumption, Smith credited his forebear with getting close to the essence of human behavior. "How destructive soever this system may appear," Smith wrote of Mandeville's *The Fable of the Bees*, "it could never have imposed upon so great a number of persons, nor have occasioned so general an alarm among those who are the friends of better principles, had it not in some respects bordered upon the truth."

Indeed, an honest look at the history of trade shows that piracy wasn't just a form of trade; it was also a potent force that drove the growth of arts and culture. In particular, piracy helped expand literacy and impacted the Western intellectual tradition in some startling ways. Starting in the 1500s, street hawkers and ballad criers (so named because they sang bawdy songs in public squares to attract buyers and make their sales) were the largest sellers of books in Europe. They pushed literacy into the countryside, carrying popular literature and almanacs, and the editions they sold were most often not authorized. By the start of the 1700s, pirate book hawkers were outselling legal stores, prompting Amsterdam's booksellers to push the city government for protectionist legislation that would ban street selling (behind the scenes, many licensed booksellers were supplying the street trade as well as crying out against it—because canny businesspeople always find a way to make a profit). Book hawkers and street singers were so common that some publishers began to issue editions designed especially for the street trade. Church groups even got in on the act. They understood that unlicensed street selling could be a useful way to spread the gospel and hired roving peddlers to sell Bibles and hand out religious tracts.

Indeed, in eighteenth-century London, it was a street hawker's pirated penny editions that restored the reputation of a long-dead Elizabethan dramatist whose plays had once been popular but had dropped from public attention. A hundred years after his death in 1616, William Shakespeare had fallen hard. His plays, when they were produced, were largely gutted through additions, adaptations, abridgments, and emendations. Contemporary dramatists routinely fashioned new soliloquies and scenes, and completely rewrote some of the plays. *King Lear* was remade with a happy ending. *The Tempest* was tricked out as an opera with special effects. One adapter created a mash-up *Merchant of Venice* with music and visits from ghosts—a proto-*Fiddler on the Roof*. *Macbeth* was staged as a musical, with singing, dancing, and flying witches—Birnam Wood come to Neverland. By the early 1700s, the bowdlerized and brightened versions had elbowed the original Shakespeare aside. Publisher Jacob Tonson put out a pricey new edition of the complete plays every fourteen years—this was enough to secure his perpetual copyright—but there were no other editions of Shakespeare on the market.

Enter Robert Walker. This small-time London printer and publisher had a big idea. Walker believed that Shakespeare would sell if the plays were published at a cheap price; in 1734, he announced a new program to bring out the entire run of Shakespeare's plays. Each play would be published in four parts. Each part would sell for a penny, and the whole play could be had for four pence. The first play he issued this way was the one he thought would be the easiest to sell: *The Merry Wives of Windsor*.

Tonson threatened to sue. He vowed to have Walker incarcerated. The renegade publisher responded with a public advertisement vowing not to back down: "These mighty men," he wrote, "think that by their great Purses they shall be enabled to pull Mr. Walker down, but Mr. Walker is a Man of Resolution, and such they'll find him, who will not be frighted by their insolent Threats." Tonson then made a backroom offer to buy Walker off, but the pamphleteer turned him down.

So Tonson decided to outhustle the hustler. He announced that he, too, would publish single editions of all of Shakespeare's plays. But Tonson decided to flood the market, distributing ten thousand copies of each play, and selling them to hawkers for a penny a play, undercutting Walker's already steeply discounted price by 75 percent. Tonson also enlisted some well-regarded literary figures to devalue Walker's books, recruiting the prompter of the Drury Lane Theatre, for instance, to write that Walker's Shakespeare offered only "useless, pirated and maimed Editions."

Walker lost the price war to the guy with deeper pockets—and ultimately dropped out of the business. But their war of printed words had an important literary result. Shakespeare's plays were suddenly available all over London at rock-bottom prices—something that had never been true even in the playwright's lifetime. For almost a century prior to the Tonson/Walker dispute, most of Shakespeare's oeuvre had neither been published in a single-play edition nor produced onstage in anything but a massively modified adaptation. Over the course of a few months in 1734, everything became available in its original form.

The result was a resurgence of interest in Shakespeare. In the first two years after the price war, the works of Shakespeare, which had almost dropped out of production, were suddenly back in vogue. By 1738, one in five plays performed on a London stage was by Shakespeare. And soon thereafter the era of adaptation and emendation came to an end. Audiences were once again ready for a King Lear who didn't live happily ever after.

If the pirate and the publisher had not sold Shakespeare's works to the masses for a penny a play, it's possible that the Bard of Avon might never have been rediscovered. He might have simply been one among the legion of minor Elizabethan dramatists. A century after the playwright's death, piracy helped make William Shakespeare a household name, helped promote literacy across the social classes (because even poor people could consider coughing up a penny a play), and helped install Shakespeare's writings as the pinnacle of English usage.

In music, too, piracy was on the scene long before the file-sharing era. Ludwig van Beethoven was typical in his relation to piracy: he both protested it and put it to use. In 1803, when a little-known arranger named Carl Zulehner started out in publishing, one of the first pieces he printed was Beethoven's—the Opus 2 Piano Sonatas from 1796. But Zulehner didn't own the rights to the works and Beethoven fought back, informing the *Wiener Zeitung* that Zuleh-ner was "a piratical engraver" who had stolen his work and introduced unauthorized changes. Yet the matter was not as clear-cut as Beethoven imagined. It turned out that the legal publisher of the Opus 2 Piano Sonatas, the Italian firm Artaria, had looked the other way when other pirated edi-tions were made across Europe and had itself pirated other works by Beethoven, apparently with the composer's consent. And although Beethoven may have embarrassed Zulehner, he couldn't stop the pirated publication from being repirated in all the major cities of the continent. Ultimately, B. Schott's Sons, a large and legitimate firm that would go on to pub-lish two of Beethoven's late masterworks—the Ninth Sym-phony and the Missa Solemnis—bought Zulehner's plates and reprinted the supposedly degraded edition. Each of the pirate editions offered minor variations in the score—and in some cases the pirates corrected errors that had escaped the proofreaders for the 1796 original. (Indeed, it was not unknown for pirates to improve the works they stole. For instance, the German novelist Hans Jakob Christoffel von Grimmelshausen, whose seventeenth-century novel *Simpli-cius Simplicissimus* was a contemporary best seller, wound up adopting some of the changes and illustrations that had been introduced in one of the pirate versions of his book when he put out an authorized third edition.)

At the same time, other publishers used the existence of piracy to try to drive down the price they would have to pay composers for the rights to their work. When Beethoven demanded that the big German firm Breitkopf pay a high fee for the right to print some new scores, the publisher rebelled. "It has unfortunately come to pass that in Germany the profit from the publication of a significantly new original work benefits many publishers but not the rightful one," the firm wrote in a letter to the composer. "Since he cannot sell his work as cheaply as the pirate reprinter can, the rightful publisher thus finds far less market for the original edition."

Breitkopf's fear wasn't misplaced. Pirates sometimes did make far more profit off their unauthorized editions than legal publishers did. For instance, in a more modern piracy row, this one in the United States, a number of the pirate publishers of the ninth edition of the *Encyclopedia Britannica* added entries that were of particular interest to the U.S. audience. All told, their versions sold twice as many copies as the legal edition did.

Culturally important piracy continues to this day. In an entertaining article in the literary magazine *Granta*, novelist Daniel Alarcón detailed how book piracy is serving to promote literature in contemporary Peru. Alarcón, who was born in Peru but lives in the United States and writes in English, reported that in Lima, more books are sold in pirated editions than in official versions. Peru's pirate publishing industry actually employs more people than the legal one and earns just as much money. The country's novelists and story writers, it turns out, don't particularly mind this, since most people can't afford to purchase legal editions, and thus they depend on piracy for readership. "Being pirated,"

Alarcón wrote, "is the Peruvian equivalent of making the bestseller list." Alarcón followed the fate of the translation of his own new book. The authorized edition retailed for fifty soles, or about $18, which might be a reasonable price in the United States, but is approximately a fifth of the average Peruvian's weekly salary, making it doubtful that any but the most devoted (and richest) readers would buy it. The pirate publishers do market research, follow the cultural pages of the local newspapers, and attend the annual book fair. Their profits depend on knowing which books generate buzz and will probably sell. So Alarcón was disappointed that, after several weeks in Peru, he hadn't found his book in the pirate kiosks. Hours before he was due to leave, he made one more venture into the marketplace and finally found a copy. The street vendor demanded twelve soles, but, hewing to street market tradition, Alarcón bargained him down to ten.

In Peru, as in much of the world, a majority of people see buying pirated bags, books, or computer programs as a necessity and not a crime. It's simply a low-cost alternative to the high cost of legal and name-brand products. Studies of consumer behavior in China have shown that people consider the pirated item as just one more choice in the marketplace, and, if they had enough money, they reported that they would buy the real thing rather than the pirated version.

To be fair, the pirates of old were different from today's pirates. Privateers like Sir Francis Drake, who plundered other people's stockpiles and warehouses, have little in common with the book pirates of Peru. Drake's business was to steal what others had produced, and he and his crew had to go out and take it by force. Today's pirates, by contrast, mostly manufacture or sell fakes. They depend on the world of patents and intellectual property protections to produce the goods they copy. And their businesses are limited only by their productive capacity. Many of today's pirates are held back only by the speed of their DVD drives.

The Business Software Alliance, an industry group that tracks unlawful copying, has estimated that global piracy in 2008 cost software companies $53 billion. That year, according to the group's statistics, 41 percent of all software installed on computers around the world was pirated. In the United States—which has tough laws against piracy and is actually one of the more law-abiding, piracy-free countries of the world—the BSA's statistics showed that one in five computer programs was pirated.

The BSA however, seems to be engaging in a bit of creative exaggeration. For instance, if you bought a program and allowed your boyfriend or your kids to copy it, you're a pirate, according to the BSA. The lobbying group operates as if there's no difference between sharing a program with your kids or purchasing a pirated copy, or even producing thousands of copies of OS X or Windows 7 or Photoshop. The BSA's piracy report doesn't distinguish among these things, so it's impossible to know where the bulk of the problem lies.

The money statistic the BSA promotes is also juiced. That's because the BSA assumes that every pirated program represents a sale not made, and that, if a buyer purchased that program, he or she would pay full retail price. But, given the high prices of many of the most popular programs (Photoshop, for instance, retails for $699), that's a debatable proposition. In most cases, it's precisely because they can't afford to buy the legitimate disks that people ask others to share their software with them or buy a knockoff disk. A decade or so ago, I got a friend to give me a pirated copy of the home publishing program Quark. It didn't matter that some of the instructions and copyright information were written in

Cyrillic, as long as I could figure out how to use it. But once I got a new computer, and the pirated software was no longer compatible with the new operating system, I didn't go out and buy Quark. Instead, I made do without it. Many computer users work like this. The genuine programs are simply too expensive to be a reasonable option. This means that that figure of $53 billion lost to piracy is unreliable at best.

Finally, buried in the fine print of the group's statistics, there's this: "Businesses, schools, and government entities tend to use more pirated software on new computers than ordinary consumers do." This is an extraordinary statement— because it means that the biggest consumers of pirated programs on new computers have nothing to do with System D. Instead, they are legal companies, doing legal work. Indeed, as the report suggests, the government—the same entity that the industry is calling upon to police piracy—is actually one of the largest patrons of pirated software.

I had a small run-in with this kind of semiofficial piracy in one of my early jobs in journalism. The publication where I worked—a formal, incorporated, taxpaying entity— composed its pages using what was then a popular text layout program. But the owners had ordered the IT staff to save money by purchasing just a single licensed copy of the program. Even so, it was installed on as many as fifty different workstations. After a few weeks of heavy use, the program crashed and the publisher had to bring in some techies from the manufacturer to fix the problem. The night before they arrived, our nervous IT chief clomped around the office removing the program from all the terminals except his own. Two days later, after the software savants had fixed the glitch and left town, our IT guy came back with the disk and reinstalled it on all our desktops. The result—at least according to the BSA: forty-nine cases of piracy.

It's simple risk-benefit economics: the high price of computer programs encourages piracy. If the price difference were equalized, piracy would be squeezed out of business. As economist Joseph Stiglitz told me, "If you have strong intellectual property rights where, in effect, there are excessive fees for use of those rights, you create an incentive for somebody to go underground."

There's a serious debate about piracy in the online world, and there are many who argue that the way to combat piracy is to welcome it, with free downloads and open source coding. This, so the argument goes, can be just as much a business model as high prices and restricted access. Indeed, Bill Gates said as much on being asked about the extent of Chinese piracy of the Windows operating system. "As long as they're going to steal it, we want them to steal ours," the Microsoft founder said.

Of course, Gates can afford to be blasé about piracy. He has amassed one of the world's largest fortunes selling legal copies of MS-DOS and the various versions of Windows. For Microsoft, building market share is a valuable thing, and if piracy means that more people are using Microsoft's programs, that's good for business, whether Gates gets dollars for each sale or not. For smaller outfits—think a small software publisher or a single book author, people who depend on royalties for their livelihood—piracy is much more of a mixed bag. Daniel Alarcón may be amused by book piracy in Peru, but if his sales in the United States were eroded by pirate publishers, he'd make no money as an author. There may be benefits to achieving the kind of market penetration widespread piracy can offer: for instance, popular bands like Radiohead have found that they can offer free downloads of their songs on the Web and build their profits from selling tickets to their concerts. But bands that don't have the huge following of Radiohead or software manufacturers whose products aren't as ubiquitous as those sold by Microsoft undoubtedly have a harder time making a decent living if people continue to pirate their works.

Still, some argue that certain highly competitive industries actually benefit from piracy. Take the business of high fashion. In a series of spirited essays, law professors Kal Raustiala and Christopher Sprigman have argued that piracy actually helps the fashion houses, because it spurs demand for new styles. The fashion industry, they note, is governed by a speeded-up version of planned obsolescence—which the professors have labeled "induced obsolescence." For the industry to make money, today's must-have designer item must become tomorrow's stale has-been. Piracy helps this process, they note, because nothing stays cutting-edge once it becomes ubiquitous. So, just as Walker's penny-a-play war with Tonson fueled demand for Shakespeare, the mass production of counterfeits helps fuel consumer demand, which forces designers to innovate and bring out new patterns and styles. And this, Raustiala and Sprigman note, is actually exactly what the fashion industry needs for continued success.

What's more, though many of fashion's biggest houses decry piracy and claim it costs them a massive amount of money, that may not be the full story either. In *Gomorrah*, his in-the-belly-of-the-beast study of the Mafia in suburban Naples, Roberto Saviano pointed out that if pouty models on runways were the only people who wore high-end items, there would be no money in high fashion. The mob makes both the originals and the knockoffs, but only the counterfeits are affordable and available in the larger sizes regular people can fit into. "Not only did the clans not create any symbolic competition with the designer labels," Saviano wrote, "they actually helped promote products whose market price made them prohibitive to the general public." Piracy, in short, mainlines high-fashion names into low-fashion people's consciousnesses. It is free brand advertising, and makes luxury items part of mainstream dreams. As an anonymous executive of a major sneaker manufacturer recently admitted in *The New York Times Magazine*, piracy is a nuisance, but it doesn't really impact the bottom line.

In my last week in Guangzhou, I went with a friend for a final visit to the counterfeit watch market behind the main train station. We entered under a giant banner advertising the market's crackdown on piracy and walked through galleries where hundreds of kiosks glinted with thousands of Rolexes and Rados—not a genuine one in the mix. It was still morning and there weren't too many people in the market. Many of the salespeople drank tea or rested their heads on the glass shelves of their kiosks.

We walked up to one brightly lit display, roused the salesperson, and asked to look at a clean-looking counterfeit Rado—no fake diamonds, just a jet-black dial set off by slender radiant hands. The clerk unlocked the display case and handed over the timepiece. "Three hundred yuan," she said with a yawn. Forty-four dollars. Then she asked if she could look at my friend's watch.

He is Chinese, but his family lives abroad, and on one of his recent trips to see them, he had bought a new watch. A Rolex. A real one. He unhooked the band and handed it over.

I fumbled with the fake. It looked good, but I was no expert. I had never even heard of Rado. I had no idea what I should look for. The clerk, by contrast, flipped the fancy watch in her fingers like a magician doing a card trick, twiddling it over and over as she inspected the metalwork on the back and sides.

After a minute or so, I handed the counterfeit timepiece back with my apologies. I wasn't ready to buy. She didn't care. She slid the genuine watch gently over my friend's wrist and fastened the metal band. "That," she announced with reverence, "is a super-high-quality fake."

Back in the 1970s, the German poet and social critic Hans Magnus Enzensberger marveled at the outsize importance luxury brands had achieved around the globe, and asked, "Will no one, not even the Congolese, be spared from wearing underpants designed by a French fashion designer?"

With people like Chief Arthur bringing pirated labels all over the world at prices people can afford, the answer, we now know, is more complex than Enzensberger expected.

Can Anybody Tell Me
How to Get to the Bridge?

Not many people are scrupulous about smuggling, when, without perjury, they can find an easy and safe opportunity of doing so.

—*The Wealth of Nations*

Juan V. Ramirez was an immigrant success story. Born and raised in Paraguay, he went to college in Massachusetts and, after graduation, got a well-paying position in information services at Northwestern University Law School in the leafy Chicago suburb of Evanston. But, after nine years in the United States, he chucked the prestige and stability of the academic life and decided to pursue a business opportunity that involved a very different relationship to the law. He returned to his native land to open a business designed to profit from the trade that smuggles goods across the Paraná River that separates Paraguay from Brazil.

"I come from a family of entrepreneurs," he explained. "My family owns a department store. Retailing's in our blood. We decided to include personal computers in our line of business, and we decided to come to Ciudad del Este to make it happen."

That was August 1991. Ramirez and his brother formed a new company they called PC Tronic and began importing major-brand computers and peripherals (touch pads, mouse pointers, printers, scanners, etc.) from Miami. Despite the fact that they dealt in respected labels like Sony, Logitech, HP, and others, fraud was in PC Tronic's DNA—in two ways. First, his business avoided all customs duties and taxes in Paraguay, often by bribing local officials. Ramirez presents this almost as a public service. "At the time, public employees, government employees, they got very low salaries," he said as he sat in PC Tronic's showroom in the Lai Lai Center, Ciudad del Este's modern computer mall. "So they needed to make extra money. And they got that extra money from us. It wasn't allowed to be honest." Officials demanded payoffs, he said, but handing over the illegal payments was worth it, because they ensured that he could import and export computers without any documentation. Bribery, he told me, made the market "very easy and very flexible." The second type of fraud was inherent in the nature of sales in Ciudad del Este. To this day, two-thirds of PC Tronic's business— approximately $4 million a year—involves smuggling: selling computers to people who illegally carry them across the border into Brazil.

Ramirez's company is actually one of the bit players in the computer market. In 2008, merchants in Ciudad del Este sold more than $1 billion worth of computers and computer components—almost all of them destined to make a clandestine trip across the border to be resold to consumers in Brazil. Add in electronics of all sorts and miscellaneous goods like perfumes, toys, and blankets, and the total smuggling trade in Ciudad del Este amounts to $2.5 billion a year—more than 15 percent of Paraguay's total economic activity.

Where there are borders, there is smuggling. Cross from San Diego, California, into Tijuana, Mexico, and you'll find yourself in a strange land of discount pharmacies. Here, everything from Ativan to Viagra and Zoloft can be had without a prescription and, by U.S. standards, for an extremely low price. Medical tourism is big business at the border. It's illegal, for sure. But it's normal. And it goes on though authorities on both sides of the border know about it. In late 2008, when gas prices in the United States heliumed to more than $4 a gallon, some enterprising California residents turned to a smuggler's version of *Pimp My Ride* to save money: they tricked their cars out with second gas tanks, then headed south of the border, where Mexico's state-run oil monopoly, Pemex, had held prices down. After a fill-up at a Mexican service station, they drove their contraband fuel back across the border. In response, at certain crossings, border agents started inspecting cars for hidden tanks.

Like piracy, smuggling has a long and noble history. Gibraltar, the rocky promontory that presides over the entrance to the Mediterranean Sea, was long a way station for smugglers moving goods from Africa to Europe. For centuries, the Pyrenees offered routes for smugglers, as did the Alps and almost every other natural boundary in Europe. And in times of conflict—wars, sieges, ethnic strife—smuggling always grew in power.

During the postmedieval period, "men and merchandise circulated and worked on the fringe of the law," French scholar Laurence Fontaine has written. "Goods were transported along routes where it was possible to avoid customs and tolls, especially when some of the goods were of smuggled origin, as was the case with raw wool and, in particular, tobacco, which was grown on a large scale (despite the ban on this) in the Alpine valleys of Lombardy and processed in the towns of the Rhine where the laws were more flexible. As soon as a new market opened up or circumstances allowed and, in particular, as soon as war began, smuggling and illicit warehouses multiplied." In fact, most wars are good for business. As Mother Courage tells her entourage in Bertolt Brecht's play about a street peddler in medieval Europe's Hundred Years' War, "I won't let you spoil my war for me. Destroys the weak, does it? Well, what does peace do for 'em, huh? War feeds its people better." While Brecht's words may sound shocking today, they're not much different from what some respected economists have said. As Joseph Schumpeter, one of the great economic phrasemakers, put it, "No bourgeoisie ever disliked war profits." Indeed, wartime profiteering extends to the modern era and to some conflicts that are considered far too noble and high-minded to have involved smuggling and profiteering. For instance, in order to channel the nation's resources for World War II, the United States instituted stringent price controls. Yet, all across the land, people and producers smuggled products across state lines and price-gouged with impunity. As much as 80 percent of the nation's meat was sold above the price the government mandated, along with 60 to 90 percent of the country's lumber and one-third of all clothing. Gas was strictly rationed, but 2.5 million gallons a day disappeared, to be sold on the black market. And this doesn't count counterfeited ration coupons. "Everyone is crooked, including myself," a meat merchant told an industry study group. As one Roosevelt administration official later noted, profiteering was the norm, not the aberration: "There can be no question that it extended throughout the entire nation, from the thief and counterfeiter to the businessman, at all levels of our economic structure, from consumer to large manufacturer." When it came to making money, the "good war" was no different from any other war: it spawned a healthy System D.

Ciudad del Este—where Argentina, Brazil, and Paraguay bump up against one another—is not a war zone. But different laws and different tax systems in the three countries have made it a mecca for organized smuggling. Essentially, Paraguay has no taxes and no customs duties, whereas in Brazil and Argentina, taxes and fees can add as much as 90 percent to the cost of a consumer item. Slipping things across the border—almost anything, from appliances to underwear to Xbox consoles—can be incredibly lucrative. And there's no shortage of demand. Brazil's population—190 million—is more than thirty times Paraguay's 6.2 million. Low prices in the small country, high prices in the big one: the equation is that simple. As one Ciudad del Este businessman put it, jerking his thumb toward the massive country just across the wide brown river, "We're here because of this giant next door to us."

This Paraguayan outpost on the banks of the Paraná was hacked out of the jungle in 1957 and christened Puerto Flor de Lis. The new city quickly rebranded itself Puerto Presidente Stroessner, in honor of army commander Alfredo Stroessner, Paraguay's dictator from 1954 to 1989. When the brutal strongman was overthrown, the city astutely changed its name once again, to Ciudad del Este. In 1965, the Ponte da Amizade, the Friendship Bridge, reached across the river to link the tiny Paraguayan border town to its sister city in Brazil, Foz do Iguaçu. The opening of the bridge gave the little Paraguayan town a chance to create a new identity. As the name of the Brazilian city implies, the main draw to the region was the jaw-dropping assemblage of two hundred and seventy cataracts called Iguaçu Falls—a waterfall so majestic that UNESCO has designated it a World Heritage site. Paraguay doesn't have any of the falls—they are shared by Brazil and Argentina—so the country looked for a distinct advantage that would pull tourists in its direction in what has come to be called the triborder region. And it found its calling in smuggling.

"Ciudad del Este wasn't supposed to be a city," said Jeffrey W. Hesler, general director of the city's office of the Paraguayan American Chamber of Commerce. "It was a frontier town that just grew in a completely unplanned way." Today, the street market surges right up to the bridge, with vendors selling the slotted silver straws and leather-clad cups that are used for sipping *terere*, the cold infusion of *yerba mate* with mint, lemongrass, and other herbs that is Paraguay's national drink. Though the city's newer buildings are stylish and modern, much of central Ciudad del Este has a shantytown feel. The Jebai Center, one of the city's older shopping malls, would look at home in a Rio de Janeiro *favela*. Its hallways are dingy and packs of exposed wiring hang off the ceilings and drape over doorways. Plumbing, too, is a challenge. The city government periodically declares the Jebai Center a firetrap and moves to close it. But it's an empty threat. The business of Ciudad del Este is business, and the government can't risk impeding it, because the smuggling in this one town with just 5 percent of Paraguay's population generates an outsized proportion of Paraguay's gross domestic product. In this landlocked country bordered by much larger and more prosperous nations, smuggling has become one of the keys to growth, and, in pure economic terms, Ciudad del Este is the most important city in the country. The city may not bring in much tax revenue or customs duty, but it generates a tremendous amount of trade, employment, and wealth.

"Ciudad del Este really doesn't require anything additional from the central government," Ramirez said. "It's the reverse. The national government needs us."

Here at the border, money talks in tongues. Things can be purchased with the local currency—the Paraguayan guarani—but also with Argentine pesos, Brazilian reais, and with the Esperanto of unofficial global trade—U.S. dollars. If you need to convert your money, or are making a large purchase and need to arrange a money transfer, there are agencies all over town. There are itinerant guys with whom you can negotiate the rate but whose currency might be counterfeit. There are crude kiosks where the rates are scrawled on chalkboards. There are well-established firms with computers and security guards. And there are a bunch of money transfer outfits, many with official-looking signs calling themselves Western Union, though some of them undoubtedly aren't. In Ciudad del Este, most businesses post their prices in dollars, though, in the smaller stores, you can often get a better deal if you pay in guarani.

Smuggling is so important to the economies on both sides of the border that it runs according to a schedule. Many Brazilian smugglers show up in Foz do Iguaçu on Tuesday mornings, engage in a series of highly public cross-border raids for the next twenty-four hours, and disappear on Wednesday evenings. They're called *sacoleiros*, and they travel back and forth across the bridge on Tuesdays and Wednesdays. Their name derives from a simple fact: they depart for the border carrying empty sacks and come home lugging those same sacks but this time overburdened and overloaded.

From all over Brazil, the *sacoleiros* take the bus to Foz do Iguaçu. It's a great national migration every week, and I decided to make the trek, too. I took the overnight bus from São Paulo, ready to interview any merchants I found. The result: *nada, nenhum,* nothing, no one. There wasn't a single merchant on the bus. Just a bunch of college students on break, a few older people going to visit relatives in the hinterland, and some Canadian backpackers heading to the falls. It was only much later, when I returned to São Paulo, my notebook still as empty as a *sacoleiro's* sack at the beginning of the great journey, that I found out what a fool I had been.

When I journeyed to Foz do Iguaçu, I took the bus from Rodoviaria Tietê, one of the city's official bus stations. But that's not how the smugglers operate. As might be expected, their bus station is totally unofficial, on a corner on Avenida Senador Queirós, just a block away from the massive street market on Rua 25 de Março where illegal street sellers do business openly. There's nothing to mark their depot—and why should there be, since it's not a legal bus station—and it operates only two days a week, one for pickups and one for dropoffs. As dusk falls on Mondays, a dozen chartered buses queue here for passengers. Several hundred people gather in the two small *lanchonetes* (luncheonettes) on the block, ready to make the sixteen-hour journey. Outside each bus, a man or a woman with a clipboard registers the name of each rider.

But it's hard to believe that this is where the famed *sacoleiros* start their journey—because these *sacoleiros* carry no sacks. Their buses, it turns out, are the sacks. The buses are chartered for the *sacoleiros* by businessmen who work closely with some of the biggest retailers along Rua 25 de Março. And the *sacoleiros*, at least in São Paulo, are no longer the brave and independent entrepreneurs of yore, who made the sixteen-hour journey to the border to get a tiny profit and a leg up on the competition. Rather, they are hired to buy goods for the big businesses on Rua 25 de Março.

When the buses—all of them marked *"tourismo"* even if they are not for tourism—arrive in Foz do Iguaçu Tuesday afternoon, they don't go to the bus station and they don't go downtown and they certainly don't go to the falls. Rather, they head straight for the Friendship Bridge. Here, just before you cross into Paraguay, are dozens of odd businesses that advertise their identity with crude hand-painted signs. They're called *"guarda-roupas"*—which, without the hyphen, means "wardrobes" or "armoires," but in this context might more accurately be rendered as checkrooms—and they are generally located next to tired little cafés, places with a smattering of food and a refrigerator full of beer and far more plastic tables and chairs than would seem to be required by the scant clientele that's around on most evenings. These businesses are virtually empty from Thursday through Monday. They make their money on Tuesdays and Wednesdays.

The buses get to the *guarda-roupas* early Tuesday afternoon. That leaves at least twenty-four hours for work. Each of the *sacoleiros* gets a shopping list and heads over to Ciudad del Este. Each person brings back the goods on his or her list: blankets, plastic trash cans, brooms, underwear, perfume, liquor, beer, toys. Tuesday afternoon and all day Wednesday, the *sacoleiros* prowl the streets and malls of Ciudad del Este, make their purchases, then take moto-taxis to the center of the bridge, where they queue in long lines to have their stuff inspected by the border guards, and then, once they're given the okay, lug the goods down the street to the *guarda-roupas*, where the coordinator with the clipboard ticks off the items that they have purchased. They stash them in the *guarda-roupas*, then head back for more shopping. In the evening, they hang out at the cafés near their *guarda-roupas*. Generally, they sleep either in run-down rooming houses near the bridge or on the buses. By Wednesday afternoon, the coordinator starts taking all the goods out of the *guarda-roupa*. He and the driver stuff all the merchandise in the luggage hold of the bus. Whatever can't fit there will have to be shoehorned in with the *sacoleiros* in the seats.

Late on a Wednesday afternoon, their final shopping trips complete, a group of *sacoleiros* sat drinking beer, waiting for their compatriots to gather so they could stuff the bus full of merchandise and make the run back to their home city. It looked like it would be a long wait. First, there's a time zone difference, and it's an hour earlier in Paraguay than it is in Brazil, so when businesses close on the Brazilian side, they're still open in Paraguay. And at this hour, the border is busy, so it may take several hours for people to get their purchases through. But this bunch had made it back to the *guarda-roupa*.

They were reddened from a full day of haggling in the hot sun. The beer bottles mounted up (they were drinking Budweiser, the U.S. beer, another product commonly smuggled from Ciudad del Este to Foz do Iguaçu) and they got increasingly boisterous. Drink now, they said, and sleep on the bus. Only the manager with the clipboard had to be alert. He still had some items that hadn't been checked off.

A *camelô* passed. He was selling pirated CDs and DVDs that had also come across the border. The *sacoleiros* called him over. They took turns flipping through the DVDs—a combination of first-run, martial arts, and hard-core porn. Finally, long after sunset and after many more beers, the bus was ready to depart. The *sacoleiros* were drunk enough to sleep, no matter how cramped the seats.

The buses leave Foz do Iguaçu Wednesday night and get back to São Paulo in the middle of the day Thursday. That way, the goods the *sacoleiros* buy will be on the streets and in the stores by the time Friday and Saturday—the big shopping days in the market on Rua 25 de Março—roll around.

This three-day round trip to the border also offers one additional advantage to the charter bus companies. Any seats not reserved for the *sacoleiros* are offered to ordinary travelers for half the price it costs to take the official bus—sixty reais instead of a hundred and twenty-nine one-way.

So why does the trade happen this way? How can it possibly make sense to pay all these people and charter all these buses just to stock up on a bunch of small-margin items like brooms and cheap Chinese carpets and plastic garbage cans? The answer involves taxation and customs duty. Paraguay essentially charges no tax in Ciudad del Este. Brazil, by contrast, has a value added tax called the ICMS—*Imposto sobre Circulação de Mercadorias e prestação de Serviços* (tax on goods and services.) The ICMS levy varies for different products, and it's hard to figure out what the actual tax rate is. This is exacerbated by the fact that different taxes are computed on top of one another. But here are some things that merchants have suggested: In Brazil, 42 percent of the price of soap powder and toys comes from the ICMS. Sheets and blankets: 37 percent. Cigarettes: beyond 80 percent. The ICMS accounts for almost 37 percent of the price of coffee and 38 percent of the retail price of underwear and sneakers. And these figures don't include state and municipal taxes. All told, the various levies in Brazil can make up 90 percent of the price of what you buy.

And then there's the policy at the border. Knowing that many families trek to the border for cheap shopping, Brazil passed a law allowing each person coming back from Paraguay to bring $300 worth of purchases into Brazil duty free and another $200 more at a reduced tariff. Anyone who buys more than $500 of goods in Paraguay is considered an importer, and must have a business license and pay customs duty, which can amount to a 60 percent markup.

So merchants from markets like Rua 25 de Março figured out how to openly scam the system. They organize the buses. They organize the *sacoleiros*. They reap the profits. And the profits are not small. If thirty people on a bus buy $500 worth of goods each, that's $15,000 worth of merchandise that can be shuttled from the border to the market on each bus. If twelve buses made the trip, that would be $180,000 worth of goods. In a year, that would mean this smuggler's channel between Ciudad del Este and São Paulo would be worth more than $9 million. And that doesn't count discounting. In my experience, prices in Paraguay were often less than one-quarter the price the same item could command on the street in Brazil. So that would boost the street value of the goods brought back on the buses to $36 million. And that assumes that the *sacoleiros* report the actual price they paid in Ciudad del Este. But there are scores of peddlers on the streets close to the foot of the Friendship Bridge who specialize in selling false receipts that mark down the value of your purchases to almost nothing. So it's likely that the value of the goods smuggled across the border is far, far higher. And this is just the trade with São Paulo. Add in almost every other major Brazilian city and the value mounts up.

The computer and electronics smugglers work differently, and are much more secretive. Several players in Ciudad del Este's computer trade told me that the bulk of their sales are not to individuals but to shady bulk purchasers known as *laranjas*, or oranges (no one involved in the trade could give me a reason why they got the name). The *laranjas* move the high-tech goods from Paraguay to Brazil—sometimes by paying off customs workers, sometimes through more creative smuggling—and earn as much as 30 percent of the value of the merchandise they bring across the border. Despite their high fee, their markup is still far less than the amount that customs duty and the value added tax would add to the price of the computers. The *laranjas* may soon face a different sort of competition, though. These days, you can buy a netbook in the United States for less than $300. If the price falls that low in Ciudad del Este, it would be possible for an individual to walk one across the border legally, tax- and duty-free. It will be interesting to see how the local computer firms, and the *laranjas* who do the smuggling, cope with the low prices computers now command.

Indeed, an individual who was willing to walk across the border several times could conceivably bring through lots of computers (or, indeed, other items) duty-free. I crossed the Friendship Bridge several dozen times, both on foot and on the public bus, and was stopped only once, when I was asked to show my passport. The border guards never asked me to open my shoulder bag, though it could have contained hun-

dreds of pirated DVDs or dozens of pairs of discount underwear, or three or four laptops.

Of course, smuggling isn't limited to this one border
crossing. It exists all over the world, even at some of the most
unlikely boundary lines. The Sham Chun River, for instance,
separates one country from itself. For decades it was a sleepy
rural outpost, a green suburb in the New Territories of the
former British protectorate of Hong Kong, the site of the last
station on the old Kowloon-Canton Railway (today known as
the MTR East Rail Line, a branch of Hong Kong's subway)
before you entered the People's Republic of China. Shenzhen, across the river, was a placid, picturesque fishing village. Between 1949 and 1979, the only legal way to cross this
border was to hike over the small bridge at Lo Wu.

Then, in the 1980s, China designated Shenzhen a Special Economic Zone, and Guangdong province, in which
the city is located, became a haven for factories. By June 30,
1997, when the British handed Hong Kong back to China,
Shenzhen was poised to challenge the capitalist city to the
south. Today, Shenzhen is almost double the size of Hong
Kong (thirteen million versus seven million.) Most of its residents are migrants from the north, and this has led to another
massive change. As in Hong Kong, the dominant street language in the old fishing village was Cantonese, but the bulk
of people in Shenzhen today speak Mandarin, China's official language. (Both Mandarin and Cantonese use the same
characters, but the pronunciation is vastly different; this is
complicated by the fact that Hong Kong uses what are called
complex characters, while Shenzhen, in keeping with the
central government's policy of modernization, uses simplified
characters, which has made for mass literacy at the expense
of some of the linguistic subtlety and etymological intricacy.)
With all this growth, the former village has become increas-

ingly cosmopolitan. Shenzhen has, in recent years, become a destination for Hong Kong's chic shoppers, attracted by many stores selling well-known brands for less than they cost in central Hong Kong. Some small Hong Kong firms have also jumped the border to Shenzhen, lured by offers of cheaper office space. It's easy for Hong Kong residents to get to Shenzhen (though Shenzhen residents and people from other parts of China still need a special permit to enter Hong Kong). A recent survey by the Chinese University of Hong Kong suggests that almost everyone in Hong Kong journeys to Shenzhen at least once a year. In general, it takes less than twenty minutes to pass through border control.

You might expect, given the ease with which Hong Kong residents can jump back and forth across the border, that savvy Hong Kong shoppers are busy sneaking cheap designer goods or knockoffs into the high-priced high-rise commercial city. But the most surprising aspect of smuggling at Lo Wu is that it goes the other way, too—bringing goods that were made in China back across the border.

The back channel exists because, though China is the manufacturing powerhouse of the high-tech global economy, it still has a highly controlled retail market. Though it makes many of the components that go into iPods, iPhones, and laptops, consumers in China often don't have the opportunity to buy these high-tech devices.

For instance, with the growth of an increasingly upwardly mobile middle class, the demand for smartphones—high-tech mobiles that can browse the Web and shoot video, among other things—has grown in China. But, until recently, the best smartphones weren't available. Smugglers came to the rescue, and police have uncovered tunnels under the Sham Chun where products moved across the border with no control.

Another aspect of Hong Kong–to–China smuggling involves laptop computers. Students and professionals who want good machines report that some major-brand laptops—particularly HP, Sony, and ThinkPad—sell lower-quality machines in China than are available in Hong Kong and the West. And these machines are also more expensive in the People's Republic. For instance, ThinkPad computers, which were once part of the IBM empire and are now manufactured by the Chinese firm Lenovo, are generally one-third cheaper in the United States and Hong Kong than they are in China. This price and quality differential has made smuggling a new distribution channel. Inside China, there are two ways of getting your hands on a smuggled laptop—and both of them are quite open. The first involves going to a store. In Guangzhou, this means going from stall to stall in the high-end computer malls of the Tianhe district. Each of the malls contains scores of different retailers—and any one of those places might stock smuggled computers. The clerks in the stores would never break out a smuggled machine for me, fearing that, as one store manager put it, I might be a spy for one of the computer companies. But one Chinese friend recounted his experience visiting kiosks in Guangzhou's Tianhe neighborhood and asking if they had *zou si*, or smuggled machines. It took all day, but he found one salesman who was willing to show him what he wanted, and he bought it. It was 25 percent cheaper than comparable new machines on display in the store and had a far faster chip and more memory.

The second route to a smuggled machine is online. Another Chinese friend bought his laptop through this route. He emailed the service to specify the exact model he wanted, and, after his clandestine contact quoted a price, arranged to make a down payment. The machine came across the border as if it were someone's personal possession. A different traveler brought through the box, packaging, and instruction manual. These items were reunited once the laptop was inside

China, and, when it arrived in his city, my friend made sure that it worked and paid the balance COD—cash on delivery.

Even in an authoritarian arena, smuggling goes on wherever there's a huge price difference (it could be due to taxes or exchange-rate differences or other factors) or a vast pent-up demand that greatly raises prices. Where profit is possible, smuggling will occur. And it exists in the United States, too. For instance, in 2008, authorities in Michigan estimated that the state was losing $14 million a year because liquor was being smuggled in from neighboring states and from Canada. That, of course, was exactly the point for the smugglers: to evade Michigan's taxes and thus make extra profit on bottles they could carry across the border. Cigarettes, too, are routinely smuggled between states, with boxes and cartons purchases in low-tax states in the south and transported to high-tax states in the north. It's illegal, but also well-known. New York's Indian reservations have a similar trade. The reservations have the legal right to sell smokes tax-free, but businessmen have figured out how to move the tax-free packs off reservation, where they can be resold at a profit.

And, of course, local laws designed to restrict products often promote smuggling by creating artificial scarcity and pent-up demand. That was the case with Prohibition—the constitutional amendment that banned the sale of all but the weakest alcoholic beverages in the United States between 1920 and 1933. Joseph Kennedy speculated on the end of Prohibition—buying liquor before 1933 and selling it immediately after the ban on alcoholic beverages was lifted—and the money helped establish a political dynasty. The Bronfman family purchased a legal liquor empire—Seagram's—with money from bootlegging. Indeed, there was so much alcohol available to those who could pay the smugglers' astronomical prices that humorist Will Rogers commented, "Prohibition is better than no liquor at all."

A few weeks before I got to Ciudad del Este, the Brazilian government decided to crack down on smuggling at the border. Instead of interrupting the *sacoleiros* or raiding the *guarda-roupas*, however, it decided to ban the Paraguayan motorcycle taxi drivers from crossing the bridge without appropriate entry papers. This meant that the *moto-taxistas* would have to have multientry visas to cross the bridge—adding a huge cost to their daily work. The drivers, however, were quick to respond. They blocked traffic on the bridge and, to clear the massive tie-up, the Brazilian government was forced to relent. Still the crazy skirmishing over smuggling continued. The government decided to try a new maneuver: enforcing the helmet law. This was easy for the drivers to handle: within twenty-four hours, most of the *moto-taxistas* in Ciudad del Este had two helmets—one for themselves and one for their passengers.

Smuggling exists because of price differences. Governments know this and often choose to put up with it—and, as in the case of Brazil, even tacitly okay it—because the people who make money from smuggling are powerful and because the public that enjoys the fruits of the smuggling would complain if this pipeline of cheap goods did not exist.

The Upside of Down the Trade

The produce of all great manufactures for distant sale must necessarily depend, not so much upon the dearness or cheapness of the seasons in the countries where they are carried on, as upon the circumstances which affect the demand in the countries where they are consumed.

—*The Wealth of Nations*

Paul Fox chose his words carefully. "No matter the legislative or fiscal structure of the country," he said, "we want to make sure these stores are financially viable."

Fox is the chief of public relations for Procter & Gamble, the $80 billion North American consumer products conglomerate that Linda Chen once dreamed of working for, and like most PR wizards, he's skilled in making hard points sound soft. What he meant, however, was this: P&G has recognized the importance of System D. To this massive company, it doesn't matter if a store is incorporated, if it is registered with its government, if it is paying its taxes, or if it is, in some technical way, breaking the law. No matter the status, Procter & Gamble wants its products to be stocked and sold in that store.

Economists hate System D. Politicians yell about tax evasion and public disorder. Nonprofits protest its low wage structure and lack of employee protections like health insurance and retirement benefits (though to be fair, in much of the world, governments and formal businesses don't offer many of these labor protections either). Sociologists debate its impact on the structure of social relations. But big business does what it always does: it figures out how to use it to make money.

For P&G this process started more than a decade ago. That was when Mariano Martin, who called himself P&G's CCO—chief customer officer (when he retired in June 2009 after thirty-three years with the firm his official title was global customer business officer)—relocated to Latin America. Like most top corporate officials, Martin, who was born and raised in Spain, had spent his professional life in the northern hemisphere, much of it in Cincinnati, Ohio, where the hundred-and-seventy-three-year-old company is based. This was his first visit to the southern hemisphere, and the experience turned the business upside down for him.

Prior to working in the developing world, Martin believed in the traditional business model favored by most multinational companies: the future was to work "up the trade"—catering to the largest retailers. The small-scale mom-and-pop shops that used to predominate in most neighborhoods in the United States and still predominate in the developing world—all the enterprises big businesses call "down the trade"—were not just an afterthought; they were no thought at all. "The idea was that they would probably disappear," Martin explained.

But Martin's time in Latin America showed how people really live outside of the West, and produced some retailing revelations. First, he learned that many of the small stores that were Procter & Gamble's good customers were not stores at all. Some of them were little more than a window cut into someone's living room or a jerry-built kiosk at the side of a dirt road. This should have been enough to drop them from consideration as a valuable market for the massive company. But P&G's market research said something astonishing about these tiny outposts. In the United States, people will make a trip to massive discounters like Walmart or Target or Kmart every couple of weeks, buying supersized boxes and packages of staple products like soap and detergent and diapers, and going home. But people in the developing world visit these tiny stores over and over, often buying a single packet of a single product each time they stop by. "These consumers actually visit these stores five and a half times a week," Martin said, still sounding amazed more than a decade later. The message was clear: unlike the big-box retailers, these small outposts offered a chance for P&G to build deep relationships with consumers. And the numbers told another story, too: "Most of the growth of consumption will come from developing markets. And these markets will not be dominated by larger retailers."

It remains true that Walmart—the Benton, Arkansas–based retailer whose network of eighty-four hundred stores worldwide rang up more than $400 billion in sales in 2009—is P&G's largest single customer, commanding perhaps 15 percent of P&G's business. But the firm that makes global brands like Ivory soap, Downy fabric softener, Pampers, Crest, and Tide has come to understand that, in aggregate, more of its customers shop in those tiny stores than shop at Walmart. (Walmart is undoubtedly hoping to change this trend by expanding into developing countries.)

"Yes, our biggest customer is Walmart," Fox said. "But in reality our largest customer is what we refer to as HFS— high-frequency stores." Indeed more than 20 percent of the company's business now comes from these tiny, less-than-three-cash-register stores in the developing world. "It is our fastest-growing customer, and, in terms of volume, it's our number one customer," Martin said.

So how does a highly formal company, traded on the New York Stock Exchange and regulated by the U.S. government, interact with System D? It turns out to be incredibly simple. When I asked economist Joseph Stiglitz how it could be done, he chuckled at my ignorance: "Basically, you would sell to a wholesaler. The wholesaler would be formal but would not have the same problem selling it through informal channels."

P&G used this exact approach to inaugurate a new distribution scheme in Morocco. The company's market research told them an interesting story: that there were seven thousand tiny villages in the North African nation that didn't have a local store. This, population data told them, represented an untapped market of 1.5 million people. And the company also knew that the trend of migration, which was bringing more young people from the rural areas to the urban agglomerations, meant that many of the same people they might sell to in these villages would at some point wind up in the cities.

The company started a pilot program in Douar Bassia, a community with just fifty households that was fifteen kilometers from the nearest bazaar where residents could make purchases. When P&G got involved, there were no stores in Douar Bassia. So the global multinational decided to create one. The company worked through a local network to pick out a likely and dedicated retailer, choosing a handicapped man and his family. He sells goods out the window of an extra room in his house.

As Stiglitz surmised, P&G did not supply the local retailer directly. Instead, they built a long distribution chain. They supplied their products to a regional distributor, who in turn supplied a branch distributor, who in turn supplied a subdistributor, who supplied a multiple village distributor (essentially a guy with a car and a place big enough to store sufficient goods for a few villages). And that person supplied the local retailer. In Douar Bassia, the village distributor delivered P&G products to stores in thirty small settlements, visiting each village twice a month.

Both the village distributor and the local retailers sell only Procter & Gamble products, but they have no direct relationship with the conglomerate—stocking their products and running contests and inducements through the distributors. Even so, P&G bought paint so the retailer in Douar Bassia could paint the outside of his kiosk to resemble a box of P&G laundry detergent.

As P&G rolled out its village store sponsorship across the country, the global multinational reported that its Moroccan turnover quadrupled. And, it adds, the investment in System D stores has led to a 30 percent increase in profits in Morocco.

Based on that success, P&G is starting to retool the company's efforts in all regions of the world. These days, P&G is developing new products, and new product lines, with those small System D stores in mind.

For instance, Martin said, P&G's staffers in Mexico alerted him to a fact he hadn't previously understood: that water is a scarce commodity in many communities. This prompted a new look at one of the company's signature products—Downy fabric softener. Market research told P&G that people in squatter communities and other areas where water is scarce wanted to use Downy. The biggest barrier to their buying it was not the cost of the fabric softener itself but rather the fact that, because it was formulated for markets like the United States, where most people have washing machines and most washing machines have several rinse cycles, Downy required several rinses to fully wash out of clothes.

Now, the company is developing a new softener specially formulated for the developing world. It hopes that what it calls "Downy Single Rinse"—which, as the name implies, would use far less water than traditional Downy—will wind up being a successful addition and could attract substantial interest in other countries, too.

And Martin suggested that there's a feedback loop that will bring products from the developing world to the developed world. "Look," he said, "not only are there low-income consumers in the developing market, but there are low-income consumers in New York and Chicago, too."

Another massive consumer goods company, the Anglo-Dutch giant Unilever (perhaps best known to Americans for its Knorr, Lipton, Hellmann's, and Dove brands) has also started to acknowledge its connection to System D. In a recent study of its operations in South Africa, Unilever noted that, though the company employs only forty-three hundred workers in the country, its ancillary operations—trucking, distribution, retailing, etc.—created thirty-two thousand System D jobs in the country. The firm estimated that those workers generated forty-three million rand ($5.4 million) in income. The report also noted that almost 75 percent of those jobs are what it calls induced—meaning that they would not exist if Unilever were not active throughout the country. Unfortunately, the report didn't attempt to put a number on the amount of Unilever goods sold through System D or the profit the company makes on those goods. Still, the report shows how closely the success of the company is tied to System D labor. Keith Hart was talking about politicians who profit from under-the-table trade, but he could just as easily have been speaking of multinationals when he told me that "the commercial heights of the informal economy are located at the top of society."

Perhaps the most strikingly visible way in which formal businesses make use of System D is in the mobile phone industry. Along every road in many African and Asian countries—on median strips, on the side streets and main drags, in the middle of highways, at almost every intersection—you can find small plastic tables with umbrellas overhead. They're called umbrella stands and they are the phone booths of the developing world. In the sparse shade offered by those umbrellas, the formal economy meets System D in an extremely direct way.

Nigeria provides a perfect case study. It's the largest country in Africa, with a mobile phone market that seems to have nothing but upside, and a variety of telecom firms are battling for market share.

MTN, a massive multinational based in South Africa and active in twenty-one countries through Africa and the Middle East, had spent years looking for a way to gain a share of the Nigerian market. With a population of close to a hundred and sixty million, Nigeria is Africa's most populous country, and one in six Africans is a Nigerian. The Nigerian market was worth a lot of money. MTN made its first move on Nigeria in 2001. "We tried to replicate the car and phone market of the United Kingdom," Akinwale Goodluck, the general manager of regulatory issues for the company's Nigerian operations, told me. "We wanted all dealers to be registered. They had to get a license from the Nigeria Corporate Affairs Commission. They had to have a business name, to be a registered company." MTN determined that it would sell airtime in three denominations: fifteen hundred naira, three thousand naira, and six thousand naira—$10, $20, and $40—which would be sold only through stores that had the MTN brand.

The result: the plan crashed and burned. Goodluck put it in gentler terms: "It became very glaring that such a 'Rolls-Royce' type of distribution network would not be feasible."

So MTN wrote off the loss and rethought its approach. It concluded that in Nigeria, where even scavengers at the garbage dump have mobile phones, the bulk of its income—perhaps as much as 90 percent—would come from selling pay-as-you-go airtime rather than selling costly monthly plans. And that meant that service had to be cheap and readily available. So MTN came back with a new plan based on umbrella stands. Almost all of its products would be sold by hawkers and street vendors. The cheapest airtime would be offered at a bargain-basement price—a hundred naira, or less than $1—and it would be available all over town. The company dropped its vision of selling phones with the MTN label. It dropped the price of SIM cards to less than $3. And it has ridden this low-priced model to a better than 40 percent share of the Nigerian mobile phone market.

In 2007, MTN had revenues of 73.1 billion rand (approximately $8.78 billion) and earnings of 31.8 billion rand ($3.8 billion), and Nigeria was a big part of that, responsible for one-quarter of MTN's one hundred million customers and 28 percent of the company's cash—or about $2.4 billion per year. And how does MTN earn that $2.4 billion? Almost all of it comes from System D.

Despite their importance to the bottom line, MTN keeps these System D vendors at arm's length. "We don't have a direct relationship with the gentleman or lady on the street," Goodluck said. "We provide merchandise and support through the dealers." What he means is that MTN's game is very similar to P&G's. It sells its recharge cards to distributors, who in turn sell to subdealers, who sell to sub-subdealers, who sell to the folks on the street, who retail the cards to the people who use them.

Most umbrella-stand operators also purchase heavily discounted contracts from MTN and other service providers. If you want to call anywhere in Nigeria on the MTN network—or any other network, for that matter—you can go to your local umbrella stand and make your call for twenty naira (thirteen cents) a minute. Most umbrella-stand operators have several phones with SIM cards from different mobile services, so you can save money by making your call on the network the person you are calling uses. Many people who have their own mobiles nonetheless use the umbrella stands to make calls—because the cost per minute is cheaper. "The umbrella market is a very, very important market now," Goodluck told me. "No serious operator can afford to ignore the umbrella people."

Margaret Akiyoyamen is one such umbrella person. She ran a stand in Lagos for several years and started in the business with just five thousand naira, or about $34, of recharge cards. She knew her customers didn't have lots of cash, so she sold denominations of between only one hundred and three hundred naira. She set up her umbrella, table, and chairs (the setup cost her two thousand naira—or about $13) on the median strip of the street where she lived, Fifth Avenue in Festac Town (in another fixed cost, she gave the local government thirteen hundred naira, or around $10, for a ticket entitling her to do business on that spot). In total, her initial working capital was just eighty-three hundred naira, or a little more than $50. It was a volume business. She got slight discounts on the cards for buying them in bulk from a large distributor, and she used a cheap handset to offer calls for twenty naira a minute.

In the first month, she reported, she recouped her initial investment. After that, Margaret pushed her business forward over the next five months. Six months in, she was buying more than three hundred thousand naira worth of cards every month—sixty times her initial load—and making a profit of forty thousand naira, or about $270—five times the government's minimum wage. Her story shows how much growth there is in the mobile phone industry, how profitable selling airtime can be for sidewalk vendors; we can only imagine how profitable it is for the mobile phone firms themselves.

"It provides a fair amount of gainful sustenance," Goodluck allowed. Indeed, he suggested, the steady profits that street hawkers make from the airtime biz have encouraged people to shift from criminality to card selling, including a number of people who had been dealing drugs. "Even beggars are selling recharge cards," he said.

MTN says it is putting together a database of the sellers and their locations. But there is one thing MTN does not contemplate doing. The company refuses to invest in these merchants who are retailing its recharge cards. "It works nicely as it is," said Goodluck, who has since been named MTN's corporate services executive. "It would not be advisable for us to go out on the street and offer them loans and credit. It's a very informal business. It would not be a safe investment."

It may well be true that hawkers and roadside salespeople are not always the most reliable investments. Some have other jobs (Margaret, for instance, had a day job at an insurance company); others may be lousy at record keeping or suffer through periods of slow sales. A few are undoubtedly fly-by-night operators. This would, indeed, make it tough to invest.

But it does seem as if the company could design a program to work with the sales force that is responsible for the bulk of its income—perhaps a college scholarship program, or a training institute designed to augment the skills of the best roadside distributors. MTN's involvement doesn't have to be limited to investing in the distribution operation. Goodluck smiled uncomfortably at the notion and repeated his mantra: "The system works well as it is."

In many other industries, too, firms have found that System D offers a secure sales force for their products. UAC of Nigeria, for instance, is a hundred-and-thirty-year-old firm with earnings of $200 million. It produces dozens of brands that would be instantly recognizable to all Nigerians and, indeed, to many across West Africa. The company has interests in food, automobiles, and real estate. The firm's stock is publicly traded on the Nigerian Stock Exchange. It's the definition of a highly formal company.

But, with at least one product, the firm makes all its money informally. The Gala sausage roll has been sold in Nigeria since two years after the country won independence from Britain in 1960. For nearly fifty years, Gala has been the go-to product for a quick energy boost. It's ubiquitous, yet you won't find it in any stores or at any snack bars, because Gala is sold almost exclusively by hawkers who line the city's congested expressways and roam the bus depots. UAC does not hire these hawkers. Indeed, the company says it doesn't even know who they are. The hawkers are independent contractors who work for distributors. And the distributors, in turn, are independent firms that buy the sausage rolls in bulk from UAC.

UAC made a conscious decision to sell Gala this way, and, without this large force of street hawkers, no one would be buying Gala, and UAC's profits would decline. But, like MTN, this venerable and profitable formal corporation does not offer any programs for the advancement and education of Gala sellers.

The global firm Inditex, headquartered in Spain, might be the best example of a company that has perfected the art of being both a formal firm and a System D pirate. With more than thirty-six hundred stores around the world, including the high-fashion knockoff chain Zara, Inditex specializes in watching what the big fashion houses have on the runway and making clothes that are inspired by famous designs. Zara's business model is based on getting the clothes from the sketch to the store within two weeks. And, the company promises, no styles stay on the racks for more than two weeks. Zara functions as a pirate in that it is stealing the high-end designs. But, rather than making an exact copy and sewing on a fake brand label, Zara prefers to eyeball the high-end creations and then make a far cheaper garment inspired by the runway. To do this, Zara sends its designers to sketch what they see on the catwalks at the fashion houses, then employs workshops that specialize in quick, cheap turnaround.

The company succeeds because it works through System D, contracting with more than a thousand workshops around the world to buy fabric and get sewing work done. These small workshops combined to produce more than six hundred million items of clothing for the firm in an average year. In a recent annual report, Inditex said it worked with 555 workshops in Spain and Portugal, 396 in Asia, 97 in what it calls non-EU Europe (most of these are in Turkey), 89 in Africa, and 40 in North/South/Central America.

Under pressure from labor activists, Inditex has started a code of conduct for its System D suppliers. But there's one thing Inditex apparently hasn't done: like the banks in Lagos and companies like Procter & Gamble, it refrains from making direct investments in the unlicensed firms with which it does so much business.

Banks, too, avoid investing in System D, though they certainly are open to deposits from unlicensed workers in every informal market in the world. Indeed, you see their branches in the midst of the cacophony of every street market. "We came from nothing, but there is big money here," said James Ezeifeoma, the dealer who has been at Alaba International Market in Lagos for three decades. "You know that because there are fifty banks here." All over the world, the banks go where the money is. The street markets do business in cash—lots of it—and they need someplace to put it. Andrew Saboru, the scavenger/trash dealer from Lagos, has an account. So does Omotola Eleshin, the white-and-green-suited *agbero* who extorts money from the public buses in Lagos. So does

Édison Ramos Dattora, the *camelô* who sells pirated DVDs on the streets of São Paulo. In each country, the banks are happy to take their deposits. But that's where bank services essentially end. The banks don't give loans to people in System D. And even if they did, they would charge their normal interest rates—20 to 30 percent. It's impossible for small merchants to borrow at these rates.

In Lagos, most bank branches are heavily fortified, as if executives were expecting Al Capone to show up with automatic weaponry—and, to be fair, thugs with machine guns do periodically attempt to bust into the branches. Unlike banks in New York, which seem determined make themselves friendlier to people, the banks in Lagos take enormous pains to keep people out. The branches tend to boast bulletproof glass and a security turnstile that prevents anyone who is not authorized from entering. I went to dozens of different bank branches in Alaba and Ladipo to try to interview local branch managers, and the response was always the same: I was accosted by security guards before I could get to the front door. The guards prevented me from going inside. Most often, they would listen to my query, duck inside, and then return after a minute or two with a brochure telling me the address of the main office and would ask me politely to leave. To this day, I have never been able to set foot inside a bank branch in the city. And though I visited all the main offices and petitioned dozens of banks through their public relations people, only one banker agreed to speak with me.

Adegboyega Adebajo is part of the investment banking group at Diamond Bank. With four hundred billion naira—or $2.7 billion—on deposit, Diamond is a solid, midsize player in the country's banking sector. Adegboyega acknowledged that Lagos was a System D city, but he contended that it would not be wise for banks to partner with merchants in the street markets.

"Yes, Lagos is largely informal and banks have noticed this," he said. "The more creative banks are looking to design products that can capture an aspect of this sector. But if we did much of our business in the informal sector, the Central Bank [a combination treasury department and federal bank regulatory agency] would be very unhappy with us. Our expectation is that roadside vendors and other informal merchants need a lot more than money. They need business development assistance and management assistance. The structures of banks as they exist today just do not make it easy to invest in the informal sector. It takes someone who they're going to see all the time and respect and trust."

Besides, he added, what System D merchants want may not coincide with what the bank wants. "Ideally, if I give the woman on the roadside a loan, I'm going to encourage her to save," he said. But this, he added, could be counterproductive from her standpoint. Like Andrew at the garbage dump, who wants to immediately quintuple his working capital, the average roadside vendor would generally want to reinvest all of his or her income into the business, with no reserve fund and no allowance for contingencies. Adegboyega continued, "These businesses have no interest in corporate governance. They're not interested in putting up the kinds of structures to sustain the business beyond the life of the sponsor. Banks try to apply the typical types of investment covenants. We, because of our business of banking, do not have the time a private equity firm would have to do the postinvestment monitoring."

So, he concluded, the banks would continue to operate in one direction only, taking money but not giving loans. Again, a conservative banker would likely approve of this: a large number of System D businesses may be too risky for bank loans. But it does seem unfair that the banks take people's money and give so little back in return.

Historian Fernand Braudel X-rayed this kind of approach a generation ago in his three-volume compendium on the growth and development of our economic system: "It is the biggest private firms which receive state aid and subsidy, whereas banks are supposed to restrict credit to small firms—which amounts to condemning them to vegetate or vanish. There could be no more dangerous policy."

Once Upon a Time in the West

In opulent countries the market is generally so extensive,
that any one trade is sufficient to employ the whole labor
and stock of those who occupy it. Instances of people's living
by one employment, and at the same time deriving some little advantage from another, occur chiefly in poor countries.

—*The Wealth of Nations*

When Emily Miranda lost her job in 2008, she treated it as an
opportunity to become her own boss. A painter with a degree
in design, she figured she would create and fabricate her own
line of jewelry. But there was absolutely no way she could
start her business through the usual route—she didn't have
the money for a business license and she couldn't afford to
rent studio space. So she headed straight to System D.

In her first quasi-legal act, she parked an old trailer in her
Brooklyn backyard. This became her studio. (It's perfectly
legal to have a trailer in your driveway, but to use it as an
unregistered location for an unrecognized business is a bit
sketchy.) Then she pirated electricity from her first-floor
apartment—a definite no-no according to the building code.
For more than a year, she sublet her apartment and lived in
the trailer—roughing it, really, because the trailer had no
plumbing and, thus, no bathroom—which made for a definite
code violation if anyone found out. Finally, she never incorporated or registered the business. When she had amassed

enough work that she needed to hire an assistant, she paid cash, off the books.

Miranda also had another System D trade that predated the jewelry biz: decorating cakes with ornate sculptures in icing (think a crown of thorns or a thatch of branches and birds made entirely of buttercream). This, too, was System D. She worked from home, with no license, no food preparation certificate, no permits (she insists, however, that cake decorating never really was a business because the price she could charge per cake could never pay for the time necessary to make her funky designs and so she wound up working mostly for friends). Still, for the past two years she has essentially run her entire life in the economic shadows.

"I'm totally off the grid," she said. "It was never an option to do it any other way. It never even crossed my mind. It was financially absolutely impossible. I just found a way to do it that would work."

Brandon Arnovick, too, stumbled into System D. A musician in San Francisco—part of what might be called the alt-hip-hop scene—he was looking for a job that would allow him to spend more time at home with his kid. That was the simple inspiration for Mission Minis, a line of minicupcakes that, he decided, would sell for a buck each. Fun food, friendly price, frolicsome name. "I was pretty sure they would cost a dime or a quarter to make," Arnovick told me. "You could basically mom-and-pop it and back-door it." What you couldn't do, however, was be legal. "I didn't have any capital or any investors. I started it in my kitchen in my house. But you can't get a health permit for a home." Still, the orders kept coming— first from little independent stores, which he could handle from his home kitchen, then regional coffee bar chains like Philz and Ritual Roasters, which he could handle with the addition of a small staff who worked in his kitchen to help him bake and ice. And then, suddenly, Mission Minis (the

name is an homage to the Mission District, the neighborhood where Arnovick lives) hit the big time: Whole Foods
was willing to stock its cupcakes in all their stores in the
region. That was when Arnovick realized: "This could potentially be awesome."

But awesome doesn't always mean uncomplicated. To
serve the big supermarket chain, Mission Minis would have
to operate on a scale that would have taken over his home
rather than simply occupying it for a few hours every day.
So Arnovick had to pry the business out of his house and
into a licensed kitchen somewhere in the city. Renting one
proved exorbitant—even a minuscule rent of $25 an hour
would amount to almost $5,000 a month for eight hours
of baking every day. Renting a fully fixtured restaurant was
even more expensive—something on the order of $6,500 a
month. The most economical option was also the riskiest:
rent a store and install a legal kitchen. This would require
him to shell out the money up front, but he would save in
operating costs. Arnovick found a good location—a former
palm reader's storefront not far from his house—which he
leased for $1,500 a month. (Part of its appeal, he recalled, was
that it was "the smallest place on the block.") So he cobbled
together $100,000 from his own savings and a few loans from
relatives and began the renovation.

Today, the bakery is complete and Mission Minis boasts
more than a dozen employees. And, since the company uses
the kitchen only during the day, Arnovick has been renting
the space to other up-and-coming System D foodies. Curtis
Kimball, a former carpenter who developed a dedicated following for his quasi-legal crème brûlées (he didn't have the
local licenses, his sales cart didn't meet local standards, and his
sole promotion was word-of-mouth and a Twitter-generated
buzz), was one of the early recruits. Natalie Galatzer, who got
her start baking pies in her home and delivering them person-

ally around the city on her bicycle—thus her business name, Bike Basket Pies—rents kitchen space from Mission Minis to produce the six dozen small pies she sells every week. Renting to System D foodsters, Arnovick notes, certainly helps defray his rent, but it also ensures that the storefront is in operation even at odd hours and helps build a community of like-minded people in the food industry.

Despite his speedy success, Arnovick hasn't quit the kitchen. He still takes a shift baking and icing his minis and makes cold calls on local businesses to get them to stock the cupcakes. "This is San Francisco," he explained. "We watched the Internet boom and bust." At the same time, he hasn't forgotten that cupcakes aren't the entirety of his life. He remains a musician—he is one-half of the Rondo Brothers and involved as a producer with the critically acclaimed hip-hop acts Dan the Automator and Handsome Boy Modeling School. "Music," he told me, "is way more dimensional than baking." His son's friends, however, give him much more street cred for his killer cupcakes. Arnovick has a solid perspective on what he's achieved. It's a job, an added income (eventually, perhaps, it'll become a really good income, once he pays off the expense of creating that storefront kitchen), but he doesn't kid himself that he's changing the world one cupcake at a time. "You don't need a cupcake to live," he told me. "You need milk and water and things like that."

Still, with the United States facing a lengthy recovery from economic meltdown, the time for System D is now. Caleb Zigas, acting executive director of La Cocina, a Bay Area organization that helps unlicensed food purveyors make the transition to legality, estimates that there are between a hundred and two hundred illegal food carts plying San Francisco's streets. He notes that licensing can be prohibitively expensive—in some cases costing more than $50,000—and the rules that people face can be almost impossible. For instance, local and state regulations often clash—and though your food cart may meet one standard, it can still be illegal under the other. And then there are the city's building codes. Mandy Harter, whose Wholesome Bakery, specializing in vegan desserts, started as a home hobby and then grew into a street business, recently opened its first retail shop. The toughest problem she faced in this transition was meeting some of the seemingly ridiculous requirements of the city codes—for example, the time the authorities wouldn't let her bakeshop open because a paper-towel dispenser had been installed at the wrong height. Even Zigas, whose organization's raison d'être is to promote legalization, concedes that "Formalizing is not necessarily a good business proposition."

Adam Smith may not have been able to imagine it almost two and a half centuries ago, but the new route to success in the economically successful countries of the world involves not one job but several—most often in System D. Whether it's working off the books, avoiding regulation, or squeezing as much money as possible out of a business before the authorities catch you, System D is an American tradition. Dick Sears, a station agent at an obscure railway crossing in Minnesota, started peddling watches to people on the trains that passed through to make some extra money—and this was the start of the business that for many years was America's largest retailer—Sears, Roebuck & Co. Frederick T. Stanley was a tinker, selling tools from a pack, before he earned enough to found Stanley Works. The roots of the company that makes Van Heusen shirts—one of the most enduring clothing brands in the United States (which today owns Bass, Arrow, IZOD, Calvin Klein, and Tommy Hilfiger)—lie in a single unlicensed pushcart run by a husband-and-wife team in Philadelphia.

As urban visionary Jane Jacobs noted, "Many a respectable American citizen of today got his education, and many a legitimate and constructive enterprise got its initial capital," from peddling, piracy, smuggling, and illegality. Indeed, she went on, "One could argue that if immigrants had derived no capital from these sources . . . the economic development of the United States would have halted."

Kids selling lemonade in front of their houses are part of System D. So are most people who grab some extra cash by selling their excess possessions in lawn or garage sales or even on eBay (depending on whether they declare all their income). A storeowner who entices you to make a purchase by offering not to charge sales tax if you pay in cash is definitely a member. As are the construction laborers who job up on urban street corners (and in the parking lots of Home Depot and Lowe's) waiting for contractors to come and hire them on the cheap. And so are the networks of families that control booths at swap meets and flea markets and pull down six-figure incomes.

For many new arrivals, System D provides a sensible way to join the American dream. Take Matilde. Born in 1943 in Jalisco, Mexico, she crossed the border into California with a coyote in 1961, when she was eighteen. She's been in the United States for half a century. At first, she worked in agriculture in the Central Valley. Then, after having four kids, she got a job in a produce packing plant. But the cold storage at the facility made her fingers and wrists stiff and it became increasingly hard for her to work. So she started a second job, purchasing things at yard sales and selling them at a local swap meet. Gradually the sales job took over. Today, she's quit the cold room and makes her living selling blankets and purses three days a week at three different flea markets. Matilde (not her real name, but one given to her by Mexican anthropologist Magdalena Barros Nock, who wrote about her in a recent essay) started her business with an investment of $4,500—$1,000 for the merchandise, $500 for the stand, and $3,000 for a van to haul everything around.

Now in her late sixties, Matilde hires local girls to help her with the work. They load and unload her merchandise, set up her stand, and handle the customers. But even after paying her employees, Matilde earns between $1,500 and $2,000 a month, depending on the season. According to Barros Nock, Matilde's income is modest. Particularly entrepreneurial individual vendors can earn $20,000 a month, while families that join forces to work several booths at different swap meets can pull in more than $100,000. Many start off like Matilde, buying locally at garage sales and reselling at the larger swap meets. But, over time, most find it more profitable to buy cheap items from China, Korea, and Taiwan—sunglasses, toys, cosmetics, purses, perfumes, plastic jewelry—just like the global rummage products sold at the market on Rua 25 de Março in São Paulo.

To attract customers, the swap meet merchants offer services that larger stores no longer provide. For instance, many offer what the Mexicans call payment *apartado*, or, as you might translate it in English, a layaway plan, allowing customers to pay little by little, and take the item home when they've made the full payment. (Though many of the merchants and their customers are immigrants from Mexico, the swap meets are not monoethnic affairs. Several of these flea markets have been around since the 1940s, and merchants include the full spectrum of ethnic groups living in southern California.) Walmart may sell things cheaper, but, if you can't get flexible terms, it may make more economic sense to pay a little more overall for the advantage of spreading your payments out over time.

Today, the ranks of System D are swelling, boosted by economic refugees—not foreigners but people pushed out of the legal economy after the downturn of 2008 and 2009. Indeed, recent census estimates have shown that twenty-seven million Americans—almost one-fifth of the U.S. workforce— report that they are working only part-time, and nine million of them say that they've been forced into part-time work because they simply couldn't find a full-time job. And one study has suggested that 3.4 million people around the country are working full-time but are classified as independent contractors so their employers can avoid the expense of providing health insurance and other benefits. And, of course, a whole lot of people are working extra jobs—off or on the books.

Once upon a time we had an honorable word for this. If someone worked a second job—it might involve after-hours hourly wages, or a self-employed situation doing something the person enjoyed more than his or her day job—we said they were "moonlighting." The word dates from the mid-1950s—etymologies differ on the exact year—and it lasted for several decades, apparently derived from Australian slang for the ancient practice of nighttime cattle rustling. The jobs that people did through moonlighting didn't have to be part of System D—but most often they were: a little pocket money, earned in cash, unreported to the government, on the side. A friend, after he retired, repaired radios and other small appliances for friends and neighbors, for a bit of scratch. Another friend still moonlights making *pasteles*—small filled pastries that are typical in Puerto Rican and Dominican cuisine—which she freezes and sells by the box to a steady list of private customers. At one time, I rewired old lamps, occasionally for cash, more often as part of a barter network. Sadly, today we have jettisoned the old cattle-rustling term. Today, people use a clinical phrase that's almost comical for its lack of passion: "income patching."

Whatever we want to call it, the truth is that formal businesses have long dabbled in System D, selling gray-market items (for instance, cameras or electronics with out-of-date or foreign warrantees) or the galleys and uncorrected publishers' proofs of new books (an editor at *Kirkus Reviews*, one of the book industry's trade publications, told me they "donate" the vast number of galleys they receive to "anyone who will pick them up," including Housing Works, an AIDS charity, and the Strand bookstore, which sells these uncorrected proofs—most of them marked "Not for Sale" or "Not for Resale"—for $1.99 each). Until 2006, it was technically illegal for a mobile phone user who had a phone that was locked to a particular provider's signal to unlock the phone so it could be used with any mobile service. No one was ever prosecuted, however, and unlocking phones became a common business all over the United States. More recently, when most networks switched to smartphones that could surf the Web, unlocking—jailbreaking, in more modern users' parlance—became a lucrative practice. Manufacturers resisted the trend, argued that jailbreaking essentially enabled users to steal the phone's proprietary programming. It wasn't until 2010 that the Library of Congress, which administers copyright, officially legalized jailbreaking—and even then, it did it only as a temporary exemption from the Digital Millennium Copyright Act, so the practice is still considered controversial.

Over the past decade, Social Compact, a nonprofit based in Washington, D.C., has been studying the size of the System D in the United States. In a series of studies, the group has shown that "unregulated economic activity" represents a significant amount of wealth, particularly in poorer communities around the country. In central Miami, for instance, this sub-rosa resource represents $850 million in undeclared income. In Baltimore, it's $872 million. In just one New York neighborhood—Harlem—it's $800 million. The District of Columbia, the nation's capital, boasts a robust alternative system that produces $1 billion of income for the people who rely on it. Houston, too, has $1 billion in System D trade. And a 2005 study by the Los Angeles Economy Project estimated that System D in the environs of the City of Angels involves almost seven hundred thousand jobs that together produce $8.1 billion in wages a year. In percentage terms, the United States may have one of the smallest shadow economies in the world—Friedrich Schneider, the Austrian economist who makes it his business to evaluate informality, puts it at somewhere between 8 and 9 percent of the gross domestic product—but, given the size of the U.S. economy, America is a System D superpower, with the largest unregistered economy in the world, worth more than $1 trillion.

Alfonso Morales, a professor of urban and regional planning at the University of Wisconsin, is perhaps one of the few academics who writes about System D who has actually experienced it from the inside. That's because he put himself through graduate school in part by selling closeout hardware on Maxwell Street in Chicago. Indeed, his experience in the market became the subject of his thesis.

The Maxwell Street Market has been a big part of the Second City's life since the 1870s. The market was municipally managed for the first century of its existence. After the urban disturbances of the 1960s, the city basically abandoned its managerial role, and Maxwell Street was run as an informal cooperative of merchants for the next twenty years. In 1994, the city forced the market to relocate and wrested back control. During that transitional period, Morales sold at the market every Sunday for a year and a half—changing stalls five times so he could experience and understand the reality of vendors who come and go, and the way long-term merchants treated new arrivals. And he returned almost every week for two years thereafter to continue his research. He found that vendors shared responsibilities—holding slots for one another, letting newcomers know the unwritten rules, policing the market. Each time he moved his booth, he wrote in a recent essay, he had to spend time establishing ties with his new neighbors. "I tested both sides of these relationships—as the interloper, finding vendors vigorously defending their neighbor's space as well as their own, and as the neighboring vendor, expected to play a role in preserving space," he said. Morales saw how tables were allocated through a customary arrangement, how people decided not to get licenses or pay taxes but nonetheless had strong opinions about the decline in city services. As at the São Paulo street market along Rua 25 de Março, there was an unofficial schedule at the market—with garage sale merchants showing up early to sell in bulk to other merchants, who could then retail the items they bought for a small markup, and an early morning magnate who, for $5, would save you the trouble of arriving extra early to claim your selling space by placing a table on your spot (according to the market's unwritten but universally accepted rules, setting up a table meant that you had claimed the space and no one else could supplant you). He credits the vendors with "a shared sense of purpose, and a willingness to engage each other on an even footing, with each participant believing the others would also cooperate in matters of vending space, but in the name of friendship." Morales suggests that through these shared efforts, the market on Maxwell Street became an unusual spot in the city—peaceful, diverse, and tolerant during a time when the rest of Chicago was tense and polarized.

As on Rua 25 de Março (and in Alaba and many other street markets), Morales discovered that vending could be quite lucrative. "People make a lot of money in these businesses," he told me. "There were a lot of Sundays I walked out of Maxwell Street with three or four hundred dollars in my pocket." (If this one-day take was typical, working just half-time, or three days a week, he could have pulled in better than $60,000 a year.) Then he lowered his voice: "And I never declared any of the income."

The city was able to push Maxwell Street from its old location in part because it won a public relations war, arguing that the market was unsafe and a haven for illegal sales, drug dealing, and gang violence. In badmouthing the market, Chicago was following a time-tested tradition that dates back at least to the Protestant Reformation. In 1509, before Martin Luther had posted his ninety-five theses and split from the Catholic Church, an anonymous author in Germany published a slim volume called *The Book of Vagabonds and Beggars* (*Liber Vagatorum*, in the original Latin). This odd little text revealed a new danger at work in the land—mendicants and street merchants. The *Liber Vagatorum* had a short run and disappeared into the medieval remainder pile. But in 1529, eight years after having been excommunicated by the pope after questioning the selling of indulgences and other suspicions of corruption in the church, Luther rescued the little volume from obscurity. He republished it with an introduction in which he asserted that street peddlers and other itinerant merchants were living proof that the devil was on the move in Germany.

The book's successful second life was odd. Traveling merchants had been fixtures in rural and urban areas for centuries. In the 1200s, vendors held impromptu Sunday markets in local churchyards. London was full of unlicensed and illegal System D workshops, and most household goods were sold on the street. In Paris, several major public plazas—including the Place de Grève, Place Jurée, and Place Saint-Gervais—were open-air public hiring halls, where workers loitered and employers could simply show up and pick people from the crowd to hire as day laborers. Yet Luther's new edition hit a nerve. The sixteenth century was a time of economic transition. Nations were just starting to boot independent farmers off the land they had occupied for generations and to recast commonly held pastures as privately owned fields. The result was an increase in economic rootlessness, with displaced farmhands roaming the countryside as vagabonds, mendicants, traders, and day laborers. There was a sense of danger in this newly emerging social order.

Perhaps inspired by the success of Luther's book, a series of authors started to publish similar screeds in other languages. In England, the parade of antipeddler pamphlets began in 1561, when John Awdeley published his "Fraternitye of Vacabondes" ("The Fraternity of Vagabonds"), a brief lexicon of these suspect citizens. Five years later, a former magistrate named Thomas Harmon proffered a longer work called *A Caveat or Warning for Common Cursitors*, a book, he promised, that would reveal "the abhominable, wycked, and detestable behavior of all these rowsey, ragged rabblement of rakehelles." Among those featured among Harmon's horrible hoards were street vendors:

> Swadders and Pedlers bee not all euyll, but of an indifferent behaviour. But for as much as they seeke gayne vnlawfully against the lawes and statutes of this noble realme, they are well worthy to be registred among the number of vacabonds; and vndoubtedly I haue hadde some of them brought before me, when I was in commission of the peace, as malefactors, for bryberinge and stealinge.

> [Swadders and Peddlers be not all evil, but of an indifferent behavior. But for as much as they seek gain

unlawfully against the laws and statutes of this noble realm, they are well worthy to be registered among the number of vagabonds; and undoubtedly I have had some of them brought before me, when I was in commission of the peace, as malefactors, for bribery and stealing.]

As proof of his bad opinion of street sellers, Harmon noted that the slang used by thieves—a lover of alliteration, he called it "the leud lousey language of those lewtering luskes and lasy lorrels" (modern rendering: "the lewd, lousy language of those loitering lushes and lazy scoundrels")—was commonly called "Peddler's French."

Over the following decades, the complaints about hawkers and peddlers accelerated and became more pointed. By 1631, when poet Richard Braithwaite published *Whimzies: or, a New Cast of Characters*, a kind of dictionary of depictions of the street denizens of London, there wasn't one positive thing he could say about street vendors. "Honest simplicity never knew the operation of them," Braithwaite wrote. "He will sell you clots for cloves, course crumms for currans . . . and compound your pepper with his earth-powder, to gull you." In less than a century, the view of street peddlers had hardened. Harmon at least allowed that they were "not all evil." For Braithwaite, that admission was gone: all street vendors were crooks.

Why were itinerant merchants transformed from honest suppliers of the goods and necessities of the nation to complete cheats? There's a one-word answer: fear. Fear of the market. Or, more precisely, fear of what the market was turning us into. As the world transitioned from feudalism, with its bonds of authority and tight-knit communities, to mercantilism, where each man was on his own, rage against street peddlers was a socially acceptable manner for people to express their fears about the new system that made economic exchange the fulcrum of the human condition.

Throughout its early centuries, the United States boasted a large cadre of peddlers and street vendors. These itinerant merchants were crucial to the nation's growth. Roving cowboys, farmhands, and laborers contributed to the nation's westward spread, and are still part of the rural scene today. Indeed, with small-scale farming on the decline, many in rural America continue to survive via System D. On the gusty Nebraska prairie, people are breeding and selling dogs off the books to earn a second income, baking cakes for parties and special events without getting licensed, engaging in off-the-financial-grid child care and schooling. One local baker who prepares and sells desserts without a license estimated that the ingredients that go into a $20 cake cost just $4, giving her a fine profit margin. Working just a few hours a day, she earns up to $500 a month from her unlicensed home-based baking business. She has thought about establishing herself in a storefront in order to grow the business, but that would mean going legit—registering and getting health department permissions and some form of insurance, and she's not sure the cost is worth it.

As important as peddlers and other itinerant and unregistered businesses have been for the nation, they have always attracted criticism. In New York City, newspapers, egged on by elite interests, long reported that pushcart operators offered substandard goods and peddlers were out to cheat people. The clamor was so great that, in the early years of the twentieth century, the city considered banning pushcarts altogether, a move that provoked anger three thousand miles away in California, because that state's citrus industry depended on New York City's army of six thousand pushcart operators to sell oranges. Still the newspapers piled on. One paper investigated what it called the Lemon Frauds—vendors who were selling a mixture of citric acid and sugary water with a few so-called "floaters"—slices of lemon—placed in the punch bowl to make it appear to be lemonade (ironically, today's bottled lemonade is not all that different from the fraudulent stuff that created so much controversy years ago).

The city formed a commission to study the problem and in 1906 it issued a surprising report. The truth, the commission reported, was that street carts were among the safest places to buy food. Only 3.5 percent of the fifteen hundred or so Manhattan food carts the commission inspected had any bad food on them, and on those carts, the rotten food made up less than one-fourth of one percent of the food on the cart. "This was in marked contrast to the little stores examined, where it was found that 20 percent contained some food unfit for human consumption," Commission Secretary Archibald A. Hill wrote in *The Independent* magazine. "The reason for this difference between the two stocks of goods is probably that the pushcart peddler has to buy in small quantities, as he has no storage room, and also for the same reason he must sell quickly, hence his goods are always fresh."

The commission also noted that the peddlers, rather than exploiting consumers, were most often the ones being exploited. On the Lower East Side, for instance, 40 percent of the pushcarts were not owned by the people who operated them but rather by brokers who leased them to the people who pushed them. Similarly, the distributors at the wholesale fruit market had contracted with a group of laborers to man pushcarts that the distributors actually owned. And the police routinely stung the peddlers for payoffs—the common bribe was $15 a month.

The peddlers tried to organize a union, but this, too, came in for criticism. Sigmund Schwartz, who for many years served as president of the United Citizen Peddlers' Association, took lots of heat for his aggressive pursuit of pushcart operators' rights. Merchants with stores led the charge against the peddlers—though a governmental investigation disclosed that they were extorting money under the table, essentially renting sidewalk space in front of their stores to the cart operators. Schwartz detailed the prices: at one Eldridge Street building, the owner of the corner store pocketed $30 a month each from soda water and pickle stands, $15 from an egg seller, $25 from a candy stand, and $15 each from six pushcart operators. That's $190 a month—or between $3,000 and $20,000 a month in current currency, depending on how you calculate the appreciation of the dollar over the past century. For his honesty, Schwartz was labeled a corrupt union boss, and accused of taking payoffs to secure city licenses for potential peddlers. In 1919, the peddlers managed to elect one of their own—Louis Zeltner, the secretary of the union—as a city alderman. But the energetic Zeltner served only one term and seems to have had very little impact on the city's peddler policy.

Only the ethnic press understood the value of street sales. The *Amsterdam News*, for instance, stuck up for street vendors in Harlem throughout the 1940s and 1950s, long after they had been pushed out of much of the rest of the city. The pushcarts, the paper editorialized, were an economic boon both for peddlers and the community.

In the modern era, we are heirs to a highly organized industrial labor tradition with set work rules and work hours, businesses that are incorporated, registered, licensed, and a market that is, in theory, regulated in order to be made fair. System D, however, exists outside these norms. So it is natural that we fear, once again, that this thriving zone of unscrupulous operators lacks morality.

This may explain why street vending remains so controversial. As they were in Martin Luther's time, peddlers and cash-in-hand laborers throughout Europe are still being blamed for all sorts of ills. On March 1, 2011, for instance, the news agency Reuters sent a shocking story over its wires: "Tackling Spain's huge black economy," its reporter asserted in a dispatch datelined Madrid, "would help plug the hole in public finances" of the southern European nation that had been teetering perilously close to default. The article reported that the value of Spain's stealth economy was two hundred billion euros (approximately $280 billion)—an amount it said was "more than double the hole in public accounts in 2010." The clear implication: reining in System D could restore the Spanish government to fiscal solvency. In October 2009, the Irish Independent published a similar story: "Illicit economic activity adds up to €6.1 billion"—or about $8.5 billion—"lost to the Exchequer annually," the reporter wrote, implying that the government could have that amount to spend on public programs if people would simply stop working for cash without reporting their wages. And, in November 2007, Swissinfo, a news website funded by the Swiss government, headlined an article on the the the activity of people working off the books with the claim that their labor "costs the Swiss economy" $35 billion a year. Again, the implication was direct: the government was being deprived of this huge amount of revenue.

The people who wrote these articles undoubtedly started off with reasonably accurate estimates of the size of the System D workforce in their countries. Where they went astray was to link those numbers to the revenues collected by their governments. In truth, of course, if the three countries were able to catch all the illicit economic activity in their tax systems, they wouldn't suddenly collect the full value of those wages. Rather, they would get a far smaller amount—the percentage they would normally be allowed to collect in taxes. Though it would gain a substantial amount of revenue, Spain would not come close to balancing its budget simply by cracking down on System D. Similarly, Ireland did not lose $8.5

billion from its treasury because of a rash of people working for cash, and Switzerland, which, as the article in Swissinfo noted, has the lowest rate of under-the-table work in the world, is not being seriously undermined by its economic underground. Indeed, in all three countries, the people who earn money off the books spend their ill-gotten gains in the national economies, so you might argue that these nations are indirectly benefitting from this cash-only work. And, since many of these people would give up their clandestine jobs if their income was taxed, you could argue that "tackling" the black economy in this way could be counterproductive.

Yet the complaints continue. Politicians routinely denigrade the street trade as the zone of illegal immigrants and criminals. Italian prime minister Silvio Berlusconi has argued that street peddlers, many of them undocumented migrants from Africa, are committing crimes and taking jobs away from native-born Italians. His proposed solution: deport many of them back to their home countries. In France, President Nicolas Sarkozy has started a series of pogroms against longtime Gypsy residents, who live and work in System D. Politicians in Switzerland and Germany, too, have campaigned against System D in part because it provides sustenance to immigrants.

But there's one thing these politicians won't admit—that System D is part of the structure of society. In Italy, for example, it's an open secret that System D is not simply fueled by migrants. In Southern Italy and Sicily, at least 25 percent of all economic activity is unreported to the government—a large enough figure that it can't be accounted for simply by illegal migration. According to local surveys, there's no social stigma to working off the books. Still, some of these silly preconceptions don't go away. In the United Kingdom, *The Independent* newspaper recently repeated the canard that the bulk of the country's off-the-books labor comes from illegal migrants. The paper reported that these migrants get their jobs through ethnic and national social solidarity and that different nationalities dominate different trades. "Ghanaians pick litter; Nigerians clean toilets in the City; Romanians and Poles work in plumbing and maintenance," the newspaper reported. The paper didn't attempt to quantify the number of native-born Britishers who were unlicensed street vendors; nor did it attempt to assess whether any of these System D workers were legal immigrants or even citizens. Even in rural villages, the existence of System D has become a tense subject. In January 2011, the picturesque British town of Brierfield—population around eight thousand—banned what the local paper called "rogue street traders" from doing business. The paper reported that the councillors insisted that the action was taken to prevent "unlicensed and unwelcome" vendors from setting up shop, and would not threaten milkmen, ice cream vendors, and what the paper called "legitimate market traders."

The value of System D has always been a matter of perception and class solidarity. Just after the Great Depression, Stanley Walker, the former city editor of *The New York Times*, penned a memoir called *The Night Club Era*. Walker had lived through what he considered a grand period in New York, and he was disgusted by the cheapening of some of its streets. "Once there were lobster palaces and cabarets; now it is cut rate," he said of Times Square, where his newsroom was located. He turned his nose up at the legions of street sellers and supported the police when they moved to round up the vendors.

At almost the same time Walker was writing his obituary for Times Square, Damon Runyon was busy chronicling the same sort of people in his stories. But where Walker found decay, Runyon found lovable rascals—Nathan Detroit, Sky Masterson, Harry the Horse, the Lemon Drop Kid, and all the other disreputables who would inspire the popular musical *Guys and Dolls*. And just five years after Runyon put out his fictionalized account, A. J. Liebling, writing in *The New Yorker*, described the doings of a lower echelon of the Times Square hemi-semi-demimonde—a panoply of composite characters he christened "heads," "heels," "boskos," "gozzlers," and "telephone booth Indians" who chiseled their way through life in the low-rent buildings just off the center of the square. Contrary to Walker, Liebling saw these folks as an important part of the soul of the city, and he reveled in the odd honesty of their conniving. They taught him the ethical standpoint of everyday economics.

Of course, this was never the dominant mode of thought in America. Eight decades later, we are still maligning members of System D. Joanne Saltzberg, head of Women Entrepreneurs of Baltimore, a business development organization, estimates that one-quarter of the people who come through her agency's door or show up at their community meetings are doing some sort of unregistered or unlicensed business on the side to add to their income. Yet policy makers ignore their needs. "There's a mind-set within economic development circles that really denigrates diverse ways of making money," she told me. "There's a built-in resistance to acknowledging that poor people work harder than anyone else on this planet. I think the real resistance is based in the long-held judgment about being poor in America—that it's a character flaw."

It's true: we tend to honor System D–ers when they are middle-class, part of an arc of success, and we tend to diminish the achievements of those who seem lower-class and are working in a more pedestrian manner. To understand that, it's useful to compare two New Yorkers who don't know each other and would seem to have very little in common: Kate Jones and Genoveva Sepeda. Kate, a graduate of the

Rhode Island School of Design, is a jewelry designer who originally hails from Maine and has been in the city since 2008. Genoveva is an immigrant from Puebla, Mexico, who has been in New York almost as long as Kate's been alive, yet still isn't comfortable speaking English.

Three years back, inspired by a former boyfriend who opened a coffee bar in Brooklyn and wanted to sell some highly individual pastries so his café could stand out from the competition, Kate started baking olive-oil cake in her home and selling it through the coffee shop. She has since stopped supplying her ex's outpost and is now distributing to a trendy coffee bar not far from her Manhattan apartment. "I don't have any health certification or licenses," she explained. "I sell to these people where I don't have to worry about packing. I just wrap it in foil and deliver it myself." Her bottom line has been helped by another one of her jobs—like many in the city, Kate's life is all about income patching—as a hostess for a popular brunch spot, which has allowed her to buy her ingredients at wholesale prices and get them delivered to her apartment at no extra charge. Her stove can handle three loaves at a time, and she bakes twenty-one loaves a week. The profits are good and, over the course of a month, the money she makes from her under-the-table cakes covers the rent on her Manhattan apartment.

For her part, Genoveva started her street business five years ago, after her husband lost his job. He has since picked up other jobs, but she has stayed on the street because the rent on their apartment in a gentrifying neighborhood of Brooklyn has risen beyond $1,000 a month, and her income is crucial to their ability to keep their home. To sell her food, she purchased a cooler and an old shopping cart. Two or three days a week, she wheels her cart to a spot in front of a bakery not far from her house (the baker, who also hails from Mexico, allows her to take shelter under his awning without paying rent), and sells tamales, mole poblano, and other regional specialties from Puebla. "My business is not big," she said as she dug into the cooler to serve a customer two foil-wrapped tamales. "It's just fifty or eighty or a hundred dollars a day." Not very much for many hours in the kitchen and on the street, but over the course of a month, if business is good, it could bring in enough to pay the rent.

Genoveva knows she could be busted by the cops for her unlicensed work. The appropriate business certificates and licenses, she told me, would cost more than $1,000, which would erase several months of income—yet getting those permissions to sell on the street wouldn't solve another city requirement: that she prepare her food in a fully approved commercial kitchen. Her home kitchen, no matter how clean, is just not good enough. And even if she managed to do her prep work in a fully legal way, it's doubtful that she would ever be able to get a city vending permit. That's because the number of licenses available for retail food vending on the street in New York City hasn't increased since the late 1970s. The maximum number is currently set at thirty-one hundred—and there's not even a waiting list, because so many people have expressed interest in getting a street food permit that the city has stopped taking names. In any event, despite desperate demand, people almost never give up their permits. Instead, when a person stops vending, he or she will simply sell or lease the permit to another vendor. The purchase price can run tens of thousands of dollars, with thousands more for brokers and middlemen.

What Kate and Genoveva are doing is, in general terms, the same. But the social milieus in which they operate are completely divergent. Kate works in private, Genoveva in public. Kate makes a product that is retailed at a high-end establishment, while Genoveva sells from a humble shopping-cart kiosk. Kate is white and highly educated; Genoveva is Mexican and still can't speak much English. And these differences perhaps are reflected in how they have been treated by the authorities. While their situations are not entirely analogous, in that Kate is not selling on the street, the fact that she makes her olive-oil cake in her home has been mentioned approvingly in several prominent local magazines. Yet her business has been ignored by the city authorities. Genoveva, by contrast, has never received any publicity. But she was recently pushed from her roost in front of the bakery. City inspectors apparently thought she was running an on-the-street outpost of the bakery and threatened to ticket the baker for operating an unlicensed outdoor café. Since he didn't want to get fined, he asked her to move. For now, she's in front of a nearby deli. But the move surely cut into her income, because she's now on a much less trafficked corner than the one she used to occupy.

This is not to blame Kate for Genoveva's situation or to suggest that city inspectors should pursue Kate as avidly as they have Genoveva. Rather, the city should be supporting both of them, regardless of how successful or mainstream or ritzy their businesses are. As Joanne Saltzberg in Baltimore put it, "We only revere success. I don't think we honor the struggle. People who have no access to business development resources. People who have to work two and three jobs just to survive. When you are struggling in this economy and still you commit yourself to having a better life, that's really something to honor."

Against Efficiency

Our merchants and master-manufacturers complain much of the bad effects of high wages in raising the price, and thereby lessening the sale of their goods both at home and abroad. They say nothing concerning the bad effects of high profits. They are silent with regard to the pernicious effects of their own gains.

—The Wealth of Nations

The man pulled a wooden handcart piled high with cardboard and Styrofoam. He refused to give his name. "I am unimportant," he said. "Just another guy." Small and wiry, his skin burnished by long hours in the South China sun, he told me he had migrated to Guangzhou from Henan province in the north and had been working as a recycler for five years. His family had migrated south with him, so he didn't have to ship his income home. None of them has the *houkou* (or residency permit) needed to reside in the city; this means his kids can't legally go to school, so he sends them to a self-organized private school on the outskirts of town.

In this megacity an hour north of Hong Kong, he said, people don't throw out their recyclable materials. Instead, the exchange is monetized: he has to buy the paper and plastic from the people who dispose of it. Everything has its price and he earns the increment. He buys cardboard for six jiao per kilo (a jiao is one-tenth of a yuan, the main unit of Chinese currency), or approximately nine cents, and sells it for one yuan, or about fourteen cents. He buys Styrofoam at two yuan per kilo and sells it for ¥3. When we met, he was arguing with a woman along his route who wanted him to pay her for a giant wad of plastic bags—but he refused, because there was no money to be made from the transaction. In the end, she walked away with her bale of bags, muttering under her breath. He turned to me in triumph. She was asking more than the plastic bags were worth, he said, and besides, the bags took up too much room in his cart. He had space for only the most valuable items. This approach earns him more than ¥1,000 (or approximately $150) a month—a reasonably respectable wage in China.

He travels six miles from the district where his routes are to the edge of the city, where the wholesaler to whom he sells his load is located. Despite the distance, he pulls his cart by hand, because City Control—the name street merchants commonly use to describe the Guangzhou municipal agency that is empowered to enforce the laws regarding street trade—has, in its own mysterious wisdom, declared that it is illegal for an individual recycler to use a bicycle. It takes a team to use a bike, the recycler said, which would dilute his profit. So he hauls his cart by hand. And he's actually lucky, because, in the municipal drive toward modernization, City Control has essentially outlawed most forms of street work.

There is an organized network of recyclers, he said, that controls who can be a recycler and what routes they can work. He works three different routes—making his deals to take away the recyclable material along each route twice a week.

The system works, but an economist would likely call it irrational and inefficient. After all, what rational businessperson would set up a recycling business in Guangzhou, a city of more than ten million people, if his entire operation depended on the brawn and the savvy negotiating skills of a bunch of illegal migrant laborers who hustled through the streets pulling homemade handcarts? It would be more efficient to organize trucks, which could haul more materials in a more sanitary manner. Since the trucks could haul far more in one trip than a single man can, it's likely that routes would be combined, and would perhaps be serviced only once a week. In addition, it would be better not to hire people who don't have their residency permit. Before the street laborers could receive their pay, the administrators would have to draw their salaries, and there would be a deduction to pay the expenses of buying and maintaining the trucks and purchasing fuel.

These are the values of the modern economic system. Outsourcing is okay because it is a rational and efficient choice: multinational companies can realize massive savings on labor costs by moving jobs to low-wage countries. Similarly, promoting big-box stores and driving out small retailers is okay because larger scale cuts down on overhead and reduces the need for redundant labor, allowing products to be sold more cheaply.

Compare this with the haphazard street market economy. Alaba International Market has dozens of merchants selling essentially identical flat-screen TVs. Each of these entities has buyers, transporters, and a sales staff. Each probably employs touts, to drag potential customers to their kiosk. In economic terms, these multiple jobs are wasteful and redundant. If all the small firms were combined, they could jettison a good number of these employees. It would be tough to let them go, but that's what's demanded by a rational and efficient market.

System D questions the value of efficiency. Why is centralized planning (a highly organized and controlled shopping mall, for instance) better than a form of trade that employs more people, even as it may divide the pie into smaller slices (a seemingly disorganized and chaotic street market)? Why is a more sober form of business better than the more cacopho-

nous? Why are locked-in prices better than the fevered nego-
tiation that goes on at a garage sale? Why is standardization
of design better than the overflowing bins and crowded alleys
of a swap meet? In System D, employment has more value
than efficiency, and the illogic of small dealers trumps the
rationality of the big retailer.

In fact, there is a spontaneous sort of efficiency in the
inefficiency of System D, something development economist
Peter Bauer outlined after one of his trips to Africa. "A colorful illustration is provided by the extensive business in used
containers," Bauer wrote. "Petty traders purchase, collect,
store, clean, repair and resell containers such as tins, boxes,
bottles, and sacks. They thereby extend the effective life and
use of these products. Labor is used and capital is conserved."
The libertarian Austrian-school economist Murray Rothbard
would have concurred with Bauer, though with his own con-
spiratorial twist: "Numerous ordinances *outlawing pushcart
peddlers* [emphasis in original] destroy an efficient market
form and efficient entrepreneurs for the benefit of less efficient but more politically influential competitors," Rothbard
wrote in his magnum opus, *Man, Economy, and State*, published in 1962. "It is easy to 'enter' the pushcart peddling
'industry' because so little capital is required."

The modern legal economy is, in a way, a closed shop.
Street peddling, and all of System D, serves to open the market to a larger group of people. It may be inefficient, and
workers like the Guangzhou recycler may earn a small increment, but at least they can earn, and in that sense, System D
makes the world a less unequal place. Growth, while it may
cause more money to pass through a market and accrue to
certain businesses, can threaten this. For instance, James
Ezeifeoma, whose firm Jinifa is one of the leading businesses
in the Alaba International Market, told me that he was worried about the downside of growth, for his business and the

entire market. With the new, massive scale of his business, he foresaw the gradual erosion of community, the drying up of the Igbo apprenticeship system that democratizes wealth—"today, it's all wage labor," he told me—and the destruction of solidarity bred from shared commercial struggle. He no longer believes that someone like him—someone who started at the bottom, with no formal education, and spent years as an apprentice—could rise in business at Alaba.

The inability to reduce the gap between rich and poor has long been a theme in writings on political economy. Gerrard Winstanley, the most famous of the Diggers—the radical egalitarian movement in seventeenth-century England—brought it up as one of his central principles in the pamphlet he published in 1651 called "The Law of Freedom in a Platform." "But shall not one man be richer than another?" Winstanley asked rhetorically, then answered, "There is no need of that; for Riches make men vain-glorious, proud, and to oppress their Brethren; and are the occasion of wars." One of the principles that Winstanley promoted to level the income disparities of his time was to liberate System D and allow farmers access to urban markets without paying tariffs or tolls for the privilege of selling their produce on city streets.

A century later, here's what Adam Smith had to say about inequality in *The Theory of Moral Sentiments*, his first book, which he published in 1759:

The rich . . . consume little more than the poor, and in spite of their natural selfishness and rapacity, though they mean only their own conveniency, though the sole end which they propose from the labours of all the thousands whom they employ, be the gratification of their own vain and insatiable desires, they divide with the poor the produce of all their improvements. They are led by an invisible hand to make nearly the same

173

division of necessaries of life, which would have been made, had the earth been divided into equal portions among all its inhabitants; and thus without intending it, without knowing it, advance the interest of the society, and afford means to the multiplication of the species.

This was Smith's first use of "invisible hand," the phrase that would become his most captivating, most enduring, and most controversial literary creation. It's a great economic fantasy: the master unwittingly shares everything equally with his slaves; lords and ladies with their servants; royalty with the plebes; bosses with their workers; and capitalism is really communism. But Smith must have known that it wasn't true. Even in his time, the rich didn't restrict their consumption to little more than the poor (King George II received an annual allotment of almost £900,000 from the national treasury to support his retinue, while the average clerk at a joint stock company earned perhaps £200 a year and the average laborer more likely on the order of £50) and, left to their own devices, didn't ensure that the necessities of life were apportioned equally among all (otherwise there would have been no need for the aristocracy to pass the Poor Laws, which treated unemployment and poverty as crimes rather than as consequences of other people's economic decisions). Perhaps this was why Smith lowered the profile of the invisible hand the single time he mentioned it in *The Wealth of Nations*.

Sixty years after Smith died, the French journalist and utopian thinker Pierre-Joseph Proudhon articulated a revolutionary plan to spur growth and reduce inequality based on superabundant credit (Proudhon proposed forcing interest rates down to between one-fourth and one-half of 1 percent), and increasing local control (his plan called for the creation of a massive number of cooperative associations to manage the economy based on reciprocity, voluntary contract, and buying and selling at a just price). A generation after Proudhon, Swiss industrialist and economist Silvio Gesell articulated a different way of addressing inequality. Gesell's novel proposal was to make money depreciate in value the same way a product or resource does if you stockpile it. "Only money that goes out of date like a newspaper, rots like potatoes, rusts like iron, evaporates like ether, is capable of standing the test as an instrument for the exchange of potatoes, newspapers, iron and ether," Gesell wrote. "We must make money worse as a commodity if we wish to make it better as a medium of exchange." Gesell wanted money to lose one-thousandth of its value every week—or 5.2 percent every year. His idea was that, if money depreciated over time, there would be no reason to hoard it. So, by this neat trick, Gesell proposed to encourage people to continually spend, and this stimulus in consumption of all sorts (two thumbs up from Bernard Mandeville!) would naturally force production to increase, thus creating jobs and sharing the wealth.

Another thirty years on—a hundred and sixty years after Adam Smith published *The Wealth of Nations*—John Maynard Keynes offered a frank diagnosis of the problems of the free-market system in the last chapter of his 1936 book *The General Theory of Employment, Interest and Money*: "The outstanding faults of the economic society in which we live," he wrote, "are its failure to provide for full employment and its arbitrary and inequitable distribution of wealth and income." Keynes believed that government could provide the leavening, leveling factor, investing in and stimulating production in order to create jobs and spur consumption, and in the process leveling the huge inequities in wages and wealth. Unlike Proudhon and Gesell, Keynes offered no utopian solution (though he did credit Mandeville and Gesell as being among the "brave army of heretics" who called into question traditional economic nostrums) and he didn't suggest that all inequities should be abolished, just that the size of the differential should be limited. "There is social and psychological justification for significant inequalities of incomes and wealth," he wrote, "but not for such large disparities as exist today."

Simon Kuznets, the great modern explicator of inequality, won the Nobel Prize in economics in 1971 for his work suggesting that inequality starts out as relatively minor in agricultural society, grows massively with industrialization, but tends to lessen in the later stages of industrial development. (As a modern example of how this might work, Bill Gates and Warren Buffett are both fabulously wealthy, but the difference between their assets and the wealth of the average American of today is likely less than the gap that existed between John D. Rockefeller or Jay Gould and the average citizen of the 1890s.) Despite this gradual leveling, however, Kuznets worried about the extent of inequality and the downsides of growth. When he was awarded the Nobel, forty years back, people perhaps expected his speech in Sweden to be dry and statistical like most of his writings. Instead, Kuznets spoke passionately about social dislocation and the unforeseen consequences of economic theories. He predicted a number of the difficulties that stem from the global impact of technology and suggested that development is not a one-way street—that it has negative results. "Concurrent with the remarkable positive achievements of modern economic growth are unexpected negative results even within the developed countries," he told the audience in Stockholm in December 1971, adding that "the less-developed countries are struggling in the attempt to use the large potential of modern technology" to gain a foothold in the increasingly interdependent world. Kuznets argued that it was pointless to expect developing nations to simply ape the actions of the

West, because the lack of highly developed infrastructure would block local production. Instead, he called for political and economic experimentation to bring the poorer countries into a more equal relationship with the already industrialized world. "A substantial economic advance in the less-developed countries may require modifications in the available stock of material technology and probably even greater innovations in political and social structure," he said—and it's possible to read this statement as a veiled plea for redistribution, a clandestine endorsement of piracy and smuggling and other techniques that lower costs and thus help bridge technological divides. Kuznets accurately predicted that technological advances would create opportunities—witness the way most developing countries no longer need to run phone wires, but, rather, have jumped directly to mobile service—but added that these technological surges would create political instability as the demands of an increasingly sophisticated citizenry bumped up against the limits of governmental capacity. "It seems highly probable that a long period of experimentation and struggle toward a viable political framework compatible with adequate economic growth lies ahead for most less developed countries of today," Kuznets stated (is this some backhanded support for System D playing a role in politics?), "and this process will become more intensive and acute as the *perceived* gap widens between what has been attained and what is attainable with modern economic growth."

These are fascinating insights—their force, sadly, is ignored by most economists—that traditional conceptions of economic growth can only go so far, that public desires often outstrip financial results, and that there are negative consequences to positive economic results. System D is one of the ground-up answers to Kuznets's fears. Piracy levels the technological divide, jettisoning the expensive regime of intellectual property rights and bringing cheap high tech to low-tech countries. Street markets like Alaba and Computer Village enable poor people to get electronics and high-tech items. At all levels, System D provides jobs, bringing people into the economy, making growth simultaneously more robust and able to reach a greater proportion of the population.

It's not clear from his writings what Kuznets would have said about System D. But four decades after his speech, the disparities and negative impacts of growth are still here. The wealthiest 10 percent of people on the planet now control more than 85 percent of global assets, according to a 2008 study by the United Nations' World Institute for Development Economics Research. If a person had just $2,138 in savings or some other form of assets—just $2,138!—he or she could be counted among the wealthiest 50 percent of the global population. And in 2010, the World Bank reported that the per-capita share of gross national income in rich countries was thirty-six times larger than that of the poor countries in sub-Saharan Africa. Whatever the merits of our market system, the planet has become a terribly unequal place—and in recent years, the gap between rich and poor, contrary to what Kuznets theorized, has once again been getting larger.

The Martinican writer Edouard Glissant, in his book *Caribbean Discourse*, traces this to a postcolonial reality that he has labeled the political economy of dispossession and pseudoproduction. For Glissant, the colonial system undermined local markets, trashed local capacity, and weakened local creativity, leading to economic stagnation and the dissolution of traditional bonds of social solidarity.

Which is exactly where System D emerges. In the colonial reality, slaves, serfs, plantation workers, even many factory proletarians were prohibited from entering the state-run economy. They could do business only on the margins. System D was their system, and potentially their liberation.

From this shadowy arena comes investment, surplus, local control, capital, creativity, and production—all of it, by law, unseen and uncounted and unappreciated by the legal world.

Beyond the postcolonial situation, System D emerges whenever people who have been passed over by the dominant economy start to act. It emerges from the bottom, starting as a rudimentary economy based on tiny and inefficient increments of profit. But over time, it scales up, creating jobs—1.8 billion of them and growing, according to the Organisation for Economic Co-operation and Development—and offers opportunities to people who have never been wealthy or well educated. David Ibekwe, the successful auto parts dealer in Lagos, for instance, dropped out of secondary school to become a trader. Alaba megamerchant James Ezeifeoma never even finished primary school. Yet, without any of the advantages of inherited money or education, both merchants are thriving in the global economy through System D.

Now, it is exactly this lack of efficiency and standardization that bothers some analysts. They push a different interpretation, arguing that System D essentially amounts to a giant blow-off preventer, intervening in cases of crisis to save the dominant system. In essence, that's the view of Princeton sociologist Alejandro Portes, who, back in 1989, edited an influential book called *The Informal Economy*. Professor Portes sees little of lasting benefit coming out of this disreputable economic arena other than perhaps the ability for a semipermanent underclass to survive for one more day. He sees System D as a kind of bastard ward of the state—a zone that is kept around because it ensures that people will have the minimum income required to survive, and thus will not revolt against the existing order. And he doesn't trust that it can scale up, exactly because it operates outside of any systemic bounds, and thus cannot function with the creativity the system allows.

"For the state, it provides a safety valve, because people find some sort of employment and that translates into relative quiescence," Portes told me. "And in the import and export sector it rebounds to the benefit of the higher-ups. It lowers the cost of consumption for the middle class and for firms that subcontract to the informal sector." At the same time, he argues, it keeps wages for the poor at a subsistence level. In this view, System D is cultivated by the state as a mechanism to keep the poor and the middle class quiet. "Without it," he concluded, "the modern state could not survive."

Though Portes remains pessimistic about System D as a long-term solution to underdevelopment—around the globe, governments are moving toward greater and greater deregulation, he noted, which will make it easier for big firms to squash smaller competitors—he also believes that incremental programs to aid these underground firms are an appropriate strategy. System D, he told me, "is a fact of life. And the best way of trying to approach it, instead of persecuting the noncriminal firms, is to create programs at the local level that engage in training and offering small business loans."

There is, however, another strand of mainstream political thinking that sees System D as an opportunity rather than an impediment to development. Roberto Mangabeira Unger, a professor at Harvard Law School who, at the time I spoke with him, was serving as what might be called Brazil's resident futurist (his official title was chief of the Secretariat of Strategic Affairs), articulated it to me in a fragmentary phrase: "If we understand the market abstractly as a system for decentralizing economic agency . . ."

It's a terrible sound bite—ugly, academic, and incomplete. It'll never make a good manifesto. (Indeed, Unger has a tendency to express himself in opaque phrases; in his writings, he has labeled economics "a nonevolutionary deep-structure social theory" that falls apart exactly because it can't grow or change and thus doesn't offer what he calls "plasticity.") Still, his splintered sentence points toward a revolution in economic thought: the market—the free market, our civic religion—can be understood as something other than an ingenious device for creating profit. "The market has no single natural and necessary legal and institutional form," Unger told me. "It's a historical evolution and a political choice." To Unger, the market can be seen as a kind of institutionalized cooperative system, in that every transaction merges the interests of the buyer and the seller. (Nietzsche anticipated this thought a hundred and twenty years ago, writing in one of his late notebooks, "The fact of credit, of the whole of world trade, of the means of transport—in all this a tremendous, mild *trust* in man finds expression.")

Economists, in the main, want to crush System D—either by banishing it to some illicit, sub-rosa, criminal zone or by forcing it to join the legal world. But, in either case, we face a serious and solemn question: if our economic system—the free market—doesn't include half the workers of the world (the people who are in System D), perhaps we need to modify our system?

And this is where that fragmentary line from the former government minister in Brazil becomes important. If we revamp our idea of the market, making its goal creating jobs, increasing incomes, reducing inequality, and elevating entrepreneurship—or, in Unger's parlance, "democratizing economic agency"—rather than creating individual profit, System D becomes a relevant part of the global economic future. For System D certainly opens access to the economy. It brings more people into the market. It enables small traders to travel and to do business internationally. It allows previously disenfranchised and disempowered people to reach a level of economic empowerment. It encourages illegal migrants—like the recycler from Henan province—to build a future in a place they are not allowed to live (and, perhaps, over time, to emerge as a constituency that can organize against restrictive rules like the five-decade-old *houkou* system).

There's no doubt that it's hard to reconsider or reformulate cherished notions like Adam Smith's invisible hand. But, as Kuznets pointed out in his Nobel speech, if those notions simply don't fit reality, and if the things the market has tried so far have not ameliorated the problem—if they had, lack of employment and income inequality would not continue to plague the world—then it's not too much to suggest that we at least should ask why the dominant economic theories and conventional market institutions are not working. System D represents half the working people of the world, and they should matter more than the continuation of an elegant yet highly unfair economic model.

Unger is under no illusion that this is easy. "The informal economy cannot rescue itself," he told me. In his view, System D is too heavily rooted in the cracks of the formal economy to take on the task of reimagining and retooling the market. He sees the strivers in System D as a hugely creative and potentially experimental bunch who are overmatched by the heavy hand of government and the restrictive force of tradition. Instead, he suggests, the job of creating a new kind of market system "requires a conspiracy within the government and agitation from outside"—that is, politicians have to think outside the box, and make alliances with System D firms, while System D firms have to figure out how to work with the government.

Any concrete proposal to revamp the market will reverberate throughout society. As John Cross, a sociologist who has studied street markets in Mexico City over several decades, told me, if governments and societies begin to recognize System D, and the important role that street markets play in development and growth, the next step would logically call for those markets and the people who work in them—who have traditionally been labeled as criminal or socially deviant—to be recognized as legitimate. At that moment, he told me, "rights are going to have to be reorganized and new rights are going to have to be recognized."

To many economists, this is a scary thought. Any articulation of new rights often appears to be a lunatic leftist fantasy. But System D has always defied easy ideological categorization. It doesn't fit neatly into the schemes of the left or the right. Karl Marx, for instance, thought the merchants and workers in System D were counterrevolutionaries. They were, he wrote in his famous essay "The Eighteenth Brumaire of Louis Bonaparte," to be lumped in with the *lumpenproletariat*: "vagabonds, discharged soldiers, discharged jailbirds, escaped galley slaves, swindlers, mountebanks, *lazzaroni*, pickpockets, tricksters, gamblers, *maquereaus*, brothel keepers, porters, literati, organ-grinders, ragpickers, knife grinders, tinkers, beggars—in short the whole indefinite, disintegrated mass, thrown hither and thither, which the French term *la bohème*." In shockingly vehement language—it may be that the philosopher of communism had his own unconscious class biases—Marx termed them "scum, offal, refuse of all classes," and labeled them as evil reactionaries who served as "the light infantry of capital." Yet, a century on, one of Marx's prominent twentieth-century disciples, the visionary psychiatrist Frantz Fanon, turned the teachings of the master on their head, asserting that the *lumpenproletariat* was "spontaneously and radically revolutionary."

The conservative/libertarian economist Murray Rothbard was as enthusiastic about System D as Fanon, but articulated his vision from a contrary pole of the political spectrum. He believed that System D merchants should have no restrictions on their actions whatsoever. He was against business licenses and driver's licenses. "Licenses deliberately restrict the supply of labor and of firms in the licensed occupations," he wrote. "Various rules and requirements are imposed for work in the occupation or for entry into a certain line of business. Those who cannot qualify under the rules are prevented from entry. Further, those who cannot meet the price of the license are barred from entry. Heavy license fees place great obstacles in the way of competitors with little initial capital." To be fair, Rothbard opposed almost any institutional attempt to rein in business. He believed that taxation made the state "a vast criminal organization far more formidable and successful than any 'private' Mafia in history," and argued that, in a truly free society, kids would have the right to run away from their parents and parents would have the right to sell their kids. He also tweaked democracy, claiming that it was destructive of economic well-being: "Looked at as a market phenomenon, 'democratic voting' (one vote per person) is simply the method of the consumer 'co-operative.' Empirically, it has been demonstrated time and again that co-operatives cannot compete successfully against stock-owned companies, especially when both are equal before the law."

Ideology, in short, is not the issue in the economic underground. You don't have to be a radical to work in System D or view System D dispassionately as a zone of opportunity for people. And the fact that System D is inefficient and irrational—in economic terms—does not mean that it doesn't have its own codes of conduct and market institutions. It is not, as Claudia Urias said of the market at Rua 25 de Março, total confusion. System D markets are governed by mutually defined norms and structures. They are communities, and the loose structures they develop over time support and stimulate growth.

Stephen Gudeman, a professor at the University of Minnesota whose academic work involves the intersection of economics and anthropology, has written about this in somewhat more nuanced terms, as a redefinition of what we mean when we speak of economic development: "Development cannot start from the reified financial sphere, nor should we expect it to be brought about by lowering trade barriers and promoting international commerce. It means more than constructing a transparent system of property rights (as the new internationalists insist is key), loaning money, or supporting projects." Gudeman suggests that development has to cast a wider net than the "logic of means-to-ends calculation" and the pursuit of profit. "It must mean recasting development in light of local dialogues about mutuality and trade." Gudeman, it seems, would favor creating some of those cooperatives and mutual aid organizations advocated by Proudhon, which could then organize and engage in some of these conversations. T-Bone Slim, a barge captain, political agitator, news paperman, and hobo poet who was active in the American labor movement of the 1920s and 1930s, put this in plainer English in one of his columns in the labor press: "Men die in hope, live in hope, but hope buys them nothing—wishing ain't ketching any fishes. It's organized economic action that brings the roof over our head."

The Honest Con Men

[S]muggler; a person who, though no doubt highly blamable for violating the laws of his country, is frequently incapable of violating those of natural justice, and would have been, in every respect, an excellent citizen, had not the laws of his country made that a crime which nature never meant to be so.

—*The Wealth of Nations*

Chris Nwaochei spoke in a whisper. I had to hold the phone hard against my ear to get the words. "There's something I have to tell you," he said. "It's a secret you need to know."

I had met Chris the week before in front of his stall in a busy market near the CMS bus station in downtown Lagos, Nigeria. As with many things in Lagos, to say CMS is a bus station is both to tell the truth and to lie. It's certainly true that CMS—the initials stand for the Catholic Mission Society, which once had an office nearby—is the terminus of many of the lines coming from the mainland, where most people live, to the historic business district on Lagos Island. But the buses drop you in a cramped outdoor mud pit dominated by throngs of salespeople hawking food, stationery, toiletries, and their cries—"Blue Band butter," "Buy butter biscuits," "Children's pencils," "Tiger blades"—mingle with the shouts of the touts advertising the destinations of the departing buses—"Mile Two," "Festac," "Apapa," "Ikeja"—which leave not on a fixed schedule, but simply whenever they get full.

And to call CMS downtown is also to tell a truth and a lie. It's true that, if there is a zone in this massive city that is urban in the sense people in the West would recognize, Lagos Island would be it, with its layered history of development, skyscrapers set in a grid of paved avenues and streets, and busy stores on street level. Yet, at the same time, this is not downtown. Many of the city's biggest businesses have vaulted across Five Cowrie Creek to Victoria Island ("V.I." in local parlance) in search of a more placid street environment. More recently, firms have been moving even farther away, south on the nouveau riche Lekki Peninsula. And there are mightier markets on the mainland, across the three bridges that link Lagos Island to the rest of the city. In Lagos, which neighborhood you call downtown depends on what you want to buy, in what kind of environment you want to buy it, and how far you are willing to go to get the best price.

To call Chris's place of business a market is also to tell the truth and to lie. Certainly, as traders in an organized place for buying and selling, Chris and his seventy-seven fellow merchants constituted a market. But their shops were made of slats and branches and odd pieces of faded lumber nailed together to support tabletops. There was nothing permanent here, and no security either. Every evening, Chris bundled up his stock—dozens of pairs of scrupulously clean used shoes— and stashed it in a nearby garage.

Finally, to say Chris and I had met is also to tell the truth and to lie. He had waited quietly on the outside of a circle of merchants who had gathered to find out what an *oyibo* or *onye öcha* was doing perusing their stalls, and grabbed my phone number when I handed out my business cards. Now here he was, calling with his furtive plea.

My friends advised me not to meet him. They thought he was a 419-type scammer looking to extort money from me. But Chris was insistent. So we set a time to get together at Tantalizers, a busy fast-food joint a block away from his stall, on the ground floor of the building that once housed the organization that gave CMS its name.

I ordered a Schweppes bitter lemon soda and a meat pie for both of us and grabbed an open booth. He dropped onto the bench seat opposite me and launched right in. His used shoes were not exactly used, he said. In fact, they weren't used at all. "When we buy them they are new," he said. "But we wash the shoes to pretend they are used." He dealt in shoes from China, he explained, and his customers considered them substandard. They expected Chinese shoes to look great at first but to fall apart almost immediately. Used shoes, by contrast, were seldom made in China, and people considered them higher quality. This attracted a higher price. "If you are selling it as used, you sell it costly," Chris noted with flawless counterintuitive logic. "If you are selling it as new, it is much cheaper."

Chinese shoes, Chris explained, were illegal under Nigerian law, and had to be smuggled into the country (the government goes back and forth on this, sometimes opening the window to importation, and sometimes banning it outright; Chris and I talked during one of the bans). But the size of the potential profit made selling these illicit shoes worth the risk. So, once a week, he traveled sixty miles to cross the border into Cotonou, the principal city of the Republic of Benin, where trade with China is unrestricted and customs duties are almost nil. There, he could choose his shoes and arrange with an agent to sneak them into Nigeria.

Chris generally bought twenty-eight pairs of shoes at a time, at a cost of about sixteen hundred naira ($12.50) per pair. He paid a lump sum of two thousand naira to the guys who knew how to get the shoes across the border, one thousand naira to his local market association as a kind of rent, and twenty naira a night to the watchman who guarded his wares through the evenings. Once he washed them, he could sell the shoes for three thousand or thirty-five hundred naira each. So, in six days of work, he shelled out perhaps $375 and took in $650, yielding $275 in profit. That may not sound like much, but it's a profit margin of 42 percent. By comparison, the forty-five-hundred-store Payless shoe chain—the dominant low-price retailer in the United States—considers it a success when it sneaks its profit margin above 5 percent. I felt bad that I had been suspicious of Chris, and I thanked him for his honesty.

Almost a year later, David Ibekwe sat behind the heavy wooden desk that took up most of the space in his tiny office in the ASPAMDA (Auto Spare Parts and Machinery Dealers Association) portion of the International Trade Fair Market in Lagos and told me about his experience importing shoes from China (though primarily an auto parts expert, David has developed a sideline business bringing in sandals and shoes). Like Chris, David ships them to Cotonou. But, as a wholesaler, he doesn't deal in dozens of shoes. He moves containers of them from China to Africa.

Who knows? I thought. David might be the guy Chris buys from. So I asked him about Chris's business model. David leaned forward and listened, his chin on his fingers, then shook his head. "He's not telling the truth," he said. "China supplies more than fifty percent of the shoes we use in Nigeria and they are sold new." David had no idea why Chris would dissemble. But he was emphatic: Chris's tale about bathing the shoes in order to command a higher price was pure hogwash.

Did Chris lie, as David suggested? It was hard to believe. He had clearly wanted me to know he was a cheat. He had volunteered all the details of his fraud. Where was the self-interest in that? Or was Chris on the level and was David too far removed from modern methods of retailing to understand a new wrinkle in the market? This seemed hard to believe, too. David is a savvy entrepreneur, and his profit depends on knowing the pulse of the market. If shoe washing was standard practice, or if it was any kind of practice at all, David would know of it. He, too, had no reason to mislead me.

So I headed back to CMS to double-check with Chris. I wanted him to take me with him to the border, so I could watch the whole process unfold.

But when I arrived in CMS, I found that a year had made a very big difference. Chris was gone, his stall was gone, and the entire market where he had worked was gone. It had been returned to its original state—as a dirt-and-gravel lot under a rust-stained highway flyover. A few brave souls had spread some blankets on the wrack and were selling a few trinkets. None of them knew Chris. I called the two phone numbers he had given me. No answer. I called repeatedly for several weeks. Each phone rang and rang, but no one ever picked up.

Chris's market was the victim of a new policy initiative. Since I had sat down with him a year before, Lagos had elected a new state governor, Babatunde Fashola, who seems to believe that street sellers and sprawling System D markets are the city's biggest nightmare. Fashola, a lawyer turned politician, has criminalized street hawking and razed dozens of spontaneous markets in paramilitary style; the merchants got no warning and certainly didn't get due process of law. The cops simply showed up and trashed and torched hundreds of kiosks. The governor called his new policy KAI—Kick Against Indiscipline—a pitch-perfect evocation of the complaints about System D that have been around ever since Martin Luther. Itinerant labor, once again, is characterized as a behavioral problem, an ethical problem (the devil footloose in the land, as Luther had it), and not primarily an economic problem.

Yet it's the economic issues that dominate people's complaints against System D. For instance, one of the largest complaints against System D is that the businesses that operate off the governmental grid don't pay taxes. And it's true. People doing their work in System D don't pay their taxes—but what most politicians and economists don't see is that there's more nuance to the problem than just asserting that all System D merchants are tax cheats.

Sir Israel C. Okonkwo, who imports parts for old Renault and Peugeot cars and trucks in the ASPAMDA market in Lagos, is a perfect example. When I met him in Lagos in 2007, I asked him about taxes. He leaned back in his chair and announced, in mock triumph, "I'm forty-four years old and I'm not paying any taxes; I haven't paid any taxes in my life." But when he elaborated on this, the picture of an unrepentant tax cheat got a little murkier. "Nobody's paying any taxes," Sir Israel explained. "Not even the banks and insurance companies. Not even the oil companies. Everybody's trying to beat the system." Sir Israel (the honorific is not courtesy of the queen of England, but by virtue of his membership in the Catholic fraternal organization called the Knights of St. Columba) insisted that he would gladly pay taxes if he could be confident that the government would spend the money on projects that were truly needed. "The government has failed," he announced. "That is why the private sector has lost confidence in the government. There is no government as far as Nigeria is concerned."

Sir Israel's System D argument about taxation is essentially the same as the argument made by the American colonists before the Revolutionary War: no taxation without representation. Taxation implies a social contract. If governments want merchants to pay their taxes, public officials have to demonstrate that they will responsibly administer the money so that the people benefit. In countries like Nigeria, where there is no water system and little electricity, where the roads that get paved first often seem to be the ones close to the homes of the rich and well connected, the government has to demonstrate its worthiness before people will even consider paying their taxes. "Let them rise up to their responsibilities," Sir Israel said. The onus here needs to be on government to increase its transparency and professionalism, so that people like Sir Israel and can see the progress in action.

So far, since he hasn't seen that progress, Sir Israel pushes a different approach: bypassing the government and investing directly in System D. "If you people feel that the government of Nigeria is corrupt," he said—and by "you people" he meant American corporations and the American government—"then come down here and visit people in the markets."

What's more, governments the world over promote job growth by offering to reduce taxes on certain businesses. New York City offers tax deals to certain real estate developments. Other countries offer tax breaks to whole swaths of industries—for instance, this is how India promoted the creation of industrial parks to house call centers and information technology firms. What's interesting about these deals is that, in essence, they legally convey to certain segments of the business community the benefits of being in System D. Of course, you might argue that these businesses are excellent investments in the long run—that New York office towers will, over the long haul, wind up stimulating the economy and producing additional tax revenues, that the workers hired by the call centers and IT firms in India are young people who will constitute the country's growing and prosperous middle class for decades to come. But, on the other side of the debate, some argue that office towers would get built anyway without any subsidy and that the tax deals promote overdevelopment. And, in the Indian arena, some economists point out that the number of people working in call centers and IT businesses is a tiny percentage of the population. Street hawking, by contrast, employs far more people, and is, therefore, far more crucial to India's economic survival.

Another economic complaint against System D businesses is that they are simply not geared to grow. As sociologist Alejandro Portes, who has written analytical works about System D since the 1980s, put it, "This is not an engine for capital accumulation and investment. In general, these firms start small and stay small."

Does size matter? Is it important to grow? The answer, of course, is that it depends how you measure success. A large business like Walmart may, in conventional terms, be more productive and efficient than several million small stores. It may, therefore, seem to offer a greater chance for economic success. But as Procter & Gamble discovered in its work in Mexico and Morocco and dozens of other developing-world countries, the profusion of hawkers, roadside kiosks, and one- or two-cashier outposts are a potent source of business. They are stores that have very close connections to their customers. On a macro level, you might argue that the redundancy of so many stores—too many people doing the same work and diluting the financial reward—is actually hugely important, because it means more people have work and therefore can survive and make purchases, which drives the economy.

And the answer also depends on what you think qualifies as growth. Is it only growth on the bottom line—profit? Or can it be on the top line—involving purely growth in the amount of business, with no impact on profit margin? And what about innovation and risk taking? Does a company have to be big to be creative? After all, it certainly was a risky move for Chief Arthur Okafor to travel to China to engage in world trade. And it was innovative behavior for Linda Chen and Juan Ramirez and Alex Wei to set up System D businesses to capitalize on this new form of world trade. Similarly, it was a major risk for Margaret Akiyoyamen to put her available cash into selling mobile phone recharge cards via the umbrella market. Every day, thousands of people risk and innovate in System D. The idea that System D firms cannot be imaginative and come up with new ideas ignores all ways in which System D creatively exploits the fissures and fault lines of borders, the looseness of the customs rules, the fractures between different levels of government. There's simply no reason a business needs to be legally registered to be generating new ways of making money.

Though we tend to anoint big firms as important, the reality is that very few of these paragons of commerce started out big. Even two of the most successful modern firms, Microsoft and Google, were once little more than garage-band operations. A company doesn't need to be supersized to be profitable and productive.

Then there's the oft-heard cavil that most System D workers have no protection against discrimination, can be fired summarily, and don't receive health insurance or Social Security. What isn't said, however, is that, in many countries around the world, workers in the legal economy don't have many of these protections, either. What's more, instead of providing more benefits, many highly formal companies— Walmart, the world's largest retailer, is the most widely cited example—are actually emulating System D. Workers and activists have accused Walmart of forcing sales associates to work many hours off the clock and without pay, doctoring time sheets, refusing to pay overtime, and declining to provide many of its staffers with health insurance. Demonizing small-scale System D businesses for not providing health insurance while Walmart remains a respected and admired company is downright unfair.

Back in Lagos, the Kick Against Indiscipline campaign made quick work of one of the largest and most entrenched markets in the city: Oshodi. In just a few days in 2009, the KAI forces destroyed most of Oshodi, overturning umbrellas, confiscating merchandise, and burning the wooden kiosks that made up that massive market. Thousands of System D merchants lost their livelihoods. Today, traffic flows relatively freely and, as several Lagos newspapers have reported, real estate prices in the area have jumped. Fashola's men have also ejected the sellers from the Carter Bridge, a move that has improved traffic but wiped out hundreds of additional businesses. And all over the city, the police have clamped down on street merchants, making them take tables off the sidewalks. They have even arrested hawkers for selling mobile phone cards and Gala sausage rolls on the streets. (By the standard of other Nigerian cities, though, it could be argued that Lagos is being lenient; a court in Abuja, the country's capital, recently sentenced seven teenagers charged with unlicensed street vending to be publicly flogged.)

The government has also cut a deal with CAPDAN, the association that runs Computer Village, to move the market to the far fringe of the city. This relocation may benefit the larger firms in the market, which will have more room and more control, but it will almost certainly lead to an economic crash for the smaller fry. The little guys will have little hope of rebooting their businesses, because they depend on walk-in trade—people seeking quick repairs or a cheap, fast way to unlock or refurbish their mobile phones. And there will be far fewer people walking around the market, since a trip there and back from many parts of the city is bound to be a full-day affair.

Many Lagosians applaud these actions. But I am queasy. There had to be a middle ground, one that would free up the roadways while at the same time recognizing the strength and importance of the market that the merchants had created. Governor Fashola claims he is determined to remake Lagos as a twenty-first-century megacity. In his heart, he may mean well. But he has fenced off the public realm, transforming vast forums of public trading into sad little spaces that allow for no true public access. Indeed, one proof of the shortcomings of the KAI drive is what the government has done with some of the land reclaimed from hawkers at highway roundabouts and interchanges. In an attempt at beautification, the city has pushed out the hawkers and replaced them with dusty plantings. Then, in fear that the street merchants would take back these small strips of land, the government immediately fenced off these faded parcels. Of course, this also meant that no one could use these forlorn pocket parks. Consider the contrast with what one System D businessman achieved. He, too, took over a small parcel between the Apapa-Oworonshoki Expressway and one of its entrance ramps. He, too, muscled a bunch of people off the land—in this case some thugs who were using the vacant patch as their domicile. And he put a fence around the parcel, just as the government has done. But, instead of installing a useless bunch of plantings, he created a tree nursery and park that is now one of the only decent green spaces in the entire city. Anyone can enter, though there is a small fee. This System D park may be privately held, but it offers public access and is an amazing respite from the choked world of go-slows and burning trash just beyond its boundaries. The contrast between this merchant's System D ingenuity and the government's feeble fenced-in gardens is telling. The traffic may move well now that the commerce is gone from Oshodi. But consider the cost—in lives and livelihoods. Why was there no attempt to work with the merchants to determine Oshodi's future?

After all, evidence of similar demolition and relocation deals around the world doesn't inspire confidence. In early 2010, the government of Luanda, Angola, razed and relocated Roque Santeiro, that country's largest System D market. The result was catastrophic for Sambizanga, the neighborhood where the market used to stand, and for the traders who moved. Most local residents couldn't afford to make the twenty five-mile round trip to work at the new market, so unemployment skyrocketed and crime escalated dramatically. Customers also avoided making the lengthy trip to Panguila, the new location, and traders report a steep decline in business. "There are no customers," a vendor told Agence France-Presse. "Before people could come to buy pants, or a CD. Now they aren't going to spend 1,000 kwanzas [close to $11] on transport to come to Panguila." In fact, business is so bad at the new market that Angola's leading microcredit bank has determined that it will no longer make loans to the merchants there. And the final sad fact is that the city has announced nothing about how it intends to redevelop the central site where the market used to be.

Similarly, when a new market was built a few years back in Nairobi, Kenya, national and local officials trumpeted it as a terrific plan to move all street hawkers off the downtown streets. Muthurwa market, adjacent to one of the busiest downtown bus depots, was supposed to include "a 24-hour market with basic facilities like water, restrooms, lighting, a hospital, a police station, multi-storied stalls, a banking hall, and an administrative office," the *Standard* newspaper reported. The new market cost seven hundred million shillings ($8.6 million) to build and opened with great fanfare in December 2007. Just a year and a half later, the *Standard* disclosed a different reality. "Muthurwa has become the epitome of chaos. The 12-hectare complex has degenerated into a den of muggers where hawkers and matatu [shared van] operators jostle for space." The newspaper's report enumerated some of the problems: "Burst sewers, dusty if not muddy roads, congestion, pickpockets, and lack of water." In September 2010, vendors protesting the horrible physical and economic conditions at the market blocked roads downtown and clashed with police.

Halfway across the world in San Salvador, El Salvador, the police and politicians have unleashed "Operation Thunder," intended to drive the city's sixteen thousand roving vendors off the streets. Though the government claims it will renovate local markets for the vendors, the drive against street selling has resulted in brawls between hawkers and the cops, because, so the hawkers claim, the new markets are far from the center of town and offer no prospect of earning a decent living. "It's not that we love selling on the streets; it's that with unemployment so high, this is the only way we have to earn a living and support our families," Martín Montoya, a leader of the United Independent Vendors Movement, one of fifty-three different organizations that represent street sellers in the Salvadoran capital, told the United Nations' Inter Press Service.

In almost every city and country, these plans to banish markets from the central streets of the cities bring up the larger issue of what constitutes economic development. In Lagos, where 80 percent of the working people make their money in System D, it's hard to see how Fashola's plan constitutes anything other than an act of civic suicide. Destroying the positive homegrown entrepreneurial fabric of the city in the name of driving out the criminals and decongesting the roads is a far too broad policy. It hurts legitimate System D businesses far more than it hits the criminals.

Sadly, the government knows better. I wound up my first

trip to Lagos in 2007 by having a long talk with Jide Sanwo-Olu, who at the time was the commissioner of commerce and industry of Lagos State. The election was a few days away. Bola Tinubu was still the governor, but it was clear that Fashola would succeed him, and, indeed, Jide was supporting the Fashola team. He was full of grand ideas for how the state government could network with System D. He wanted to see *okada* drivers and bus drivers working in cooperatives. "If they do that, the government will give some incentives," he told me. He indicated that the government was ready to create partnerships with the informal markets to improve infrastructure and trade. "In our tax net, we have less than a million people. But we know that in the informal sector we have at least two million people. So, how do we bring these people into the net? Even our tax collectors are also corrupt." Jide had a variety of proposals. A small flat tax of 5 percent of a firm's income or perhaps a flat tax of fifty thousand naira. Arranging lump payments through the market associations or meeting directly with the associations to find out the exact kind of government projects they would need to begin feeling like they would like to support public initiatives. But the administration he works for (he remained in government in the Fashola administration) decided on the opposite approach. Though System D is responsible for 80 percent of the employment in Lagos, the current administration has approached it in a punitive manner.

Univinco, the nonprofit that claims it wants to preserve and enhance life on Rua 25 de Março, seems poised to make the same mistake in São Paulo. It hired an architect to design a new streetscape for the twenty-first century. The renderings adorn the walls of the organization's office. Unfortunately, what's most interesting about the drawings is what isn't in them. People. There are no customers in the drawings of this street market that draws a million shoppers a day on holidays.

Instead, Univinco's proposal for a brave new street market of the future shows a line of identical vendors' carts, spaced uniformly down the block. In the guise of saving the street market, this plan would throttle the street's vibrant commercial life by imposing the dispiriting, overplanned reality of a food court. Univinco seems determined to kill the market in order to save it.

As in Oshodi, the plan for Rua 25 de Março would likely benefit the bigger businesses and landlords in the area, who could expect higher property values and higher rents. Perhaps the street would become home to a perfume retailer selling genuine Calvin Klein rather than a *camelô* with a barrow full of cloned cologne. But in terms of the ground-level businesses and the people who come from all over the city to buy and sell, the loss of cacophony would be a disaster.

Nonetheless, in early 2010, São Paulo police started the process, making several raids on Galeria Pagé, one of the malls connected to the street market at Rua 25 de Março. The authorities claimed they collected more than a ton of pirated goods, including mobile phones, video games, and digital cameras, with a street value of perhaps R$10 million—or about $5.7 million. The *camelôs*, understandably, were worried about their livelihoods. But, within a day, most of them reportedly moved one stop farther out of town to the streets around the train and subway station in Brás (interestingly, this was another location where some of the smaller merchants opened up shop a century ago when the development of the office zone pushed traders off the downtown streets).

Fashola and Univinco and all others who seek to drive out the System D merchants seem to be deliberately ignoring what Ghanaian economist George B. N. Ayittey recently tweeted: "Every social need is a business opportunity." In their quest to make their cities saner and more understandable to outsiders, both Fashola and the planners at Univinco seem wedded to an economic strategy that deifies efficiency over employment and criminalizes the chaotic marketplaces that have defined the cities of the developing world. These informal markets, we are relentlessly told by most economists and politicians, are inefficient and can't scale up. In his writings, Ayittey has cited an Igbo proverb: *Enyene Idem ofiok oto nte Mfat edebede enye*—only an organism knows best its own needs and can best serve them. "Yet," he continued, "the pretentious state never consulted African 'organisms' and sought to determine and serve their needs." To Ayittey, as to development economist Peter Bauer, most officials wear the blinders of the West when confronting the businesses of Africa, Latin America, and Asia. Yet when you look at them from within, System D businesses turn out to be extreme examples of efficiency in action: they are organisms that know their own needs.

Significantly, Fashola has adopted Ayittey and Bauer's approach with regard to one powerful System D agglomeration: the *okada* industry. A number of years back, in a move designed to cut down on crime, the government decreed that *okada* drivers would be banned from working at night. Though this was a serious blow to some drivers' incomes, the *okada* men largely accepted the move. More recently, when Fashola negotiated with the unions that represent the drivers to restrict the bikes to a single passenger and to require that drivers and passengers wear helmets, System D sprang into action. Dozens of businesses in ASPAMDA started importing different styles of helmets in all sorts of cool colors. The cost was reasonable (I bought several for less than $3 each).

Of course, Fashola may have been motivated by the massive political might of the *okada* business. With as many as a million bikes operating in the city, and thousands more people involved in importing the bikes and bringing in parts to service them, and actually doing the repairs, there would have been a serious political price if Fashola had simply outlawed the industry, or forced all the drivers to get expensive licenses. You can't put a million people out of work and expect to get reelected. Still, in working with the *okada* industry, Fashola demonstrated the wisdom of engaging in a dialogue with the local entities that have long been filling social and economic needs.

If other System D groups are going to avoid being wiped out by misguided but well-meaning officials like Fashola, they're going to have to organize to maximize their power and figure out how to interact with the political system. And if the political leadership wants to harness the entrepreneurial spirit—the very thing that helps their country thrive—they're going to have to work with System D. What's needed is a kind of shotgun wedding.

Why Not Formalize the Informal?

It cannot be very difficult to determine who have been the contrivers of this whole mercantile system . . . The interest of our manufacturers has been most peculiarly attended to; and the interest, not so much of the consumers, as that of some other sets of producers, has been sacrificed to it.

—*The Wealth of Nations*

Since the city's birth as a safe haven for smugglers, Ciudad del Este's computer and electronics operations have all been part of System D. This was not an impediment. Icompy, Alex Wei's family-owned firm, routinely bought from well-known suppliers in the United States, including, staffers at his company told me, Bell Microproducts, Ingram Micro, Intcomex, Tech Data Worldwide, Encore Technical Sales, EVGA, Ma Laboratories, and Soyo. With a hundred employees, Icompy was such a respected dealer that, as one Paraguayan economist who knows the city well put it, "his firm could buy one hundred million dollars in products with the agreement that he will pay in thirty days. They operated for ten to twenty years in a highly informal market with absolute trust."

Essentially, the business model involved two acts of smuggling—or what Alex calls "camouflage." First the firms smuggled computers, peripherals, and other electronics into

Paraguay. Then they smuggled them out to buyers in Brazil. This was a great business, when computers were luxury items and prices were high. But as computers increasingly became a mass-market item, the dynamics of the business changed. In the 1980s, Alex told me, when his father founded the family business, selling a desktop computer in Brazil generated 100 percent profit for a Ciudad del Este dealer. His father quit the business a decade later when profit margins tumbled below 10 percent. Now, Alex reported, prices have fallen so low that the profit margin has dropped to 4 percent. Over the years, Brazil wised up to the disproportionate number of computers in the country that originated in Paraguay, and started to steer tax breaks to a local firm called Positivo, so it could sell computers at a price that would rival the Paraguayan firms. As recently as 2004, according to local merchants, three-quarters of the computers and computer components purchased in Brazil came through Paraguay; today, the cross-border trade supplies just 10 percent of the Brazilian market. So it was understandable that Ciudad del Este's information technology companies started to fret that their operating system was about to crash.

So, five years ago, they decided to go legit. Every single one of the computer dealers in Ciudad del Este is now a legal, registered, taxpaying company (indeed, Alex reported with a kind of perverse pride that Icompy is now the fiftieth-largest taxpayer in Paraguay), and their imports are all open and on the record and on the books.

On the surface, this appears to be a major vindication of the idea advanced more than two decades ago by the Peruvian economist, entrepreneur, and think-tank leader Hernando de Soto. De Soto is one of the pioneers in thinking about System D. His book *The Other Path*, issued in Spanish in the mid-1980s and in English in 1989, was, essentially, the first mainstream volume to acknowledge the vitality, validity, and value of System D. He offered a simple and intuitive response: simplify the workings of regulations and legal codes to make it easier for System D businesses to join the licensed, registered, incorporated world. In short, make it possible to formalize the informal (interestingly, though de Soto usually gets credit for this idea, officials in his hometown, Lima, Peru, have been legalizing informal squatter communities since at least 1961).

In *The Other Path* and its later companion volume, *The Mystery of Capital*, de Soto correctly recognized that System D businesses and neighborhoods are a hugely important part of the economy, yet the proprietors of these firms and residents of these neighborhoods were denied access to the tools of the formal system—loans, mortgages, bank accounts, government aid, etc. These items, he wrote, represented a massive increase in capital that could lift people out of poverty. Money locked in System D, he contended, was essentially dead capital. Allowing System D to formalize would be a simple, win-win solution. Owners of previously informal firms would be able to get loans—and that injection of capital would work wonders. "As soon as the poor become accountable under formal law, they will be able to afford low-cost housing and thus escape from the topsy-turvy world of the extralegal sector," de Soto wrote. "The elites will then begin to collect their rewards as well: Builders and construction material manufacturers will find their markets expanding, as will banks, mortgage companies, title agencies, and insurance firms."

In the real world, however, things are seldom so simple. Indeed, follow-up studies have suggested that most squatter communities in Lima that received private title to their homes didn't experience any ramp-up in mortgage lending. The squatters-turned-owners and formerly informal businesspeople felt more secure and were willing to invest more of their meager savings in their homes and businesses. But their dead capital remained dead, because no banks were willing to accept their now-legal homes and businesses as collateral for a loan.

Likewise, the successful formalization of the computer businesses in Ciudad del Este also proves that de Soto's one-size-fits-all solution won't necessarily work the way he thinks it will. That's because the computer businesses of Ciudad del Este didn't actually want to formalize and certainly didn't need to formalize. They had no problems accessing cash and no problems buying from reputable suppliers in the formal world. Instead, they were led to formalization by an outside economic agitator named Reinaldo Penner, who figured out how the firms could actually save money by joining the legal world. Penner runs Paraguay Vende, a nonprofit based in Asunción, the country's capital. Funded by the Agency for International Development—the economic arm of the U.S. State Department—and operated by a private Washington, D.C.–based consulting firm called Chemonics, Paraguay Vende's job is to engage in business development in the small, landlocked South American country.

Like everyone else in the country, Penner had long been aware of the economic value of the smuggling corridor along the border with Brazil. Alone among all the politicians, bureaucrats, and economists, he looked for a way to improve it. His "aha!" moment came when he read the fine print of the Mercosur treaty (the *Mercado Común del Sur*, called Mercosur, is the Southern Common Market agreement that links Argentina, Brazil, Paraguay, and Uruguay). Here, he discovered something irresistible: in an incentive to get Paraguay and Uruguay—the two poorer and less populous countries—to join a free-trade network with the two behemoths on their borders, Mercosur stipulated that information technology and electronic devices that can be considered educational in nature can be imported duty-free into the two smaller countries. In other words, smuggling the computers into Paraguay, which was costing Ciudad del Este businesses big bucks in bribes to customs officials, was no longer necessary.

Penner took his findings to the people running the computer companies in Ciudad del Este. They could save money, he told them, if they made their businesses legal. To Juan Ramirez, who runs PC Tronic and was the head of the chamber of commerce of the information technology firms at the time, the idea made sense. The computer businesses evaluated the proposal, and decided it would be interesting as long as the Paraguayan government would offer an additional inducement—a deal to lower the amount of taxes they would have to pay once they were legally incorporated and registered. Essentially, they wanted to swap the unpredictable and unknowable costs of hoodwinking the Paraguayan government for the completely predictable cost of paying taxes. "Things had changed a lot since we started in business," Ramirez said. "The market share was much lower than it used to be. Essentially what we were saying is, 'Lower taxes and we will make it all legal.'"

In an odd but understandable twist, there were some powerful portions of the Paraguayan government that were against the plan. "The biggest problem was the officials," Penner explained. "The customs officials opposed formalization." Though they made all sorts of arguments against the plan, the biggest issue was this: customs officers didn't want to lose the payoffs that the informal industry was paying them.

Despite the official opposition, the deal was cut and signed in 2005. In the quiet, air-conditioned offices of the chamber of commerce, Alex Wei scrawled the costs and benefits on a dry-erase board: the computer businesses are guaranteed to pay a reduced tax, the IVA (or *Impuesto al Valor Agregado—*

Tax on Aggregated Value) of 1.5 percent, a *valorización* tax of 0.5 percent, and what Alex called, in a blend of Spanish and Portuguese, *Imposto La Rata*, an additional tax of 0.6 percent, making for a total tax bite of 2.6 percent. Normal businesses in Paraguay pay approximately 10 percent in taxes. Essentially, in exchange for formalizing, with zero tariffs guaranteed by the Mercosur agreement, the information technology companies were guaranteed a tax savings of almost 75 percent. The effects were almost immediate. The year the deal closed, the value of imports into Paraguay that were reported to the government jumped by 66 percent, rising to $5 billion from $3 billion. Penner says the bulk of the increase was due to the formalization of the computer firms.

So what's the problem this presents for advocates of de Soto's plan to formalize the informal? It's just that Alex Wei and his fellow computer merchants admitted to me that, if not for the squeeze in the computer market, and the dual advantages of the quirk in the Mercosur treaty, and the extremely generous tax arrangement offered by the Paraguayan government, they never would have made the deal. De Soto assumes that things will automatically be advantageous for businesses if they leave System D. But the choice between becoming formal or remaining in System D, Penner told me, was a brutally direct question of costs and benefits. The questions the computer firms had to answer didn't involve their sudden ability to get loans or have bank accounts. Instead, Penner said, they asked, "What is the cost of bribing people? What is the cost of being exposed to blackmail? And how does that compare to the cost of paying taxes?"

There's another problem with using Ciudad del Este as the proving ground for de Soto's thesis: despite the fact that they formalized with regard to Paraguay, the computer businesses in Ciudad del Este are actually still part of System D. That's because, though one half of the business—bringing the machines into Paraguay—may now be open and aboveboard, the other half—bringing the machines out of Paraguay and into Brazil—remains clandestine and underground. As Alex put it, "We may no longer be informal, but the people who buy from us are." And those people—the shady network of large-scale smugglers known as *laranjas* who specialize in bringing computers on the cross-border journey—are still doing business.

Moreover, the IT industry got Paraguay Vende's attention and received special government action, because it accounts for more than 7 percent of the country's economic activity. The electronics industry in Ciudad del Este, which is currently trying to strike a similar deal, may also get some attention, because it is an equally large sector of the economy (all told, these two sectors in Ciudad del Este are responsible for an amount of trade equal to one-sixth of Paraguay's gross domestic product.) But what of most of the other businesses in Ciudad del Este—the ones selling underwear and socks and cheap consumer goods and those slotted straws and leather-swathed cups for drinking *tereré*? Unfortunately, they don't have power. They can't boast $1 billion in sales. They can't show that they are a huge chunk of the country's GDP. This means they will never be able to wrangle the kind of favorable agreement that will allow them to formalize. Instead, they will continue to smuggle their goods into Paraguay and smuggle them out again.

Formalization, indeed, is no magic bullet. Many businesses do better if they avoid the regulatory apparatus entirely, no matter how stripped-down and simplified the authorities make it. As Penner explained, the decision of whether to go formal involves more than cutting the licensing fees and the time required to incorporate. "This is not just avoiding the high costs of bureaucracy," he told me. "The key question is to find a competitive advantage in being formal." Or, as Gilles

Deleuze and Félix Guattari asked in *Anti-Oedipus*, their antic yet serious examination of the schizophrenic desires that spawn under capitalism, "How can people possibly reach the point of shouting: 'More taxes! Less bread!'?"

De Soto is certainly correct that the antiquated rules and procedures that make registering and incorporating and paying taxes a time-consuming and frustrating process should be trimmed back. There's simply no reason to have bureaucracy for the sake of bureaucracy (in the 1980s, de Soto documented that it took two hundred and eighty-nine days to get a business license in Peru, and he estimated that the cost of going through all the official procedures amounted to more than two and a half times the annual salary of a minimum-wage worker). Even the most proregulatory zealot would probably concede that this is excessive. It is absurd that that it can take months to get your goods out of Apapa port in Lagos, when you can often access them within twenty-four hours if you ship them to Cotonou. It is demented that there are active disincentives to doing business legally. But de Soto is wrong to suggest that simply pruning the out-of-control bureaucracy and bloated make-work rules will induce System D businesses to join the formal sector. In fact, most System D entrepreneurs make money precisely because they work off the books, evade registration requirements, or engage in smuggling or piracy. These things are part of the DNA of their system—and, like the Ciudad del Este computer dealers, any merchants who do business at the side of the road will need to see some serious and direct incentives if they are going to consider going legit. The idea that formalization offers an automatic avenue to commercial and social success is captivating, but it hasn't worked. Even when countries have adopted de Soto's paradigm, growth has remained elusive. As Princeton sociologist Alejandro Portes told me, "The promise of

Hernando de Soto's 'Other Path,' that you would open the markets and lift regulations and the economy would take off because of the energy of these small enterprises, has not materialized."

The main issue here is that de Soto and most other economists view System D from the outside. When your world involves incorporation, registration, and licensing, you see the barriers to achieving these things as the key problem. Those who know System D from the inside, however, have a different perspective. To them, there's nothing intrinsically more desirable about registration or licensing, if getting a registration or a license doesn't add anything to a business's bottom line. While getting incorporated may serve some businesses, it offers no occult power to extract profit from a particular business. Indeed, it simply protects a firm's owner from personal liability in any legal challenge. From the perspective of System D, then, the importance of the legal business world starts withering away. I would have liked to have gotten de Soto's thoughts on these issues, but he did not respond to my repeated requests for an interview.

Martha Chen, a lecturer at Harvard University's John F. Kennedy School of Government, who also works with informal enterprises through her position as coordinator of Women in Informal Employment: Globalizing and Organizing (WIEGO), a network of advocates and traders that is active in thirty-five countries, suggests that de Soto's idea that all businesses should be registered and incorporated and formalized arises from this same outside perspective. To the modern economist, incorporation, registration, and regulation may seem like eternal verities. And, she notes, they have indeed been spectacularly successful tools for development in post–World War II Europe and North America, which have economies that, until recently, were dominated by labor-intensive heavy industries. But before the past two generations, the United States and Europe had a more mixed economic picture. And the developing world today mimics that kind of structure. Economic power in the developing world is more fragmented, more reliant on small-scale businesses, family farms, local traditions, and extended social and regional networks, which may or may not be part of the legally recognized economic structure.

Chen wants us to consider that, contrary to de Soto's prescription, the best thing for many of the entrepreneurs of the developing world might be to stay in System D and grow. For a midsize dealer in recycled materials like Andrew Saboru, there's little benefit in incorporating or registering his business. No matter what he does, it's unlikely he'll get financing to grow, which is his major need. Similarly, it doesn't make sense for a street seller in Ciudad del Este to get a business license: it only costs money and cuts down on profits. For these merchants, the answer lies not in groveling at the altar of formalization but in creating a middle ground in which the flea market is a fine model for productive economic activity.

"We need to come up with models that allow the street trader to coexist along with retail shops and along with large malls," Chen told me. "The informal economy is not the problem. It's part of the solution. Street traders, waste pickers, market women: these people really do contribute to the economy and to their cities. How can we manage our cities in a way that has space for them? What we need to do with the informal economy is to figure out how to help it become more productive, more efficient, and more effective."

Freedom to Trade

Political œconomy . . . proposes to enrich both the people
and the sovereign.

—*The Wealth of Nations*

John Ebeyenoku stepped outside the shed that housed his
grinder. He stood amid piles of plastic containers, flip-flops,
and synthetic hair that his workers were steadily feeding
into the maw of the machine. Every few minutes, the motor
changed its frequency, as if it were thinking about the new
load of plastic before it could digest and spit out the same
plastic carved into tiny pellets of nylon that other workers
would bag for resale.

Above his head, modernity reached out to the people of
Lagos: an illuminated highway billboard powered by a massive diesel generator depicted smiling, clean, well-groomed
people—an advertisement for the mobile phone service
MTN with the catchphrase, "Yes, you can!" He pointed to
a small utility pole not far from the oversize advertisement.
This was the notable achievement of the merchants of Ojota
Mechanic Village. For years, the transformer on that pole
had been broken, and no power ever came to Mechanic Village. Though the traders mobilized and protested, neither
the city nor the utility responded to their complaints. So
they took action. Seven merchants got together, purchased a
transformer, and had it installed. It cost more than two mil-

lion naira (close to $15,000), but it was worth it. Now, when power surges through the wires, John and his fellow businessmen can use it.

Unfortunately, though, the utility doesn't have enough power to feed the city, and the electricity is off in Lagos more than it is on. In 2007, it was routine for some neighborhoods to be without power for days at a time. One day in Festac Town, the neighborhood where I was living, the power had been off for about sixteen hours when it suddenly surged to life. People scurried to turn on their light fixtures and plug in their mobile phones. But the power died after twenty seconds and remained off for another twenty-four hours.

Most people have ceased to get angry about this. Instead, they shrug their shoulders, stare at the sky, and, in a tone of regret and exasperation, say, "NEPA" (pronounced "nay pah"), which stands for the National Electric Power Authority, the former name of the government-controlled utility that is now known as the Power Holding Company of Nigeria. (An old Nigerian joke is that NEPA stands for "Never Expect Power Always.") Then, after this bittersweet exclamation, they run to set up their System D power sources—personal generators that have been brought into the country by traders like David Obi. In Alaba, there are generators at every price point and for every purpose: tiny motors the size of Dustbuster vacuum cleaners that can power a few feeble bulbs, devices the size of lawn mowers that can run a roomful of computers or power the refrigerator at a local bar, tractor-size models that can power an entire house, and even locomotive-size behemoths that can power whole office buildings. All over the city, residents and merchants alike sang the same song: though they paid their NEPA bills every month, their generators were their primary power supply, while NEPA offered only an occasional backup source of electricity.

The trade in diesel generators has been ingenious, innovative, and incredibly profitable. It has also been good for the country. Without those System D generators, the mobile phone system wouldn't operate, Internet cafés would cease to function, the city's crowded luxury hotels—the Sheraton and the Eko—would be dark and dank, the banks would have no ATMs, the international airport would have no ability to allow planes to take off and land at night, and, of course, the merchants in Ojota Mechanic Village would not be able to run their recycling machinery. The entire economy of the city would stumble. At the same time, the generators have also been bad. All companies operating in Lagos need generators to provide electrical power (indeed, most large firms have two generators, one to run most of the time and the other to serve as a backup in case the first generator breaks down), and this has greatly restricted the country's economic progress. The profusion of generators has also added to the environmental catastrophe of the city. Though diesel engines emit fewer toxins than gasoline engines do, they pump out an amazing amount of soot and grit, and the thousands of generators that run almost twenty-four/seven in Lagos have created an additional layer of grime and pollution in a city where the air already seems hazardous. And there's a cost to the political culture, too: the fact that people like John Ebeyenoku must buy a generator and the fuel to operate it has made them cynical about the ability of government to do anything. There is no public movement in the city to get the power company to provide more for the people.

Dozens of individual small generators provided the background noise of Ojota Mechanic Village. A group of scavengers dozed on their carts, awaiting the dealers who would weigh their haul of plastics and metals. Across the road, a vast pile of burning car tires—property of a recycling firm that recovers and resells the carbon black and steel reinforcing belts—emits an acrid cloud that floats above the valley day and night.

John's ten employees grind and bag almost a ton of nylon every day. They work in two shifts—five during the day, five at night, seven days a week. "We cannot keep up with the demand," he said. "We need financial assistance. We need an expert to come here and check our income and expenditures. And we need an expert to advise us on new technologies. If we had good machines, we could get twenty tons a day." Another recycling merchant, whose firm has been treating and crushing polyvinyl chloride for better than twenty-five years, added to the list. "Give us the land. Give us roads. Give us water. Give us electricity. Give us loans. Importation of PVC should be abolished." (A policy of "no PVC except recycled PVC" would ensure that businesses like his would have a monopoly on the market and thus could command a higher price.) He shook his head and repeated, almost word for word, something that Sir Israel Okonkwo had said when I met him in the auto spare parts market: "There is no government here in Nigeria."

Moved by necessity, these merchants had done something important. They had banded together in mutual aid to buy the transformer, a fine example of joint action. Yet they were still complaining. It remains questionable whether a big city with big aspirations like Lagos can survive without a stable power grid. Yet, at the same time, those seven cooperating merchants in Ojota Mechanic Village have not joined to pressure the government for power. Nor have they pooled their money to buy a bigger generator that might serve all of them while saving on fuel consumption. There was no continuing organization, no attempt to approach other issues collectively. Despite the improvement they had made through mutual aid, they hadn't used the experience to take on anything bigger. Each owner still complained about government, and the market's larger needs—infrastructure, training, access to innovative technologies, positive economic policies, etc.—still seemed beyond its reach.

Even in places where merchants have formed strong market associations, their development was limited. The Auto Spare Parts and Machinery Dealers Association (ASPAMDA) market, where Sir Israel and David Ibekwe both do business, is an inspiring example of System D's knack for self-organization. A bit more than a decade ago, the auto spare parts market was spread through the decaying buildings of Idumota, at the foot of the Carter Bridge on Lagos Island. The streets were so jammed that they couldn't get container trucks in to deliver their imports—and when they did, they often had to make payoffs in order to avoid violence from the local miscreants called area boys. So they came together and made a deal with the government to take over an unused wing of the International Trade Fair complex, ten miles away out the Badagry Express Road. ASPAMDA today remains a System D market, but there are no touts shouting at you, no street hawkers hitting you up to buy their goods. In an unusual move, the association actually created set hours for the market and decreed that all businesses must be closed on Sundays. ASPAMDA is orderly, organized, and ready for shipping, delivery, and world trade. And it is booming. Yet the association has no control over anything beyond its front gate. To get to the market, you have to exit the Badagry Express Road and enter the trade fair compound. And that short trip has become an opportunity for perpetual corruption. Someone has taken over the entry to the compound and turned the access point into a privately controlled tollbooth. Every time they drive into the market, every time they get a delivery, the merchants of ASPAMDA are strong-armed to pay that toll. Every customer who comes to see them pays it, too. It's a huge frustration and a huge cost, and market leaders say they have no ability to get rid of the fellow who has taken over the bridge. Indeed, some merchants told me, they don't feel they even have the power to complain, because the toll taker slips lots of money to local and national politicians, and if any merchant or group of merchants made noise about this, the consequences could be catastrophic. The market association—all-powerful in its own domain—insists that it is powerless to do anything about this governmentally approved patronage ring.

The toll taker at ASPAMDA is a true heir to the tradition of piracy exemplified in the doings of Sir Francis Drake and his near contemporaries, the Barbary corsairs, whose daring and violent exploits disrupted the traders of the Mediterranean. At the trade fair complex, one man has seized a location and extorts his massive profit by force and intimidation. When I passed by, several of the toll takers who work for him left the long line of cars and massed around me after I pulled out my camera and prepared to take a photo of the list of toll charges that was posted at the side of the road (only in Lagos, I think, will a brigand post a price list.) The show of force worked and I quickly shoved the camera back in my shoulder bag without having gotten the snapshot. The massive amount of money collected here is of no benefit to the market or the trade center complex—and that's the difference between this toll and the informal payments collected by market associations, or the daily dues *okada* drivers must pay to government officials for the ticket that ensures they won't get arrested. In the latter two underground transactions, the money pays for certain concrete benefits—the improvement of the market, the possibility of doing business without impediment. If a market association's leadership simply pockets their dues and does nothing to make the market better, the rank-and-file merchants can rise up to depose them. If the police refuse to honor the local government's daily tickets, the motorcycle taxi drivers will stop paying. But here at the trade fair complex, there was no exchange involved in the transaction. Sure, money changed hands. But the people in the vehicles that paid got nothing in return. This wasn't a productive business; it was an extortion racket.

Kate Meagher, a lecturer in development studies at the London School of Economics who has spent much of the past decade researching unlicensed and unregulated manufacturing clusters in eastern Nigeria, has seen the limitations of System D self-organization in action. "The major demand at this point is not credit," she told me. "It's infrastructure, roads, electricity, skills of cooperative development, exporting and marketing expertise. Small-scale producers aren't going to get these things just by saying so. They need to organize truly powerful associations. But they haven't got the social capital to do that." Without the solidarity to create structures that can influence things beyond their immediate environment, the merchants are looking to government for salvation—and unfortunately, Meagher suggested, the government, which often operates like a corrupt entity itself, is unlikely to provide the necessary support. "The state's not going to do this on its own. And the international lobby is pushing the opposite of what they need."

We live in an increasingly System D world. As urban visionary Jane Jacobs predicted back in 1969, the cities of the future "will not be smaller, simpler or more specialized than cities of today. Rather they will be more intricate, comprehensive, diversified and larger than today's, and will have even more complicated jumbles of old and new things than ours do." Without ever having seen them—and even if she had, Lagos, Ciudad del Este, and Guangzhou were comparatively tiny outposts four decades back—Jacobs described exactly how these cities and scores of others around the world would develop. Even troubled cities in unstable nations have become outposts of global trading circuits. In Harare, Zimbabwe, one young mother told the *Standard* newspaper that she could make multinational transactions without ever leaving town. "I'm on my way to the Gulf complex [a popular discount shopping center] where I will buy two bags of socks and napkins from the Nigerians then sell them to the Indians and Chinese downtown," this homegrown System D merchant explained.

To move forward in this increasingly chaotic environment, the businesses and markets of System D must reinvent themselves, creating structures in which they can pool their talents and extend their reach and power, thus taking on some of the characteristics of a system. And the formal world must also find ways to reinvent itself—making itself more nimble and adaptable, and, in a sense, less of a system. Governments need System D markets, because they are creative and questing and are where the jobs are. And System D needs government because it needs the goodies—infrastructure, organized ports, currency with a relatively stable exchange rate—that only government can provide. This tension offers an opportunity to forge a creative and productive space in which System D can develop and thrive. This dynamic global future won't involve free trade in the classic neoliberal sense—the destruction of barriers and tariffs and regulations so major global firms can suck up more profit. Rather, this new market system will involve the freedom to trade for System D.

Though it may sound libertarian, freedom to trade does not simply involve a Rothbard-style approach that would dismantle all rules that rein in business. Indeed, associations like the one at ASPAMDA have built power and stimulated trade by creating bottom-up edicts, directives, and rules for their marketplaces. Market associations intuitively understand what free market absolutists don't—that you don't end nefarious practices like illegal dumping or child labor by making it easier for firms to do business without oversight. The association at ASPAMDA understood that it needed to regulate its market to clean it up.

What would a world in which System D and the dominant system cooperate look like? How can System D make itself simultaneously more productive and more accountable? How can it gain stature with government without destroying itself through formalization? What would it take to give street markets more autonomy and control over their local environments and trading activities, while at the same time ensuring that the merchants feel a greater sense of social inclusion and responsibility? There have been a few tentative steps forward, some initiated by System D markets themselves, some that could be created by government fiat, and some coming from nongovernmental groups that are helping to organize the self-employed workers of System D. Taken together, these feeble first steps are beginning to unlock the potential of this parallel world of trade.

The sweltering, dusty kiosk was stuffed with rows of church pews. A dozen people lolled in the antique stillness, waiting to testify. Five men entered and took their seats around a battered table at the front of the room. This was the start of the meeting of the Alaba case settlement panel, a System D community court that meets twice a week to adjudicate conflicts in the market.

The first dispute involved a customer who said she received degraded merchandise and a dealer who was absolutely outraged that she would accuse him of deceit. The board members listened to the complaint and the response— sometimes voiced softly, sometimes at high volume. Then they concocted an agreement. The merchant was to take the defective item back, but instead of a refund or compensation for her lost time in making the complaint, the customer would get a simple replacement. What if that one, too, failed to work, the frustrated buyer shouted. The board was not impressed. A new television, one member declared, would be sure to satisfy her. The merchant grumbled, the customer grumbled—unhappiness all around. Justice delivered, case closed.

During a short recess in the proceedings, Wilfred Nwankwo, secretary of the panel, took a moment to talk. Under the previous market leaders, he said, Alaba was a fractious place, and justice in commercial disputes was hard to come by, which made shoppers fearful of buying. Though he is a merchant, and thus perhaps more inclined to believe the word of one of his fellow traders, he also was studying law at Lagos State University. In keeping with his training, he told me, he wanted the panel to be objective and not adversarial. "Arbitration is our work," he said. "Most often we arrive at a peaceful solution. This is how we have harmonized the market."

Disputes have been around as long as there has been commerce. Every society develops mechanisms to deal with them. In ancient Greece, each market—the *agora*—had a popularly elected manager—the *agoranomos*. In Muslim North Africa, every commercial district had a *muhtasib*. Roman merchants established their own arbitration panels. Britain had Piepowder. This odd term—the word has nothing to do with pie and only a bit to do with powder—dates back to the twelfth century, when the tradition started that every local market had to be accompanied by a tribunal that could render justice to offended buyers and sellers. The panels were called Piepowder courts—a corruption of the French *pieds poudrés*, or dusty feet—an apt metaphor for the speed with which justice needed to be rendered. In a street market setting, cases have to be heard almost as soon as they are brought, because peddlers can easily pack their wares and skip town long before a traditional court could even convene. Piepowder tribunals operated for as many hours as the fair was open and could hear cases as quickly as an hour after a dispute arose. If a merchant failed to show up or respond to a charge, the court could order his or her goods seized, in a kind of primitive bail bond. The goal was to have cases presented, argued, and settled within twenty-four hours (though many actions lasted much longer). Surviving court records show that the Piepowder judges offered mediation, arbitration, and hearings. After one proceeding dragged on for the full duration of the local fair, the judge convened what he called a "love day," on which the plaintiff and defendant should come together and solve their dispute.

Piepowder tribunals were the lowest courts in the land, and were often lampooned, their judges pilloried as buffoons (Ben Jonson's 1614 play *Bartholomew Fair*, for instance, was a comic take on the doings of a Piepowder judge in London's largest street market). Despite their low public regard, however, Piepowder courts were also early adopters of some judicial innovations that we take for granted today. Trial by jury, hearing testimony, adjudicating matters based on evidence and not just sworn oaths: these practices arose in Piepowder cases and seem to have leaked upward into the higher courts. These tribunals declined as industrialization took hold. But the requirement that every local market in the United Kingdom have a Piepowder court remained on the books until 1971.

The Alaba case settlement panel is a kind of Piepowder court—and these types of institutions should be the norm in every major System D market all over the world. As in Alaba, these courts can be set up on an ad hoc basis, by associations of merchants. Or they can have the force of law, and be written into statute, as has been done at Tokyo's Tsukiji market, where sushi-grade tuna is bought and sold. High-end tuna is costly, and judging its quality is a kind of art. Disputes are common, even between buyers and sellers who have worked together with mutual trust for years. Adjudication must be swift, since fish spoils rapidly, and the evidence can't be stored but needs to be carved up and resold. The tuna court at Tsukiji doesn't have a single law school–trained judge. Instead, it's run by the auctioneers themselves. Yet its decisions have the force of law, since the power of the court has been written into the city's municipal statutes. Participants get a hearing, and one appeal—which is essentially a chance to reargue the case before the same judges, because there's no higher market tribunal. Like the Piepowder courts of history, the tuna court generally handles disputes, no matter how complex, the day they arise.

If markets establish Piepowder-type tribunals, they may receive more benefits than simply the possibility of crafting swift and sure solutions to individual market disputes. In joining to create a court, the merchants in a System D market create something bigger than themselves. They don't need white-wigged barristers or learned jurists to tell them what to do. Informally, haphazardly, they build their own social contract, based on fairness, equity, and justice. Forming a market court means that they have taken an initial step toward collective organizing and cooperative action. Once a market creates a court that endures, it is possible to look toward other tasks: perhaps an infrastructure bank, or a local sanitation department (a few merchants wielding brooms can make a big difference), or a market security force. If System D merchants can consistently work together to solve problems in their markets, their power and prestige will be greatly extended, and, as Wilfred suggested had happened in

Alaba, their businesses will grow, because more people will trust their dealings.

In professions that don't have an organized location for buying and selling—which often face the most discrimination and repression from municipal authorities—System D workers turn to mutual organization for protection and security. Thirty years back, Sérgio Bispo dos Santos walked from the rural north to the big city. During the three-month trek, he slept outside, kept away from people, and lived mostly on bananas. Bispo (like Brazil's popular ex-president Luiz Inácio Lula da Silva, who is known as Lula, he has chosen to go by his last name) made it to São Paulo, the country's biggest city, and cut a new life for himself as a *catador de lixo*—an unregulated itinerant garbage recycler. Brazil has three hundred thousand *catadores*. São Paulo alone has twenty thousand. The *catadores* roam the streets collecting any castoff items that have value and reselling them to distributors.

For his first two decades in the big city, Bispo worked alone from a corner of the Largo Sete de Setembro, a plaza on the edge of São Paulo's business district where a large number of recyclers had set up camp. Though they occupied the same location, they hustled their routes and sorted and sold their pickings separately. Ten years back, however, the city government decided to evict the *catadores* from the downtown plaza.

The move drove the *catadores* together. Bispo joined with a few others to seize a small unused parcel under one of the city's radial highways. But instead of welcoming their action—after all, this new site meant the garbage recyclers were truly off the street—the city government treated it like a declaration of war. The police shot at the scavengers and roughed them up. Every day he wheeled his cart out into the city, Bispo risked being harassed or arrested for the simple act of recycling trash. Nonetheless he and his fellow co-op members kept at it, and won a nervous truce with the city.

Today, the members of his group of scavengers are well entrenched on the lot they seized seven years ago. It is now the headquarters and sorting station of the cooperative that they have named after the neighborhood where it is located: Cooper-Glicério.

As darkness fell, he returned to the compound to sort the waste he had collected. Even the humblest materials—napkins, for instance—have value: they can be turned into newsprint. But Bispo shook his head as he wadded up a bunch of tiny plasticized papers. He tossed them over to me. "Unhappily," he said, "there's no way to recycle candy wrappers." The members of Cooper-Glicério also collect used cooking oil from nearby hospitals and restaurants, cardboard and white office paper from downtown firms, old computers from office buildings, and almost anything else that they think has any value (interestingly, Bispo noted, there's particularly strong underground demand for undamaged empty Johnnie Walker whiskey bottles, because there's a clandestine business that refills them with mass-produced rotgut).

Cooper-Glicério is a successful business. Its three dozen members collect a total of one hundred tons of recyclable materials every month. But even at that scale, they can't afford to buy compressors or shredding and baling machines, or even a battered old truck to transport the sorted stuff to buyers. The cooperative cannot sell to the big manufacturers who are the end users of recycled materials. Instead, Cooper-Glicério must sell its pickings to the city's big carting companies, which Bispo contends are part of a mob-linked cartel of firms that control the recycling industry. Given their size, the cartel dealers have almost total control over prices. For instance, Bispo told me, the cartel will pay his cooperative only twelve reais per kilo (about $7) for copper, while they collect thirty reais per kilo (or almost $18) when they resell the copper to metal fabricators. That's a profit margin of 150 percent that the cartel companies earn simply because they are bigger than the cooperative. And the markup on *papelão*, or cardboard, is even worse: the cartel makes a profit that is thirteen times larger than the amount it pays Cooper-Glicério.

Cooper-Glicério is itself part of a national organization called the Movimento Nacional dos Catadores de Materiais Recicláveis (MNCR), the National Movement of Collectors of Recycled Materials. This cooperative of cooperatives has the potential to help its members win national recognition as a kind of parallel provider of city services. Still, despite a commitment from the Brazilian government to work with this well-organized group, only about thirty-five thousand of the three hundred thousand *catadores* in the country, or a shade more than one in ten, have chosen to join the national union. Sonia Maria Dias, an activist academic who has worked with the *catadores* in her hometown of Belo Horizonte and throughout the country for several decades ("I really became a garbologist, not a sociologist," she joked), admits that the membership numbers are dispiriting. Recyclers, she suggests, are generally classic individualists and prefer to work alone, outside of bureaucracy, and away from the glaring eye of the government.

Whether organized or solo operators, all the *catadores* were recently hit by something out of their control. Demand in China has been helping to fuel the boom in recycling, but in 2009, overzealous Chinese firms, eager to suck up waste from all over the world, bought up too much paper and cardboard, and, when demand died, prices crashed worldwide. In Brazil, the price of *papelão* dropped 80 percent in just two years. Street scavengers in India have reported a similarly catastrophic price crash. Dias found some black humor in the devastation wrought by the fall in prices: "I guess you might call that the invisible hand of the market," she said.

Though it's not clear when prices will return to sustainable levels (there was a rebound in 2011 for large scrap dealers, but street recyclers still reported depressed earnings), this much remains true: recyclers are doing important work, helping to save the planet from drowning in garbage that could otherwise be reused and repurposed. By organizing into cooperatives they increase the amount they can recycle and resell and ensure that more of the money goes to the people who do the recycling labor, and doesn't get siphoned off to endless layers of middlemen, brokers, and corrupt cartel corporations. In cooperatives, they can also create safer and better working conditions. If more countries emulated Brazil, and established policies to encourage the creation of recycling cooperatives, it would provide an incentive for street recyclers to organize, and, ultimately, to skip the middleman and sell their pickings directly to those who pay the highest price.

Two important groups in India—the Self Employed Women's Association (SEWA), and Chintan, an urban nonprofit dedicated to sustainability and the environment—are leading the way in cooperative development. They organize scavengers, recyclers, and others, and they are trying to reinvent the market, bringing women into the forefront of leadership (though men tend to control the market associations and the larger System D companies, women constitute a massive portion of the System D labor force, particularly in garbage scavenging; with organizing, sisterhood can be economically powerful), creating better working conditions and higher incomes, starting insurance pools and loan funds, and engaging in cooperative action to create more job security for informal workers. Through these organizations, women, and by extension all System D workers, are starting to have a voice in politics.

Jua Kali means "hot sun" in Swahili, and it is the local term of art for System D in many nations in East Africa.

Merchants from several of these countries have founded an annual *Jua Kali* expo, a chance for artisans and merchants to show off their products and trade ideas. Outside of the *Jua Kali* network, other street vendors from Zambia, Malawi, and Kenya have convened an organization dedicated to sharing strategies and building a network that can provide mutual support so they can resist government efforts to destroy their markets. Maker Faire Africa—an annual conference of the continent's inventors and entrepreneurs—is another example of this kind of activity. These local efforts could be expanded on a regional and ultimately a global basis.

There are scores of such System D efforts throughout the world. In San Francisco, La Cocina is providing technical assistance to unlicensed food businesses in the hope that they will make the jump from System D to the formal world. In New York, the Street Vendor Project is mobilizing licensed and unlicensed street merchants to press for their rights. A Dutch nonprofit called the PharmAccess Foundation has rolled out a pilot program for an HMO health care network for System D workers, working in partnership with a local hospital and a group of female auto mechanics in Lagos. In Cambridge, Massachusetts, WIEGO, a nonprofit with global membership, is advocating for System D. All of these groups are pushing for a world in which System D assumes an important role. Some or all of these groups could come together to highlight the positive role System D has played in the global arena, creating a worldwide event where thousands of artisans and traders could network, trade, learn, and organize, and where outsiders could learn about the benefits of their work.

Bispo's cooperative, Wilfred's Piepowder tribunal, the self-made associations that govern the street markets of the world, the well-established rules that keep Rua 25 de Março functioning, the efforts of women who work in System D to create joint insurance plans, better their working conditions, and share methods and tactics: these are all forms of cooperative organizing. Still, forming System D coops is no panacea, as Alexander Chayanov, the great modern theoretician of cooperative economics, understood quite well. Chayanov, a noted Soviet economist, was purged by Stalin—arrested in 1931 and executed in 1937—for arguing that a linked system of market-based cooperatives made more sense as a development strategy than collective farms. He cautioned, however, that it would be impossible for these local cooperatives— joint marketing groups, credit cooperatives, insurance pools, and consumer buying clubs—to join into a gigantic supercooperative. That's because their economic interests are different: no matter how cooperatively organized, dairy farmers want to get the highest price they can for their milk, while families that buy the milk want to pay as little as possible, and the companies that provide cash simply want to ensure the money they invest is used wisely and ultimately repaid. Still, he argued, cooperatives with divergent interests could come together on issues of governance and public policy. If today's System D markets can engage in this kind of self-mobilization and self-empowerment, they can bolster the cooperative tendencies of their markets and greatly improve their autonomy and their power, giving them a dynamic role in local politics and decisions about trade policy. Then they can join with groups in other cities and other countries to assert their force in the global arena. This kind of awakening would go a long way toward giving System D a voice worthy of its size and importance. Through cooperative organizing, System D can help determine the world's economic future.

In an outdoor bar by the National Theatre, five people reenacted a scene that could have come straight from *L'Elisir d'amore (The Elixir of Love)*, Gaetano Donizetti's comic opera of 1832. A sweet-talking vendor extolled the ink-black herbal tonic he had in his bag for its vital efficacy in warding off many kinds of diseases and, he noted in a suggestive whisper, increasing sexual potency. The four men at the table were educated, intelligent, and totally transfixed by his spiel. In the end, three of the four bought bottles of the tincture.

On a packed bus ensnared in a go-slow not far from Mile 2, the scene repeated itself with a slightly different flavor. A man suddenly stood. For ten minutes, he sounded off about good behavior, the power of positive thinking, being healthy, and getting right with God. Then he got down to business. His diction remained ministerial, but his pitch was pragmatic. He passed some boxes of tablets around the bus. This preacher was selling deworming medication. In the end, more than half the people on the bus bought his nonprescription prescription.

There's nothing particularly new about these vignettes. People have been selling patent medicines since long before Donizetti wrote his opera. From a modern medical perspective, we tend to view all these street merchants as fraudsters making miraculous claims about spurious snake oil. In truth, however, many potions that are still common in today's medicine cabinets started their commercial life as questionable and untested remedies. Vicks VapoRub and Pepto-Bismol (both now owned by Procter & Gamble) originated as patent medicines. So did Bromo-Seltzer, Angostura bitters, milk of magnesia, and Luden's cough drops.

The people who sold these unregulated elixirs, unguents, emollients, and exfoliants have long been considered charlatans. Yet, contrary to the pejorative meaning the word has in contemporary parlance, there once was a time when being a charlatan was an honorable profession. In Renaissance Italy, charlatans were actually licensed medical practitioners. Each city-state created its own independent commission called a *protomedicato*. The board generally included the most distinguished and respected physicians of the town. Each potion, each lineament, each tonic and rub that was offered for sale in the town was subject to review. The *protomedicato* listened to the claims a street seller made, studied the products, did assays, and, if they could determine that the tonic or lotion had some beneficial effect and wasn't harmful in any way, approved the person as a charlatan licensed to sell that concoction. Over the years, *protomedicato* tribunals licensed thousands of charlatans to distribute their potions.

Nigeria has a bureaucracy that is ready-made to handle its elixir sellers—the same bureaucracy that is involved in regulating the production of those heat-sealed plastic baggies of H_2O called Pure Water. Every company that produces Pure Water must be registered with Nigeria's National Agency for Food and Drug Administration and Control (NAFDAC) and keep to a set of rules. According to NAFDAC's regulations, each borehole must reach down at least a hundred and fifty feet, and the water must be filtered, chemically treated (if necessary), and sterilized before it can be fed into machines that fill the baggies and scald them with heat to seal them. Each company must be inspected and receive a license before it can sell any water, and NAFDAC reinspects each firm every six weeks, to make sure the equipment is well maintained and the water is safe to drink. Also, according to the agency's rules, it is illegal to sell Pure Water that has remained in its bag for more than two months—because in that amount of time, chemicals from the nylon bag can leach into the water. This stripped-down version of regulation has been a success. The Pure Water companies obey the rules, and all of them print their NAFDAC license number on their bags, though they may still camouflage their profits and evade other governmental requirements.

Regulating elixir sellers would be similar to what NAF-
DAC already does with Pure Water—testing to ensure public safety, and allowing vendors to sell on the streets as long
as they follow the minimal set of rules and offer only the
products they are certified to offer. The agency could even
recruit eminent traditional healers to monitor the street sellers, allowing them to evaluate each patent medicine before
it could be offered for sale. The elixir sellers given permission to market their products by this modern version of the
protomedicato needn't be forced to get incorporated or have a
business license. The goal of this modest form of regulation
would be limited. It would not stamp out traditional medical
practices; nor would it eradicate street sales. Rather, it would
use the skill of modern medicine to bolster traditional heal-
ing. This would, of course, extend the government's bureaucracy. But if the elixir sellers and traditional practitioners paid
a small fee to get NAFDAC certification for their tinctures,
the program might pay for itself. The benefit to the public
health would be worth the price.

Around the world, thoughtful politicians are looking to
engage System D. In the Philippines, where three-quarters
of the nation's workforce—24.6 million people—work in
System D, progressive legislators have introduced a bill that
would establish "a Magna Carta for the informal sector." This
bill would not force unregistered, unincorporated, or unlicensed firms to become formal, but it would give System D
workers a package of governmentally recognized rights—
such as safe and humane working conditions, the right to
form a union, and access to channels of alternative dispute
resolution—that would greatly improve conditions for workers. At the same time, the bill would create an inducement
for informal firms to get business licenses by giving firms and
workers access to an affordable health insurance program
and to Social Security. In return, informal firms would pay

modest registration fees and annual dues to the government, increasing the public coffers by $25 million to $50 million. Officials in Kenya, too, have been pressed by an organization of street vendors to consider extending labor protections to street vendors and market workers. While these proposals seems unlikely to pass anytime soon, the simple fact that legislatures are considering them represents a significant advance for System D.

In Bolivia, where more than two-thirds of all jobholders work in System D, President Evo Morales has announced a new plan to offer retirement benefits to System D workers. The populist leader hopes to enroll a hundred thousand of them in a new pension program this year. The program would be funded through contributions from street marketeers and other System D workers, but it would be augmented by a surcharge of half of 1 percent on workers' salaries and a 3 percent tax on formal-sector employers. This money would be dedicated to what Morales has called a solidarity fund, which would pay for pensions for low-wage workers. Over the next few years, the Morales administration hopes, a large percentage of System D workers will sign up.

A different kind of law that is friendly to a set of people working in System D recently came into effect in New York State. The Domestic Workers' Bill of Rights, which became state law on November 29, 2010, establishes minimum employment standards for the state's two hundred thousand nannies, home attendants, and housecleaners. For the first time, their workweek will be limited to, at most, six days; they will have the right to higher wages if they work more than forty hours in any week; and they can qualify for an extremely short paid-vacation time (three days of vacation after twelve months of work, as guaranteed by the law, is skimpy by almost any standard). The Bill of Rights even applies to people who work off the books. Sadly, however, the legislature rejected a broader set of proposals that would have guaranteed domestic workers two weeks' notice before they could be dismissed, severance pay, and the right to join a union and engage in collective bargaining.

Alfonso Morales, the planning professor at the University of Wisconsin who financed his graduate degree by selling cut-price hardware at Chicago's Maxwell Street Market, offers another in-between proposal that would enable governments to recapture some off-the-books cash without preventing people from surviving in difficult times. He suggests that street markets are crucial for development, and that municipal, state, and national governments in the United States and elsewhere have to learn how to work with them. "We need to go from a purely enforcement mentality to a mentality of 'let's try to enlarge the pie and increase people's share of it,'" he told me. "We should allow vendors to incorporate themselves incrementally into the system. If we do this, there's lots of room for growth." The mechanism he proposes is simple—a strategy that doesn't force formalization on unwilling entrepreneurs, but doesn't allow System D firms to operate with no civic responsibilities either. Rather than making merchants incorporate and pay taxes, Morales proposes that government offer business licenses to informal merchants, but hike the licensing fees so that these firms are contributing to the public coffers without paying taxes. The benefit of getting a license is clear: merchants could no longer be arrested or harassed by the police for selling on the street. Yet, he argues, the licensing procedure should not force them to formalize and declare all their income. This, he asserts, represents a win-win approach—giving informal merchants a stake in the legal world while adding to government revenues.

A further route for governmental intervention in System D involves direct investment. Robert Pollin, an economist at the University of Massachusetts at Amherst, has led a team looking to create "pro-poor, employment-focused economic policy" prescriptions for both South Africa and Kenya. In these economists' estimation, lack of employment is one of the key problems facing Africa (and, by extension, much of the developing world). Their idea is that government should stimulate certain sectors of the economy that have a good chance of producing lots of jobs.

In addition to a major push to fund infrastructure—in South Africa, the economists have proposed allocating thirty billion rand (approximately $4.3 billion) more per year than the government has budgeted, and funding the expansion by raising taxes and royalties—the group recommends the creation of a new policy that would require banks to hold back 25 percent of their assets from general lending in order to use the money to target loans to companies the government was already assisting to create job growth. The government would guarantee these loans, and this pool of reduced-interest credit would offer a double spur for action—multiplying the impact of government subsidy with mortgage money. The economists suggest that these doubly subsidized firms should account for somewhere around one-fourth of the economic activity of the country.

Pollin and his colleagues are adamant that the companies the banks and the government should aid must be formal—and this seems to make sense given the official statistic that just 2 million of the 12.9 million working people in South Africa earn their income off the books. (Indeed, South Africa has long boasted the lowest rate of cash-only labor in Africa.) But Adcorp, an employment services firm, has recently challenged South Africa's narrative about the number of people working in the economic underground. Comparing domestic expenditures, capital formation, and the circulation of bank notes, Adcorp extrapolated that an additional 6 million South Africans are economically active but remain uncounted in the country's employment statistics. Brian Kantor, an economics professor and investment strategies with Investec Securities, told the *Financial Mail* newspaper that the government's assessment of the number of people working in System D was far off the mark. "Our official measurement of the informal sector is about 5%-6% of GDP," he told the paper. "That's a nonsense number. In Italy, it's 15% and in the US and Britain it's far higher."

Indeed, officials in countries that acknowledge large numbers of people working in System D are not afraid of looking to government to invest in off-the-books businesses. For instance, Arjun Sengupta, an MIT-trained economist who served as the head of India's National Commission for Enterprises in the Unorganized Sector, recently called for a fiscal stimulus plan for System D that would pump $8.2 billion into the country's unrecognized and unregulated businesses. Sengupta, who died in 2010, promoted the idea of development as a human right and was one of the rare economists who was not afraid to engage with System D. "The idea is to introduce a fiscal stimulus programme in the form of public investment and expenditure specifically aimed at the informal economy, on which 880 million people depend, for their livelihood and purchasing power," he wrote in *The Economic Times* newspaper in 2009. This kind of loose-knit joint operation between government and System D is exactly what is needed to ensure that the majority of the Indian population continues to survive and thrive.

Finally, governments could also benefit System D by using their power as the regulators of national and local banks. In a recent article published by the Himalayan News Service, one of the governors of the central bank in Nepal put the problem in stark terms: "The money is in the informal sector." Bank director Yubaraj Khatiwada called this "a chronic problem." It's only a problem, however, if you believe that businesses exist to serve banks. After all, the banks are quite willing to take deposits from System D merchants. The problem is the other half of the equation: banks will seldom give loans to these depositors.

If banks exist at least in part to serve their customers, then we have to reverse this mind-set. What would it look like if banks had to satisfy their local market? After all, the status quo is not necessarily bad for banks. They make money on deposits, no matter where the money comes from, but System D merchants who put their money in local banks get little benefit, other than a secure place to store their cash.

It's time to start negotiating a global consensus on appropriate banking. The principle should be this: banks should be expected to serve the needs of their communities, and if a System D market is their community, it should be incumbent on the banks to come up with ways to assist that System D market. One way to push this forward: require banks to open their books and to show how much each branch has on deposit and how much it loans out to the local community. If information truly is power, then knowing these details might encourage System D workers and firms and even entire markets to boycott certain banks that are unresponsive to their needs. And these kinds of organized consumer actions would spur banks to further reevaluate their practices.

These proposals, involving diverse countries, developed and developing, offer a modest blueprint of the kinds of government policies that can create an in-between zone, where System D firms and workers can be recognized and can have rights without being forced to formalize. If implemented, they could help ensure that System D works for the national and global good.

Engagement with System D can also help solve some of the more difficult, devious, and conflicted aspects of the global economic underground. For instance, for most of 2007, Monsurat Aro spent her mornings at the bus stop at Mile 2 in Lagos, Nigeria, selling bags of Pure Water. But unlike most of the vendors, she used the sums she earned to pay for her education. For four hours a day, she carried a plastic bucket full of bags of drinking water on her head and chased after the buses, trying to sell as many bags as she could. The profit she made was small—Monsurat bought in small quantities, and so earned only two naira per bag, compared with the three and a half naira that many other Pure Water sellers earned—but on an average day, she took in a hundred and twenty naira (or a little less than $1), enough to help buy the uniform, notebooks, and knapsack she needs for school.

When I interviewed her, Monsurat was thirteen. She should not have to work, but the government offers no help. Nor do the distributors who are buying the water cheaply and selling it to Monsurat at a profit. Nor do the dozens of companies that pump the water from the ground and seal it in the bags and make the real money. Nor, to be honest, did I. Yet, if she stops working, chances are she will be thrown out of school, because students are required to have books and a book bag and a uniform, and if she breaks those rules, she will likely be expelled. So she must continue to work. "Pure Water," Monsurat shouted as she charged after another dented yellow van. The blue bucket on her head bobbed and the sweat dripped down her neck and arms and soaked into the slowly thickening wad of creased and dirty five-, ten- and twenty-naira bills that she clutched in her hand, her ticket to a better education and a better life.

There's no question that child labor is heinous. It should

be against the law everywhere and it should be prosecuted. People who abuse children (or adults, for that matter) in order to make a buck are criminals. And, undoubtedly, some System D merchants are guilty. Companies that produce pirated products, in particular, have been accused of engaging in widespread child labor abuses. But, as we crusade against child labor, we have to confront the contradictions inherent in Monsurat's story. If we prevent Monsurat from working we will prevent her from going to school—a truly upside-down result. And, of course, the practice of child labor is not limited to System D businesses. Back in the 1990s, Nike and other global brands routinely had their goods made at developing world factories that employed children. The practice continued until activists exposed it and made it a global concern. More recently, China lied about the age of one of the gymnasts on its team in order to bolster its scores at the Beijing Olympics. Misusing kids is not solely the domain of System D. Governments and well-respected corporations are in on it, too.

Still, when we drive these jobs underground, we miss an opportunity to confront the powerful moneyed interests behind them and to craft real-world rules to restrict the worst labor practices. Perhaps the best approach for everyone— workers, owners, government, advocates, children—is to recognize that System D workers exist. That way, when government officials and inspectors barge into informal workplaces, the workers and the managers who coordinate their work won't fear criminal prosecution and will be more likely to cooperate with prosecutors and investigators.

Without government engagement, System D also offers simple and unfortunate ways for businesses to evade important environmental regulations. For instance, huge caches of old computers and mobile phones—products that should be recycled where they are used—are being shipped around the globe, often with falsified manifests. Once they get into a country, they become almost impossible to track, as they are distributed to local markets where manual laborers rip them apart, taking only the most obviously valuable materials, and leaving the other toxic compounds—mercury, plastics, and other polluting chemicals—to rot and leach into the groundwater, or to be burned, polluting the soil and emitting toxic fumes.

Not all the operators in this illegal economy are part of System D, but the proliferation of out-of-date computers and discarded cell phones in China, Africa, and India has become a major problem. An environmental group called the Basel Action Network (BAN)—the name comes from the location where the global e-waste treaty was negotiated and signed, Basel, Switzerland—has exposed much of this toxic dumping. Through surreptitiously collecting materials from unauthorized dump sites, BAN has found that hard drives and other equipment from U.S. and European governments, universities, and private businesses are being chopped up, dumped, and burned in Nigeria and China. (Following in BAN's footsteps, I toured the outer reaches of Alaba, Ladipo, and Computer Village, and in each market I saw workers raking masses of circuitboards, plastic computer bodies, and shards of other components into piles and setting them alight.) In Seelampur, on the fringes of Delhi, a recent exposé by the news magazine *Tehelka* showed the awful downside of this underground trade. "Why should we go to school when we can make up to Rs. 200 every day by segregating copper from plastic," a fifteen-year-old boy told the weekly. A mother who has been ripping the copper from e-scrap for twelve years but is still earning less than half what the teens make, described her family situation this way: "My kids are naked ghosts in this pile of trash." Though the weekly's reporter saw "heaps of motherboards burning steadily" in the market, an official of the government's Central Pollution Control Board told him that "there is no burning of motherboards in Seelampur." If nongovernmental advocacy groups like BAN could work openly with the leaders of System D markets like Alaba and Computer Village, these markets could be incorporated into the global monitoring system, and together, System D and environmentalists could put pressure on unscrupulous operators to change their ways. This would be great for laborers who are exposed to toxic residues and would make it harder for American and European dealers to bolster their profits by using these markets as dumping grounds so they can avoid expensive recycling costs.

People concerned about the labor conditions and environmental regulations in System D might gain hope from the innovative policy created by Inditex, the highly formal global clothing company based in Spain. Inditex is a low-price, high-style retailer, and it keeps its cheap-but-chic reputation by sticking to a just-in-time business model—getting limited quantities of new designer-inspired knockoffs into stores within two weeks after each runway show. The firm keeps its costs down and its business vital by contracting with more than a thousand unlicensed artisans and workshops around the world. These System D operators sew and stitch and cut and weave fabric and garments. In 2007, Inditex inked an agreement with the International Textile, Garment and Leather Workers' Federation, a global union, which guaranteed it would audit its System D suppliers and hold them to a set of workplace standards. Among other things, Inditex promised that it will not work with any firms that engage in child labor or forced labor, and that it will require all its subcontractors to institute a forty-eight-hour workweek. The first year the agreement was in operation, Inditex disclosed that though 90 percent of its European and American work-shops and 80 percent of its Turkish suppliers scored high on its audits, only 50 percent of its Asian suppliers met the test. And the number was even lower in Africa—43 percent. Though the company refused to discuss specifics, the first year after the audits began, Inditex dropped two hundred and forty-seven firms it had worked with, almost one-quarter of its global suppliers.

Inditex's policy is a positive example of how a formal company can interact in a reasonable and healthy way with System D firms. Inditex's program of conducting workplace audits of its suppliers—without forcing them to be subject to what could be inflexible oversight by government regulators—is a creative means of ensuring that companies provide decent working conditions while not forcing System D businesses to get registered or to report their income to the government, two paths that could easily jeopardize their operations (and, of course, Inditex's profits) and ultimately put them out of business. It's the kind of program that Procter & Gamble and other consumer goods companies that sell their products through System D stores could implement in their contracts with their business partners.

Two barrel-chested men stood in front of an obscure, unmarked doorway on a side street in Ciudad del Este, pointing military-issue assault rifles out into the street. Neither of them had a uniform. But they eyeballed passersby like soldiers. Ciudad del Este generates more than $8 million in cash every day; someone has to guard it.

A cash-only economy naturally attracts organized crime. Law enforcement authorities allege that Ciudad del Este's smuggling trade has been organized by a Middle Eastern Mafia that funnels the profits to support global terror. Initially, the Paraguayan businesses stood accused of being a funding base for Hezbollah and Hamas. Shortly after September 11, 2001, U.S. authorities added a new bogeyman to the list: Al-Qaeda.

It is undeniably true that tens of thousands of people of Lebanese descent live and work in the triborder region of Argentina, Brazil, and Paraguay. But it's crucial to be aware of what the vast majority of them are doing: living legally as citizens. The Lebanese migration to South America began more than a century back. Today, there are more Brazilians of Lebanese descent (seven million) than there are Lebanese living in Lebanon (four million). The children of the original immigrants are knit into the local fabric of life. São Paulo mayor Gilberto Kassab, for instance, is of Lebanese descent. But he is 100 percent Brazilian, born and raised and educated in São Paulo, and has been a part of the local political scene for two decades.

Perhaps the most well-connected merchants in Ciudad del Este are members of the Hammoud family. They own the Monalisa department store, a windowless building painted deep blue, where you can find Italian suits and leathers, designer perfumes, and other luxury products for a fraction of the price they would carry in Brazil. The roar of Ciudad del Este—the shouts of the street merchants, the whining of the two-stroke motorcycle engines, the bustle of the delivery trucks, the slick sound of unspooling packing tape—disappears the moment you walk inside. It's all marble and mirrors and spritzes of perfume and hushed grandeur—Bloomingdale's for the cross-border bargain hunter. Take the escalator up a few flights and there's a café where you can purchase a cappuccino or a glass of champagne and admire your purchases while listening to the soft sounds of a cocktail pianist playing a lounge version of "The Sound of Silence."

After years of whispered allegations, the United States

became openly interested in the Lebanese community in Ciudad del Este and Foz do Iguaçu after the attacks on New York and Washington on September 11, 2001. In early 2002, the United States joined with the three countries whose borders come together in the region to create an investigative unit called the 3+1 Group on Tri-Border Area Security. Its mission was to delve into the accusations that the region is a financial and operational hub for terrorists. In 2006, the Department of Homeland Security ponied up $2.2 million for a deeper investigation. There were some isolated suggestive news stories that emerged from these probes—for instance, the BBC reported that in 2006, one money transfer agency in the city, which reported what seemed like a skimpy annual turnover of $50,000, was found to have been sending as much as $10 million a year to Lebanon (though this may sound suggestive, $50,000 amounts to one-half of 1 percent of $10 million, the standard fee a high-volume money-transfer enterprise would charge, and there was no evidence that the money had gone to any nefarious purposes). A new national law mandating that money-transfer agencies must keep records of the senders and receivers of all transactions with a value of more than $10,000 seems a sensible way to ensure at least a degree of transparency in the movement of currency.

Still, without presenting any public proof, the U.S. government has designated the Ciudad del Este shopping center Galeria Pagé (though it has the same name as a mall in the São Paulo street market on Rua 25 de Março, there's been no official suggestion of any direct connection between the two shopping pavilions) a Specially Designated Global Terrorist Entity. The government says that the businesses in Galeria Pagé pay a percentage of their profits to Hezbollah. The U.S. Treasury Department's Office of Foreign Assets Control has stated that the shopping mall and all the businesses in it are part of a network affiliated with Assad Ahmad Barakat, who, law enforcement authorities assert, is the Hezbollah ringleader in the region. But it's hard to know exactly what evidence the United States has—because it hasn't revealed any on the record. In one of the few public statements the United States has made, Charles Allen, then undersecretary of the U.S. Department of Homeland Security, speaking at a conference in 2006, offered this: "During a raid on Barakat's apartment, police discovered Hizballah propaganda praising martyrs as well as several speeches by Hizballah leader Hassan Nasrallah."

A few tapes and several speeches, and nothing on the link between Barakat and the shopping mall. That's the only material that's been presented in the open. Still, because it has been named as a Specially Designated Global Terrorist Entity, any American firm that can be shown to have done business with any company in Galeria Pagé can be charged with conspiracy to commit acts of terror. And, indeed, in February 2010, the U.S Attorney for the Southern District of Florida indicted three Miami businessmen—one electronics dealer and two freight forwarders—after they sent several hundred thousand dollars' worth of video games and digital cameras to Jomana Import Export, an electronics reseller in Galeria Pagé. According to the indictment, the freight forwarders worked with the Paraguayan company to create false paperwork to cloak the final destination of the shipments (this, of course, is standard operating procedure for all businesses in Ciudad del Este, because, if they're not dealing in computers, the economy of the entire Paraguayan city operates in System D, and thus doesn't exist for tax purposes).

Michael Tein, a lawyer who represents Khaled T. Safadi, whose Miami company was accused of selling the gaming equipment to the Galeria Pagé firm, made light of the case. "Believe it or not, this indictment actually charges these gentlemen with supporting Hezbollah by shipping them Sony PlayStations," Tein told the *Miami Herald*. "I guess that's a new type of weapon of mass destruction." Despite his sarcasm, his client and the others named in the indictment were ordered held without bail.

Development consultant Reinaldo Penner, who works under contract with the U.S. Agency for International Development (an arm of the State Department), admits that many of the businesses in the city do have problems with transparency, but insisted that he knew of no links between the merchants he has worked with and terrorism. He didn't deny that some merchants may be laundering proceeds from drug sales (authorities allege that lots of illegal drugs also make their way across the Paraná River into Brazil), but he insisted, nonetheless, that Ciudad del Este is relatively clean. "If there is money laundering," Penner said, "it's not happening in Ciudad del Este. They're bringing the money out of Ciudad del Este into Brazil and Argentina and laundering it there." What's more, he and several others pointed out, the tales suggesting that the Lebanese merchants in Ciudad del Este was simply a network of terrorist financiers could be investigated very easily. A number of prominent merchants of Lebanese descent in the city—including members of the Hammoud family that owns the Monalisa department store—are United States citizens, and it would be easy to arrest them and charge them under U.S. law if there was sufficient evidence against them.

Whatever the merit of the charges, Ciudad del Este's Lebanese retailers have started to shy away from reporters, fearing that each news story will simply amplify the old accusations, thus giving the tales of terror more credibility. Their denials, they complain, make it into the press only as an afterthought. Though I wanted to speak with executives of Grupo Monalisa, they referred me to Jeffrey W. Hesler, the director general of the local office of the Paraguayan American Chamber of Commerce.

I met him in his office, up an uneven flight of stairs in a quietly deteriorating building next door to the sleek corporate headquarters of Grupo Monalisa. The contrast is stark. For all the luxury of the Monalisa establishment, the chamber of commerce office looks like a stage set for a spy movie set in a backwater banana republic. The lock and peephole are missing from the front door, and the two empty "O"s allow you to peer into the offices before entering. Most of the furniture is decrepit. Strips of veneer peel off the oversize conference table. The chair rails are covered with dust. The carpet is frayed and threadbare. The walls are festooned with cheap posters of kitschy American views—all of them faded, stained, and curled, and dangling at odd angles.

Hesler, a U.S. citizen who arrived in the region three decades ago as a backpacker and never left, seemed a spy movie character, too—Our Man in Ciudad del Este, soaked with sweat and still speaking with a Southern accent. He giggled a bit too long when I asked about the mysterious guys with guns I had passed on the way to his office. "Let's be honest," he said when he caught his breath. "Ciudad del Este is a border town—and every border has its Mafia." Then he launched into history. "The arms, the drugs, the money laundering: it all comes from the Stroessner times. It was a feudal society. And you had to pay off the military to do anything." He emitted another overlong cackle. A cash-only economy attracts lawbreakers, he admitted. But he insisted that, contrary to all the allegations, Ciudad del Este's biggest problem was simply bad press due to the fact that lots of the most successful merchants were originally from the Middle East. "There's been a lot of slander. It's easy to accuse Ciudad del Este of a lot of things. But there's never been any proof."

Indeed, despite the prosecutions and terrorist designations, the U.S. State Department has admitted, in writing, that it has no knowledge of any terror cells in Ciudad del Este, and no proof of terrorist fund-raising either. In a 2009 report signed by Secretary of State Hillary Clinton, the State Department acknowledged that, after seven years of investigations and allegations, it could offer no evidence of any nefarious actions in the trading city. "The United States remained concerned that Hizballah and Hamas sympathizers were raising funds in the Tri-Border Area by participating in illicit activities and soliciting donations from sympathizers in the sizable Middle Eastern communities in the region," Clinton's report stated, adding that "there was no corroborated information, however, that these or other Islamic extremist groups had an operational presence in the region."

The charges against the merchants in Ciudad del Este are reminiscent of the attacks against peddlers in the United States before the Revolutionary War. In the early 1770s, citizens throughout the colonies that would become the United States became increasingly aware of the activities of peddlers—and they didn't like what they saw. It wasn't that they didn't like the peddlers or thought that peddling was immoral. Rather, the colonists were engaged in an economic war with Britain and didn't want roving street merchants to break the embargo they had imposed on goods from anywhere in the British Empire. In 1774, a year after the Boston Tea Party, the *Connecticut Courant* reported approvingly that people from several towns in the Boston area had found "those Gentry, called Pedlars" selling tea, and had seized the offensive merchandise and burned it. And in 1775, just a month before the hostilities that would become the Revolutionary War commenced, the Provincial Congress of Massachusetts (the renegade body that, prior to the Declaration of Independence, declared itself free from British control), in a decree signed by John Hancock, ordained that local officials had the authority to search the packs of all peddlers, in order to prevent the strolling merchants from "selling East-India goods and teas." As India was part of the British Empire, the Provincial Congress declared, selling Indian spices and teas served to "interrupt and defeat" the effort to "secure the rights and liberties of the inhabitants of these colonies." In selling British goods, the peddlers were seen as providing aid and comfort (and money) to the enemy and, in the process, jeopardizing the revolution. As Thomas Jefferson later noted (he was writing about all businesses in general, and not just peddlers), "Merchants have no country. The mere spot they stand on does not constitute so strong an attachment as that from which they draw their gains." Adam Smith, too, made it clear that the commercial morality of most merchants was not to choose sides in a conflict, but rather follow the "pedlar principle of turning a penny wherever a penny was to be got."

Of course, you don't have to be in System D to break laws or violate trading bans. Formal firms commit crimes, too. In Ciudad del Este, legally established businesses also use the back-channel wire transfer agencies so they can save money and camouflage overseas transactions. In China, in 2008, a dairy company was caught selling powdered milk that had been cut with melamine, a cheap resin used in making Formica. This awful act of adulteration caused at least six deaths and made tens of thousands of kids seriously sick. Yet the firm responsible had all its licenses, was part-owned by a well-respected New Zealand dairy, and even had strong connections to the Chinese government. Similarly, the outfit that manufactured the cheap but corrosive Sheetrock that was used extensively in home construction in some areas of the United States over the past decade was a fully licensed joint venture between a well-connected Chinese corporation and a German construction firm. Finally, in perhaps the most extreme example of formal-sector crime, between 2001 and 2007, one stable and respected company paid out 4,283 bribes worth $1.9 billion—$1 million in bribes every business day—to win contracts and curry favor with officials all over the world, from Venezuela to Vietnam. The corporation with this dubious distinction was highly regarded, heavily regulated, and extremely formal: the German firm Siemens, a global electronics and engineering giant whose shares are bought and sold on the Frankfurt Stock Exchange and in London, New York, and Zurich.

Still, governments may have legitimate worries about the growth of unrecorded transactions. Consider cassava, the root vegetable that is crucially important for millions of people across Africa, both as a cash crop and as food. The cassava harvest is currently threatened by a devastating blight. A virus that corrupts the valuable and nutritious tuber has been spoiling the crop in Uganda. So far, the blight hasn't moved out of East Africa. But health officials fear it will migrate— and not for biological reasons. Pollen may know no passport, but, for this virus, the problem is more likely to be the pursuit of cheap seedlings than the inadvertent action of the wind. With a few dollars to an impoverished border guard or a trek through the bush to avoid the authorities entirely, traders could easily move infected tubers across national lines. The biggest fear of agricultural and health authorities is that unwitting merchants will transport the virus to West Africa, ultimately contaminating the crop in Nigeria, the world's largest producer of cassava. This would be a catastrophe, and would cause a famine and a local economic crash with global repercussions.

No array of penalties, or attempts to seal-off wide-open borders, will succeed. With or without regulation, some businesses will continue to seek out the shadows. If governments want to crack down on the funding of nefarious causes, if they want to prevent the cross-border trade in contaminated products, they will have to engage with System D.

Vitalis Okwudili Ikedi lolled on a large woven bag stuffed with clothes. He and eight other men were relaxing in e-domain, a freight-forwarding business in Guangzhou. They passed the hours swapping stories, making mobile phone calls, and occasionally grabbing the store's single beat-up old laptop so they could check their e-mails on the sly. Vitalis let everyone else talk. The bag he lay on was about to be sealed up tight and shipped off to Africa.

When I left the store, after an hour of conversation, he followed me down the block. He insisted that I hear his story. Everyone else had been boasting of how good the trading life was. Vitalis promised that his tale would provide a different vision of African life in Guangzhou, that his experience ran counter to the narrative of trade and profit all the other businessmen had provided.

While he said the tales of criminality in System D were largely exaggerated, Vitalis wanted me to understand that there were real difficulties in the life of an unlicensed trader. For every merchant like David Ibekwe, who insists he likes life in Guangzhou better than in Nigeria ("This is my country," David had said as we sat in his stall in the ASPAMDA market in Lagos, surrounded by stacks of Chinese-made products. "But I cannot lie to you. It is too rough. I prefer being in China"), there's a Vitalis—broke, sick, despondent, and unable to go home.

Vitalis hailed from Port Harcourt, in the oil-rich south of Nigeria. Like most of his fellow African traders in Sanyuanli, he had overstayed his three-month tourist visa. When I met him, he had been in Guangzhou for nine months. He came to

South China to do business, and he thought he would be able to make his way in trade, but there has been no redemption in his story, no deal that turned around his fortunes and made him a success. His life in Guangzhou has been a succession of failures. With no money and no backers, he was living by his wits, doing odd jobs for chump change from various Nigerian merchants. He pulled some bills from his pocket and counted them—fourteen yuan, or about two dollars. That was all he had left, he said. He felt abandoned by the system, abandoned by the Chinese he did business with, abandoned by his fellow Nigerians.

And now, he said, he was being hunted like a cane rat. In the month before I met him, he had been forced to move three times because the police had started conducting sweeps to nab Africans who had overstayed their visas. "They beat your door down while you're sleeping," he said. "Here there are no human rights. If they catch you, they put you in prison. These people are very wicked. I don't know why. But they don't want our color here."

To Vitalis, everything had become a racial slight. Chinese businesspeople sold him substandard goods and then bad-mouthed him as an ignorant foreigner when he complained. Passersby were offended if he jaywalked instead of using the pedestrian bridges the government has built all over the city. His neighbors called the cops if he and his friends stayed up late.

Some of the bad feelings undoubtedly come from cultural misunderstandings. For instance, Nigerians are used to bargaining in taxis and they insist on bargaining in Guangzhou even though drivers can be prosecuted if the police catch them not using their meters. Then, because the fares are obscenely high compared to similar rides in their home countries, the Africans I spoke with accused the cabbies of deliberately driving in circles to run up their meters.

But there is also a very real undercurrent of racism in the city. Even Linda Chen, who does 90 percent of her business—better than $1 million—with merchants from Nigeria and counts many of them as her friends, said she was not comfortable with the number of merchants from south of the Sahara who had come to live in Sanyuanli. "This area looks like a tiny Africa," she said, "and I don't like these people staying in China. They can spoil the life very easily." Too many Africans, she suggested, would corrupt the business environment and wreck the social fabric: "These people don't get to know their business partners and don't get to know the culture." Linda, whose business depends on good relationships with Africans, told me she supported police efforts to round up those who had overstayed their visas.

In order to avoid being arrested during a recent raid, Vitalis said, he had simply fled out the back of his apartment while the police were beating on the front door. In his haste, he had left his documents behind. So now he no longer had his passport and invitation letter (this is a requirement for Africans to get a visa). He felt there was nothing he could do, as he was afraid that if he went to the police station, the authorities would throw him in jail. Not only was he in China illegally but he now had no proof of his own identity.

Vitalis and thousands like him are caught in a bind. "People like this will tell you that they want to go back today," one successful Nigerian who was also hanging out in e-domain that afternoon told me. "But first they have to pay a fine [currently set at five thousand yuan, or more than $700] and then they have to buy a new air ticket and the total will cost them more than two thousand dollars." In other words, they can't make money in China, but they have to pay money—more than what most of them have—to leave the country and head home.

Vitalis insisted that Africans should not establish themselves permanently in Guangzhou. "Should you come to China to trade?" he asked. "I would say, 'No.' China is no good. If you have the money, you come here and buy what you want and leave. That's all."

Doing business overseas necessarily involves risk. James Ezeifeoma, the big importer from Alaba International, remembers that his first two trips abroad were successful. But the third time he tried to make a deal to import goods back to Nigeria, he got taken by a scammer who sold him counterfeit dollars, and he lost $13,500, a huge sum at the time. Today, he's able to laugh it off as a learning experience, but at the time it was devastating. Still, James was already settled and established as a dealer when he started in international trade. He had no intention of staying for months overseas. As Vitalis suggested, he traveled, bought, and came home. Unfortunately, most of the successful Nigerian merchants I met in Guangzhou had little sympathy for Vitalis. David Obi, who spent his first few months in China living like Vitalis, surviving from one small deal to the next, offered some tough advice. With the Chinese, he suggested, the key to success in business is this: "Keep their rules and give them what they want." Still, turning deals in System D involves risk—and some people are better at assessing risk and surviving loss than others. Vitalis, sleep-deprived and racked by a hacking cough, doesn't want to be a casualty of System D.

Fortunately, there's a possible solution for Vitalis and other System D merchants caught in his bind. Their home countries and the United Nations should discuss the feasibility of creating a globally agreed upon regime of multientry three-year traders' visas that would retroactively legalize all the African traders in Guangzhou, and allow them to travel home (and back to China, if they so choose). It would recognize that System D is global. What's more, making it easier for traders to get visas would also give them greater security and accountability, because there would no longer be any reason for traders to travel illegally as tourists and to disappear into the underground, where they can be harassed and threatened and hounded by the authorities when they overstay their visas.

These efforts and ideas aimed at building a productive in-between zone for System D are admittedly small. Some are succeeding and some are failing and some have yet to be tried. But, considered together, they hold out hope that this massive realm of trade that employs half the workers of the world and creates as much value as a superpower will grow and strengthen itself in the coming decades. They offer an alternate vision of globalization—a vision of empowerment, employment, and global equity based, not on the abstraction of the free market, but on the concrete principles of the flea market.

Keith Hart, the anthropologist who "discovered" the informal economy four decades ago, thinks development through System D processes is possible, and even, perhaps, inevitable. "Yes, the informal economy is a potential source of growth," he told me. But, he added, the powers that be will resist this kind of sub-rosa power. "I don't think it can be taken for granted or extrapolated indefinitely into the future. Distribution is a major source of capitalist expansion and I can well imagine there might be pressure coming from well-established supply chains to try to reduce competition from roadside vendors. The voices for a bureaucratic crackdown on this stuff are likely to be heard quite strongly." Still, Hart insists that, in the region where he started his studies—the one he still knows best, Africa—underground economic activity will win out. "In the next fifty years Africa will have something of a major economic miracle," he told me, and "some sections of the existing informal economy will take off." If System D markets in Africa move to strengthen their cooperative institutions, they will build greater autonomy, greater control and stability, and greater access to information, and will further their access to politics. Then they will truly be ready to seize the initiative to grow in this coming economic boom.

Roberto Mangabeira Unger, the Brazilian political philosopher who teaches law at Harvard, doesn't go quite that far, but he, too, suggests that the entrepreneurial operators in System D are fertile ground for economic innovation and expansion. This realm, he said, can be "a hotbed of micro-experimentation, mixing the small-scale with economies of scale through pooling of resources." The strivers involved in System D, he said, can become a serious global force with the potential to create transformative change, if they are willing to expand their cooperative tendencies.

Our current system has created lots of wealth but has made the world an alarmingly unequal and unfair place. We still have yet to confront the twin problems that have plagued the dismal science of economics since its outset—unemployment and inequality. Despite hundreds of years of theorizing and pontificating, these two devastating issues seem as far from being addressed as they were before the invention of the free market.

In the face of such stasis, business leaders, economists, and government officials should not be surprised that System D is coming up with its own solutions (after all, this is what System D always does). These efforts—provisional and haphazard though they may be—are not being developed in the West or in the privileged halls of governmental buildings, or in the august offices of multinational nonprofits, or anywhere where economists talk of rational and efficient markets. Instead, they are being concocted in the street—in the oil-slicked lanes of Ladipo, on the dusty streets of Ikeja Computer Village, in the crowded stalls of the International Trade Fair Market, among the touts and global traders of Alaba International Market, in the run-down storefronts of Sanyuanli and on the Friendship Bridge between Ciudad del Este and Foz do Iguaçu, and in the hypercrowded street market on Rua 25 de Março—wherever the merchants of System D are scheming, planning, meeting, trading, exchanging, and, in innumerable small ways, building a better world, one deal at a time.

Exchange is creation.

—Muriel Rukeyser

My Stealth Family

The vices of levity are always ruinous to the common people, and a single week's thoughtlessness and dissipation is
often sufficient to undo a poor workman for ever.

—*The Wealth of Nations*

If anyone had bet me, five years ago or so, that I would write
a book that had anything to do with economics and have a
great time doing it, I would have taken that wager, and I'd be
paying out big-time.

I started this book as a beggar—with nothing in my cup,
putting myself at the mercy of total strangers. I am fortu-
nate that some incredible people reacted to my abject need
with generosity and spirit. They embraced my work and
shared their insights and contacts and friendship. They
are my System D family—and I could not have made any
headway without them. This stealth group includes Mosudi
Olanrewaju, Chika Okafor, Olayemi Adesanya, Sesan Awo-
jole, Ricardo Peres, Jonas Hagen, Dai Men, George and Eva
Lian, John Kennedy, Henry Yang, Chuks Obunseh, Engineer Pwol, Micheal Iluobe, Chukwuma Agwu, and Abiodun
Awolaja.

Many others helped out with friendship, advice, and support. Among them: Sérgio Bispo dos Santos, Uche, Sylvain
Souchaud, the crew at the Festival Suites Hotel & Bar (Aus-
tin, Demola, Ubong, Anita, Emily, and Queensly), Ladislau

Dowbor, Asoro, Taye Adesanya, Emeka Okafor, Gabriel Ponce de Leon, Sergio Palleroni, Ugo Okafor, Tunji Lardner, Alfred Adefila, Tobi Obuseh, Wale Yaro, Wale Dudu, Vanderlei Canhos and his family, Bei Feng, Jack Qiu Linchuan, Qiu Liben, Ai Xiaoming, Haitao Huang, Kevin Ming, Zhixin Deng, David Ibekwe, Laura Tompkins, Jan Van Esch, Li Xiaoming, Ariela Martinez Legal, Julie Zhong, Yao Zhang, Nzefili Macaulay, David Bandurski, Shina Loremikan, Felix Morka, Joe Melara, Jim Puckett, Sharon Francis, Alfredo Brillembourg, Hubert Klumpner, Adi Ignatius, Vera Titunik, Taye and Lukman (the "drop-car" drivers who hang out at the entry to A1 Close on Fifth Avenue in Festac Town), Adam Kleinman, Joy and Gift (at the Internet café on A1 Close), Sarah Boulos, Ify and her family, the Bale of Bariga, Sean Basinski and his colleagues at the Street Vendor Project, Amaka Joseph (for keeping me healthy with her wonderful bitterleaf, egusi, and oha soups), the folks at Thrillers and Mr. Biggs on Fourth Avenue in Festac Town (who couldn't imagine why anyone would drink so much Nescafé), the whole gang at "last bus stop" (which, in true Lagos form, isn't even a bus stop), and the Summer Garden restaurant in Festac Town (you haven't eaten till you've tried their *isi ewu*, stewed goat's head).

Hundreds of hawkers, street vendors, *mototaxistas*, System D importers, and market merchants opened their lives to me. I salute the risk they took in trusting an outsider with their stories, ideas, and creative spontaneity. A number of academics also shared their thoughts, research, and conclusions. Their willingness to talk was valuable and encouraging. If my work has failed to live up to any of their expectations, let me quote something Ludwig Wittgenstein wrote: "Even to have expressed a false thought boldly and clearly is already to have gained a great deal."

Jennifer Carlson, my agent, was a continual quiet force for good. I am glad she puts up with me.

My editor, Andrew Miller, approached this book with patience and guts. He let me raise my own roadblocks and make my own mistakes. Then he piled on and forced me to be broader, deeper, and more coherent than I thought I could be. Yea, Andrew.

My colleagues and friends Michael Ashkin, John Bartelstone, Bryan Finoki, Annette Fuentes, Karen Lowe, and Justin Nobel helped even when they didn't know they were helping. Brian Connell read an early draft of the manuscript and his feedback allowed me to see what I was writing about in a new light. George Garneau had a knack for calling at the right time with the suggestion of beer and falafel.

A grant from the Fund for Investigative Journalism supported some of the reporting.

This book owes a big debt to two of the world's great collections—the New York Public Library and the Columbia University Libraries—and to the dollar carts (now sadly $2 per hardcover) and uncorrected proofs section of the Strand Bookstore.

My parents, Marilyn and Frank Neuwirth, and my brother Dave and his family—Hattie, Henry, and Eva—were always there when I needed them.

Andrea Haenggi is, now and forever, the center of my System D.

All acts of peddling, smuggling, haggling, higgling, hawking, street selling, bootlegging, forestalling, copying, pirating, dashing, shoe washing, and showing appreciation contained in this book—as well as all errors, omissions, and insufficiencies—are the sole responsibility of the author.

Finally, as Macedonio Fernández elegantly put it, "I repudiate all the blank pages published here as forgeries."

Stealth Sources

Before the invention of the art of printing, a scholar and a beggar seem to have been terms very nearly synonymous.

—*The Wealth of Nations*

Achtenberg, Emily. "Bolivia: New Pension Law Lowers Retirement Age, Raises Expectations." *NACLA Report* (Jan. 11, 2011).

Alarcón, Daniel. "Life Among the Pirates." *Granta*, vol. 109 (winter 2009).

Alexander, Christopher. *A New Theory of Urban Design.* New York: Oxford University Press, 1987.

Amsterdam News. "Harlem Pushcart Markets Provide Colorful Spectacle and Give Small Tradesmen Chance," Nov. 5, 1930.

Anderson, Chris. *Free: The Future of a Radical Price.* New York: Hyperion, 2009.

Ayala, Edgardo. "Street Vendors Warn of Fight Against Urban Removal," *Inter Press Service*, Dec. 22, 2010.

Ayittey, George B. N. http://twitter.com/ayittey/status/26949643735

———. "The Failure of Development Planning in Africa," in *The Collapse of Development Planning,* ed. Peter J. Boettke. New York: NYU Press, 1994.

Azam, Jean-Paul. *Trade, Exchange Rate, and Growth in Sub-Saharan Africa.* Cambridge, UK: Cambridge University Press, 2007.

Bang, Peter F. *The Roman Bazaar: A Comparative Study of Trade and Markets in a Tributary Empire.* Cambridge, UK: Cambridge University Press, 2008.

Bauer, Peter. *The Development Frontier.* Cambridge, MA: Harvard University Press, 1991.

———. *From Subsistence to Exchange and Other Essays.* Princeton, NJ: Princeton University Press, 2000.

Berger, John. *Lilac and Flag: An Old Wives' Tale of a City.* New York: Pantheon Books, 1990.

Bhattacharya, Sabyasachi, and Jan Lucassen. *Workers in the Informal Sector.* Delhi: Macmillan India, 2005.

Bierce, Ambrose. *The Devil's Dictionary*. New York: Dover Publications, 1958.

Bishop, Elizabeth. *The Complete Poems*. New York: Farrar, Straus, and Giroux, 1984.

———. *Edgar Allan Poe & the Juke-Box*. New York: Farrar, Straus, and Giroux, 2006.

Blondé, Bruno, Peter Stabel, Jon Stobart, and Ilja Van Damme. *Buyers and Sellers: Retail Circuits and Practices in Medieval and Early Modern Europe*. Turnhout, Belgium: Brepols, 2006.

Braithwaite, Richard. *Whimzies*. London: Bull's Head, 1631.

Braudel, Fernand. *The Perspective of the World*. London: Phoenix Press, 2002.

———. *The Wheels of Commerce*. New York: Harper & Row, 1982.

Brecht, Bertolt. *Mother Courage and Her Children*. New York: Grove Press, 1966.

Brook, Barry S. "Piracy and Panacea in the Dissemination of Music in the Late Eighteenth Century." *Proceedings of the Royal Musical Association*, vol. 102 (1975–1976).

Brooklyn Eagle. "Fish and Fruit Pedlers," May 21, 1859; "The Peddling Nuisance," June 16, 1860; "Important to Peddlers," Nov. 5, 1882; "Local Candy Peddlers," July 31, 1887; "They're No Good in Brooklyn," Feb 8, 1890; "Says Police Graft on Pushcart Men," June 23, 1895; "A Raid on Peddlers," June 23, 1895; "Coal Cart Peddlers," March 11, 1897; "About Peddlers' Licenses," October 18, 1899; "Raid on the Peddlers," Jan. 17, 1900.

Brotton, Jerry. *The Renaissance Bazaar: From the Silk Road to Michelangelo*. Oxford, UK: Oxford University Press, 2002.

Brown, David, ed. "The Autobiography of a Pedlar," in *Midland History*, vol. XXI. Birmingham, UK: University of Birmingham, 1996.

Business Software Alliance. Sixth Annual BSA-IDC Global Software Piracy Study, May 2009.

Carcopino, Jérôme. *Daily Life in Ancient Rome*. New Haven: Yale University Press, 1940.

Chamoiseau, Patrick. *Solibo Magnificent*. New York: Pantheon Books, 1997.

Chayanov, Alexander. *The Theory of Peasant Co-operatives*. Columbus, OH: Ohio State University Press, 1991.

Chicago Tribune. "Maxwell Street Merchant Pardoned for Selling 'Toy' Rolexes in 1984," Dec. 24, 2008.

City of New York, Department of Investigations. "DOI Undercover Operation Exposes Illegal, Black Market Trafficking in Mobile Food Vending Permits and Results in the Arrest of Six Individuals." Press release, June 30, 2009.

Clinard, Marshall B. *The Black Market*. New York: Reinhart & Co., 1952.

Confucius. *The Four Books: Confucian Analects*. New York: Paragon Book Reprint Co., 1966.

Connecticut Courant. "At a Meeting of the Inhabitants of the Town of Farmington," Sept. 3, 1770; "Boston, February 17," February 15, 1774.

Connecticut Courant and Hartford Weekly Intelligencer. "In Provincial Congress," March 6, 1775.

Cross, John, and Alfonso Morales. *Street Entrepreneurs: People, Place and Politics in Local and Global Perspective*. New York: Routledge, 2007.

Davidson, Basil. *The Black Man's Burden: Africa and the Curse of the Nation-State*. New York: Times Books, 1992.

Deleuze, Gilles, and Félix Guattari. *Anti-Oedipus: Capitalism and Schizophrenia*. Minneapolis: University of Minnesota Press, 1983.

de Soto, Hernando. *The Mystery of Capital: Why Capitalism Triumphs in the West and Fails Everywhere Else*. New York: Basic Books, 2000.

———. *The Other Path: The Invisible Revolution in the Third World*. New York: Harper & Row, 1989.

Dias, Maria Odila Silva. *Power and Everyday Life: The Lives of Working Women in Nineteenth-century Brazil*. New Brunswick, NJ: Rutgers University Press, 1995.

Dionne, Craig, and Steve Mentz, eds. *Rogues and Early Modern English Culture*. Ann Arbor: University of Michigan Press, 2004.

Doya, David Malingha. "Jua Kali Artisans Told to Focus on the Needs of Export Markets." *The East African*, December 6, 2005.

Duby, Georges. *The Early Growth of the European Economy: Warriors and Peasants from the Seventh to the Twelfth Century*. Ithaca, NY: Cornell University Press, 1974.

Dugas, Don-John. *Marketing the Bard: Shakespeare in Performance and Print*. Columbia, MO: University of Missouri Press, 2006.

Edgcomb, Elaine, and Tamra Thetford. *The Informal Economy: Making It in Rural America*. Washington, D.C.: Aspen Institute, 2004.

Enzensberger, Hans Magnus. *Critical Essays*. New York: Continuum, 1982.

———. *Political Crumbs*. London: Verso, 1990.

Feldman, Eric A. "The Tuna Court: Law and Norms in the World's Premier Fish Market." *California Law Review*, vol. 94 (Mar. 2006).

Fernández, Macedonio. *The Museum of Eterna's Novel*. Rochester, NY: Open Letter, 2010.

Fernández-Kelly, Patricia, and Jon Shefner. *Out of the Shadows: Political Action and the Informal Economy in Latin America*. University Park, PA: Pennsylvania State University Press, 2006.

Financial Mail (Johannesburg). "Employment, Sharp Eye on Stats," Feb. 11, 2011.

Fisman, Raymond, and Edward Miguel. *Economic Gangsters: Corruption, Violence, and the Poverty of Nations*. Princeton, NJ: Princeton University Press, 2008.

Fontaine, Laurence, ed. *Alternative Exchanges: Second-hand Circulations from the Sixteenth Century to the Present*. New York: Berghahn Press, 2008.

———. *History of Pedlars in Europe*. Durham, NC: Duke University Press, 1996.

Gentilcore, David. *Medical Charlatanism in Early Modern Italy*. Oxford: Oxford University Press, 2006.

Gerhard, Peter. *Pirates of the Pacific, 1575–1742*. Lincoln, NE: University of Nebraska Press, 1990.

Gesell, Silvio. *The Natural Economic Order*. http://www.utopie.it/pubblicazioni/gesell.htm, accessed March 9, 2011.

Glenny, Misha. *McMafia*. New York: Alfred A. Knopf, 2008.

Glissant, Édouard. *Caribbean Discourse*. Charlottesville, VA: University of Virginia Press, 1989.

———. *Poetics of Relation*. Ann Arbor, MI: University of Michigan Press, 1997.

Goodman, Emily Jane. "Landmark State Law Protecting Domestic Workers Takes Effect." *Gotham Gazette*, http://www.gothamgazette.com/article/Law/20101129/13/3420, accessed 12/1/2010.

Gorz, André. *Farewell to the Working Class*. Boston: South End Press, 1987.

———. *Strategy for Labor: A Radical Proposal*. Boston: Beacon Press, 1967.

Gramsci, Antonio. *Selections from the Prison Notebooks*. New York: International Publishers, 1971.

von Grimmelshausen, Johann Jakob Christoffel. *Simplicius Simplicissimus*. Indianapolis: Bobbs-Merrill Co., 1965.

Gross, Charles. "The Court of Piepowder." *The Quarterly Journal of Economics* (Feb. 1906).

———. *Select Cases Concerning the Law Merchant*, vol. 1. London: Selden Society, 1908.

Grupo Inditex, *Annual Report 2007*, http://www.inditex.es/en/downloads/Annual_Report_INDITEX_07.pdf.

———. *Annual Report 2009*, http://www.inditex.es/en/downloads/Annual_Report_INDITEX_09.pdf.

Gudeman, Stephen. *Economy's Tension: The Dialectics of Community and Market*. New York, Berghahn Books, 2008.

Hanawalt, Barbara A., and Anna Grotans. *Living Dangerously: On the Margins in Medieval and Early Modern Europe*. Notre Dame, IN: University of Notre Dame Press, 2007.

Hart, Keith. *Formal Bureaucracy and the Emergent Forms of the Informal Economy*. Paper presented at the EGDI –WIDER conference in

Helsinki, Sept. 17–18, 2004, http://thememorybank.co.uk/papers/emergent-forms/, accessed March 22, 2011.

He, Xin. "Why Do They Not Comply with the Law?" *Law & Society Review* (Sept. 2005).

Heyne, Paul. *"Are Economists Basically Immoral?" and Other Essays on Economics.* Indianapolis, IN: Liberty Fund, 2008.

Hill, Archibald A. "The Pushcart Peddlers of New York." *The Independent* (Oct. 18, 1906).

Horn, Zoe Elena. *Coping With Crises: Lingering Recession, Rising Inflation, and the Informal Workforce.* Inclusive Cities Report, January 2011, http://wiego.org/gec_study/2/GEC_2_English.pdf, accessed March 22, 2011.

Hürriyet. "Turkey Ranks 95th on the Black Economy List," Dec. 27, 2010.

Ibn Khaldùn. *The Muqaddimah: An Introduction to History.* Princeton, NJ: Princeton University Press, 1969.

The Independent (Dublin). "The Black Economy Is Back in Business," Oct. 18, 2009.

International AntiCounterfeiting Coalition. Submission of the International AntiCounterfeiting Coalition to the United States Trade Representative, Special 301 Recommendations, February 17, 2009.

Jacobs, Jane. *The Economy of Cities.* New York: Random House, 1969.

Kapstein, Ethan B. *Measuring Unilever's Economic Footprint: The Case of South Africa.* Durban, South Africa: Famous Publishing, 2008.

Keynes, John Maynard. *General Theory of Employment, Interest, and Money,* http://www.marxists.org/reference/subject/economics/keynes/general-theory/.

Klamer, Arjo *Speaking of Economics: How to Get in the Conversation.* London: Routledge, 2007.

Koolhaas, Rem. *Mutations.* Barcelona: ACTAR, 2000.

Kropotkin, Petr. *Mutual Aid: A Factor of Evolution.* Boston: Extending Horizons Books, 1955.

Kruse, Paul. "Piracy and the Britannica." *The Library Quarterly*, vol. 33, no. 4 (Oct. 1963).

Kuznets, Simon. Prize Lecture, December 11, 1971, http://nobelprize.org/nobel_prizes/economics/laureates/1971/kuznets-lecture.html, accessed March 9, 2011.

Lancashire Telegraph (UK). "Clampdown on Rogue Street Traders in Pendle," Jan. 10, 2011.

de La Pradelle, Michèle. *Market Day in Provence.* Chicago: University of Chicago Press, 2006.

Lemire, Beverly. *The Business of Everyday Life: Gender, Practice and Social Politics in England, c. 1600–1900.* Manchester: Manchester University Press, 2005.

Liebling, A. J. *Liebling at Home*. New York: PEI Books, 1982.
————. *The Telephone Booth Indian*. San Francisco: North Point Press, 1990.
London Times. "The Book-Hawking Union," Oct. 3, 1850; "Book Hawking in England," Oct. 23, 1856.
Los Angeles Times. "County Licenses," June 6, 1883; "Human Chattels," Mar. 18, 1891; "Tamales Calientes," Sept. 25, 1894; "Push Carts in a Bad Way," June 25, 1905; "Push Carts Go, Stands Come," July 16, 1905.
Luther, Martin. *The Book of Vagabonds and Beggars*. London: John Camden Hotten, 1861.
Mace, Nancy A. "Litigating the 'Musical Magazine.'" *Book History*, vol. 2 (1999).
MacGaffey, Janet, and Rémy Bazenguissa-Ganga. *Congo-Paris: Transnational Traders on the Margins of the Law*. Oxford: International Africa Institute/James Currey, 2000.
Malliet, A. M. Wendell. "'Flowers! Flowers!' Harlem Hears Street Hawkers Shout," *New York Amsterdam News*, July 3, 1937; "Pushcart Markets Under 'L' Thrive by Pleasing Buyers," July 10, 1937.
Mandeville, Bernard. *The Fable of the Bees*. Oxford: Clarendon Press, 1924.
————. *A Modest Defence of Publick Stews*. New York, Palgrave Macmillan, 2006.
Marx, Karl. *Capital*, vol. 1. New York: International Publishers, 1967.
————. *The Eighteenth Brumaire of Louis Napoleon*. New York: International Publishers, 1963.
Mayhew, Henry. *Henry Mayhew's London*. London: Spring Books, 1900.
Meagher, Kate. "Social Capital, Social Liabilities, and Political Capital," *African Affairs*, October 2006, 105 (421): 553–582.
————. "Social Networks and Economic Ungovernance in African Small Firm Clusters," Queen Elizabeth House, paper for the QEH fiftieth birthday conference, n.d., http://www.qeh.ox.ac.uk/dissemination/conference-papers/meagher.pdf/, accessed March 14, 2011.
Milanovic, Branko. *The Haves and the Have-Nots: A Brief and Idiosyncratic History of Global Inequality*. New York: Basic Books, 2010.
Morales, Alfonso. "Public Markets as Community Development Tools," *Journal of Planning Education and Research*, 28 (2009).
Mörtenbach, Peter, and Helge Mooshammer. "Trading Indeterminacy—Informal Markets in Europe, *Field*, vol. 1, no. 1, http://www.field-journal.org/uploads/file/2007_Volume_1/p%20mortenbock.pdf, accessed March 20, 2011.
Myers, Robin, Michael Harris, and Giles Mandelbrote, eds. *Fairs, Markets, and the Itinerant Book Trade*. New Castle, DE: Oak Knoll Press, 2007.
Nace, Ted. *Gangs of America*. San Francisco, CA: Berrett-Koehler, 2003.

Naím, Moisés. *Illicit: How Smugglers, Traffickers, and Copycats Are Hijacking the Global Economy.* New York: Doubleday, 2005.

New Democrat (Monrovia, Liberia). "CBL Contradicts Jobless Figures," March 21, 2011.

The New York Times. "Invaded by Filth and Dirt," July 20, 1893; "Back at Push-Carts Again," Aug. 26, 1893; "The Day's Interesting Testimony," June 30, 1894; "Lexow Committee Report," Jan. 18, 1895; "A Vegetable Trust, Now," Sept. 29, 1900; "How the Poor Are Robbed by the Use of False Scales," June 28, 1903; "Park Row Peanut Panic," Sept. 27, 1903; "Giving the Pushcart Men a Place of Business," July 3, 1904; "Pushcart Men in Court," July 23, 1904; "Police and Pushcart Men in East Side Row," July 28, 1904; "In the Business World," Aug. 10, 1904; "Pushcart Men to Fight," May 1, 1905; "Peddlers Want to Strike," Aug. 21, 1905; "Peddlers Tell of Graft; May March on City Hall," May 24, 1906; "The Push-Cart Peddlers," June 4, 1907; "Sweet Potato Men Revolt," Nov. 14, 1910; "Peddlers Prepare Appeal to Gaynor," July 1, 1912; "Aldermen Indorse Pushcart Markets," July 10, 1912; "The Romance of the Picturesque Pushcart," July 14, 1912; "Zeltner for Alderman," Aug. 2, 1919; "Louis Zeltner, 77, East Side 'Mayor,'" May 13, 1953; "Virus Ravages Cassava Plants in Africa," May 21, 2010.

New York Tribune. "The Pushcart Legions," Apr. 25, 1900; "The Wary Buyer and the Wily Greek," July 1, 1900; "Fruit Trade a Vast One," Aug. 5, 1900; "Extortion Charges Made," Sept. 11, 1900; "The Greek Pedler's Woes," Sept. 16, 1900; "Pedlers Plead for Rights," Sept. 29, 1900; "Wiskinkie of Pedlers," May 6, 1902; "Picturesque Markets," May 25, 1902; "The Pushcart Women," Sept. 29, 1902; "Discharges Pushcart Men," Feb. 9, 1903; "Blackmail Crushed Out," May 5, 1903; "War on Basket Peddlers," Aug. 8, 1903; "The London Coster," Nov. 26, 1905; "Paris Push Cart Men," October 21, 1906; "Pushcart in Politics," Sept. 16, 1907; "Put S. Schwartz Out," Oct. 1, 1908, "Schwartz Won't Tell," Oct 13, 1908.

Nietzsche, Friedrich. *Daybreak: Thoughts on the Prejudices of Morality.* Cambridge, UK: Cambridge University Press, 1997.

———. *Human, All Too Human: A Book for Free Spirits.* Cambridge, UK: Cambridge University Press, 1986.

———. *Writings from the Late Notebooks.* Cambridge, UK: Cambridge University Press, 2003.

Nock, Magdalena Barros. "Swap Meets and Socioeconomic Alternatives for Mexican Immigrants." *Human Organization* (Oct. 1, 2009).

Nordstrom, Carolyn. *Global Outlaws: Crime, Money, and Power in the Contemporary World.* Berkeley: University of California Press, 2007.

———. *Shadows of War: Violence, Power, and International Profiteering in the Twenty-first Century.* Berkeley: University of California Press, 2004.

The Observer (London). "Sale of Game in London," May 19, 1829; "The Street Stalls Revolution in Tottenham Court-Road," Apr. 3, 1853.

Organisation for Economic Cooperation and Development. *Is Informal Normal*, March 31, 2009.

Parilla, Josephine C. "Benefits Workers Will Get from the Magna Carta," *The Manila Times*, Sept. 23, 2009.

Perry, Guillermo E., William F. Maloney, Omar S. Arias, Pablo Fajnzylber, Andrew D. Mason, and Jaime Saavedra-Chanduvi. *Informality: Exit and Exclusion*. Washington: The World Bank, 2007.

Petit, Pierre, and Georges Mulumbwa Mutambwa. "Lexicon and Economy in Lubumbashi." *Africa*, vol. 75 (2005).

Polanyi, Karl. *The Great Transformation*. Boston: Beacon Press, 1957.

———. *The Livelihood of Man*. New York: Academic Press, 1977.

Pollin, Robert, Gerald Epstein, James Heintz, and Léonce Ndikumana. *An Employment-Targeted Economic Program for South Africa*. Amherst, MA: United Nations Development Programme/Political Economy Research Institute, 2006.

Portes, Alejandro. "The Informal Economy and Its Paradoxes," in N. Smelser and R. Swedberg, eds., *The Handbook of Economic Sociology*. Princeton, NJ: Princeton University Press, 1994.

Portes, Alejandro, Manuel Castells, and Lauren A. Benton, eds. *The Informal Economy: Studies in Advanced and Less Developed Countries*. Baltimore, MD: Johns Hopkins University Press, 1989.

Proudhon, P. J. *General Idea of the Revolution in the Nineteenth Century*. Mineola, NY: Dover Publications, 2003.

Raustiala, Kal, and Christopher Jon Sprigman. "The Piracy Paradox: Innovation and Intellectual Property in Fashion Design." *Virginia Law Review*, vol. 92 (2006).

———. "The Piracy Paradox Revisited." *Stanford Law Review*, vol. 61, no. 5 (2009).

Remer, Rosalind. "Preachers, Peddlers, and Publishers." *Journal of the Early Republic* (Winter 1994).

Report of the Mayor's Push-Cart Commission, City of New York, 1906.

Reuters. "Analysis—Faltering Economy Boosts Spain's Black Market," March 3, 2011.

Reyneri, Emilio. "Illegal Immigration and the Underground Economy," National Europe Centre Paper No. 66, February 2003, accessed March 8, 2011.

Rimbaud, Arthur. *Complete Works*. New York: Harper & Row, 1976.

Rothbard, Murray N. *The Ethics of Liberty*. New York: New York University Press, 1998.

———. *Man, Economy, and State*. Auburn, AL: Ludwig von Mises Institute, 2009.

Roy, Ananya. "Why India Cannot Plan Its Cities." *Planning Theory* 8, 76 (2009).

Rukeyser, Muriel. *The Life of Poetry*. Ashfield, MA: Paris Press, 1996.

Sachs, Joel. "Hummel and the Pirates." *The Musical Quarterly*, vol. 59, no. 1 (Jan. 1973).

Saro-Wiwa, Ken. *Sozaboy*. Essex, UK: Addison Wesley Longman Limited, 1994.

Saviano, Roberto. *Gomorrah*. New York: Farrar, Straus and Giroux, 2007.

Schmidle, Nicholas. "Inside the Knockoff-Tennis-Shoe Factory," *The New York Times* (Aug. 19, 2010).

Schneider, Friedrich. "Shadow Economies and Corruption All Over the World: Empirical Results for 1999 to 2003." *International Journal of Social Economics* (2008).

———. "Shadow Economies and Corruption All Over the World: New Estimates for 145 Countries." *Economics: The Open Access, Open Assessment E-journal* (July 2007).

———. "Shadow Economies around the World: What Do We Really Know?" *European Journal of Political Economy*, vol. 21, no. 3 (Sept. 2005).

Schumpeter, Joseph A. *Capitalism, Socialism, and Democracy*. New York: Harper & Row, 1950.

Sengupta, Arjun. "Modify Schemes to Push Demand," *The Economic Times*, Feb, 10, 2009.

Slim, T-Bone. *Juice Is Stranger Than Friction: Selected Writings of T-Bone Slim*. Franklin Rosemont, ed. Chicago: Charles H. Kerr Publishing Company, 1992.

Smith, Adam. *The Theory of Moral Sentiments*. Amherst, NY: Prometheus Books, 2000.

———. *The Wealth of Nations*. Amherst, NY: Prometheus Books, 1991.

Social Compact, DrillDown Reports, http://socialcompact.org/index.php/site/drilldown/category/introduction/, accessed Nov. 30, 2010.

Stiglitz, Joseph E. *Making Globalization Work*. New York: W. W. Norton & Co., 2006.

Stroh, Patricia. "Evolution of an Edition." *Notes*, second series, vol. 60, no. 1 (Sept. 2003).

Swissinfo. "Moonlighting Crackdown to Recover Lost Revenue," Nov. 29, 2007.

Tangires, Helen. *Public Markets*. New York: W. W. Norton & Co., 2008.

Tehelka (New Delhi). "Where Computers Go to Die," Jan 15, 2011.

Thomas, Dana. *Deluxe: How Luxury Lost Its Luster*. New York: Penguin Press, 2007.

Tinker, Irene. *Street Foods: Urban Food and Employment in Developing Countries*. Oxford: Oxford University Press, 1997.

Turner, John F. C., and Robert Fichter, eds. *Freedom to Build: Dweller Control of the Housing Process*. New York: The Macmillan Company, 1972.

Unger, Roberto Mangabeira. *False Necessity: Anti-Necessitarian Social Theory in the Service of Radical Democracy*. London: Verso, 2001.

———. *Social Theory: Its Situation and Its Task*. London: Verso, 2004.

———. *Plasticity into Power: Comparative-Historical Studies on the Institutional Conditions of Economic and Military Success*. London: Verso, 2004.

Venkatesh, Sudhir. *Gang Leader for a Day*. New York: Penguin Books, 2008.

———. *Off the Books: The Underground Economy of the Urban Poor*. Cambridge, MA: Harvard University Press, 2006.

Viles, Edward, and F. J. Furnivall, eds. *The Rogues and Vagabonds of Shakespeare's Youth*. London: Chatto and Windus, 1907.

Walford, Cornelius. *Fairs, Past and Present: A Chapter in the History of Commerce*. London: Elliot Stock, 1883.

Ward, Ned. *The Second Volume of the Writings of the Author of the London-Spy*. London: J. How, 1706.

Wasserman, Suzanne. "The Good Old Days of Poverty." *Business and Economic History* (Winter 1998).

Weber, Max. *The City*. New York: The Free Press, 1958.

———. *General Economic History*. Glencoe, IL: The Free Press, 1950.

———. *The Protestant Ethic and the Spirit of Capitalism*. New York: Charles Scribner's Sons, 1958.

Whiteman, Maxwell. "Notions, Dry Goods, and Clothing." *Jewish Quarterly Review* (Apr. 1963).

Winstanley, Gerrard. *The Law of Freedom in a Platform, or True Magistrcy Restored*. New York: Schocken Books, 1973.

Wittgenstein, Ludwig. *Culture and Value*. Chicago, IL: University of Chicago, 1980.

The World (New York). "Minister Gets After Peddlers," June 13, 1902; "Why He Harries the Peddlers," Jan. 10, 1903; "The Push-cart Peddler," Mar. 27, 1903; "Pushcart Men Surrender at Last," Mar. 30, 1903; "Another Blow at Push-cart Plague," July 1, 1903; "The Pushcart Men's Grievances," May 31, 1904; "Push-carts and Markets," Sept. 16, 1906.

Wright, Daniel R. "Moonlighting," *The Wall Street Journal* (Mar. 22, 1954).

Wright, Richardson Little. *Hawkers & Walkers in Early America: Strolling Peddlers, Preachers, Lawyers, Doctors, Players, and Others, from the Beginning to the Civil War*. Philadelphia: J. B. Lippincott Co., 1927.

Zimbabwe Standard (Harare). "Informal Trade Oils Underground Economy," Jan. 4, 2011.

Index

Aakoo, 67
Abuja, Nigeria, 195
academia, System D criticism in,
    20, 179–80
Accra, Ghana, 20
Adcorp, 236–7
Adebajo, Adegboyega, 142–3
Adesanya, Olayemi, 22
Adesanya, Taye, 22
Africa
    Chinese trade with, 68, 69, 72–4,
        75, 83, 84, 89, 188–9, 252–5
    crop smuggling in, 251
    economic development in, 65–6,
        256–7
    Italian street peddlers from, 163
    labor issues in, 243
    mobile phone marketing in,
        135–9
    Muslim conflict resolution in, 222
    smuggling from, 115
    smuggling into, 73, 188–9
    System D organization in,
        228–9, 234, 257
    System D's role in, 25, 66
    toxic dumping in, 241
    unemployment in, 236
    see also Nigeria
agberos, 49–50, 54
    see also bus system, Lagos
Agence France-Presse, 197
Agency for International
    Development, U.S., 206

Ahmed, Alhaji Rasaq Olusola
    "Decency," 48–9, 50
Ajegunle, Lagos, Nigeria, 29, 30
Akiyode-Afolabi, Abiola, 75
Akiyoyamen, Margaret, 138, 139,
    194
Alaba International Market, 55–8,
    171
    conflict resolution in, 221–2,
        223, 225
    growth of, 71–2, 172–3, 225
    power supply in, 214
    products sold at, 57
    touts at, 57
    toxic dumping in, 241
    value of, 58
Alarcón, Daniel, 105–6
Allen, Charles, 246
Amsterdam, Netherlands, street
    selling in, 101
Amsterdam News, 161
Anari, Patrick, 42, 43
Angostura bitters, 231
Aniekwu, Sunday, 63
Anti-Oedipus (Deleuze and
    Guattari), 210
Anyika, Jude C., 55–8
Apapa (port of Lagos), 76, 92, 210
apprenticeship, Igbo system of,
    74–5, 172
Argentina
    Lebanese population in, 244
    smuggling into, 116, 117

Aristotle, 98
Armarinhos Fernando, 9, 10, 15
Arnovick, Brandon, 146–8
Aro, Monsurat, 239
Artaria, 104
Asia
  labor issues in, 243
  mobile phone marketing in,
    135–6
  see also China
Astron, 23
auto industry, 33, 62, 63, 64, 69,
    74, 76, 77, 79, 84–5
Auto Spare Parts and Machinery
    Dealers Association
    (ASPAMDA), 74, 201, 217–18
Awdeley, John, 157
Ayittey, George B. N., 200, 201
Azam, Jean-Paul, 92

Balogun, Tunji, 61
Baltimore, Md., System D income
    in, 154
  women in business in, 165
banks, System D's relations with,
    41, 141–4, 206, 236, 237–8
Barakat, Assad Ahmad, 246
Barros Nock, Magdalena, 150,
    151
Bartholomew Fair (Jonson), 223
Basel Action Network (BAN), 241
Bauer, Peter, 172, 201
Bazaaristan, 27–8
BBC, 245
Beethoven, Ludwig van, 104–5
Beijing Olympics, 94, 240
Bell Microproducts, 203
Berlusconi, Silvio, 163
Better Life Water, 43
Bierce, Ambrose, 88
Bike Basket Pies, 148
Bispo dos Santos, Sérgio, 225–6
Bolivia, System D in, 234

Book of Vagabonds and Beggars, The,
    156
bookselling
  piracy and, 101–4, 105–6
  sale of uncorrected proofs, 153
Braithwaite, Richard, 158
Braudel, Fernand, 70, 144
Brazil
  business tax breaks in, 204
  cooperatives in, 226, 227, 228
  economy of, 15
  Lebanese population in, 244, 245
  minimum wage in, 10
  population of, 117
  recycling industry in, 225–8
  smuggling crackdown in, 129
  smuggling into, 9, 113–14,
    116–24, 204, 206, 207, 209
  taxation in, 122–3
  see also Rua 25 de Março; *specific
    cities*
Brecht, Bertolt, 116
Breitkopf, 105
BRIAN Integrated Systems, 61
bribery
  in Nigeria, 31, 56, 76
  in global business, 251
Bromo-Seltzer, 231
Bronfman family, 128
B. Schott's Sons, 104
Budweiser, 122
Buffett, Warren, 176
bus system, Lagos, 47–52
  description of CMS station of,
    186–7
business
  child labor in, 240
  credit-based, 24
  crime in, 250–1
  growth in, 194
  labor issues in, 194–5, 242–3
  profit motive in, 98–9, 100, 181
  regulation of, 220, 221

software piracy in, 108
System D–generated profit for,
135, 137, 138, 139, 140, 141
System D interaction with, 9,
12–13, 16, 26–7, 28, 77, 94,
130–44, 152–3, 208–9, 242–3
tax deals for, 192–3, 204, 207–8
Western model of, 131, 171,
172, 193, 211–12
see also economics
Business Day (Lagos), 61
Business Software Alliance, 107

Canton Fair, 75, 88
CAPDAN, 195
capitalism, 99–100
Carcopino, Jérôme, 35
Caribbean Discourse (Glissant), 178
cassava, 55–6, 251
catadores, 7, 225–7
*Caveat or Warning for Common
Cursitors, A* (Harmon), 157–8
CDs, pirated, 5, 122
charlatans, 230–2
Chayanov, Alexander, 230
Chemonics, 206
Chen, Linda, 77–8, 79, 92, 95, 194,
254
Chen, Martha, 211, 212
Chicago, Ill., street market in,
154–6
children, 20, 150, 239–40, 241
China
African smuggling from, 73,
188–9
African trade with, 68, 69, 72–4,
75, 83, 84, 89, 188–9, 252–5
child labor in, 240
consumerism in, 80, 94, 126
corporate crime in, 250
dominant business model in,
95–6
economic policy in, 94, 99

employment in, 19
factory work in, 83
high-end brand production in, 96
language in, 125
mobile phone exports from, 90
Nigerian trade with, 63, 64,
67–70, 71, 72, 73, 75–9, 84,
86–7, 88, 95, 188–9
piracy in, 86, 88–91, 92–7, 106,
109, 111
public health system in, 81
recycling industry in, 227
Rua 25 de Março merchants
from, 7–8
smuggling from, 125–6
smuggling into, 126–8
System D's role in, 25
tax paying in, 78, 80–1, 82, 94
technology retailing in, 126, 127
toxic dumping in, 241
2008/2009 financial crisis effects
in, 96, 97
U.S. trade with, 80
see also specific cities
China Plaza, 93, 94
China Southern Airlines, 71
Chinee Water, 42
Chinese University of Hong Kong,
126
Chintan, 228
cigarettes, smuggling of, 128
Ciudad del Este, Paraguay, 116–19,
121–5
business formalization in, 204,
206–9, 212
computer and electronic trade
in, 124, 203–4, 206–9, 246
crime in, 247, 248, 250
currency trading in, 118–19
economic activity in, 114, 118,
123–4, 209, 243
Lebanese community in, 244,
245, 246, 247

Ciudad del Este, Paraguay *(cont.)*
  money transfers in, 245
  policing in, 124–5, 129
  street market in, 118
  System D in, 24
  taxation in, 122, 207–8
  terrorism allegations against,
    243–9
Clinton, Hillary, 249
Computer and Allied Products
    Dealers Association of
    Nigeria, 61
computer industry
  Chinese trade in, 126–8
  falling prices in, 124, 204
  illegal dumping in, 240–2
  Nigerian trade in, 58–61, 195
  Paraguayan trade in, 113–14,
    203–4, 206–9
  poor workmanship in, 83
  smuggling in, 113–14, 124,
    127–8, 203–4, 206, 207, 209
  see also Ikeja Computer Village
computer software, piracy of, 107–9
conflict resolution, 221–5
Connecticut Courant, 249
construction industry, 150
cooperative development, 225,
    227, 228–9
  limits of, 230
  criticism of, 184
Cooper-Glicério, 226–7
copyrights, 153
Correct Technologies, 58, 59
Cotonou, Republic of Benin, 33,
    85, 92, 188, 189, 210
courts, as an institution in street
    markets, 221–5
crime, 20, 27, 217, 218, 219, 239,
    243, 247, 248, 250–1
Cross, John, 182–3
Crusades, 70
currency, *see* exchange rate

Dairo, Ogun, 64–5
danfo, see bus system, Lagos
Dattora, Édison Ramos, 5–6, 13,
    14, 15, 142
Davidson, Basil, 30–1
débrouillards, 17
Deleuze, Gilles, 210
de Soto, Hernando, 204–5, 206,
    208, 210, 211
Deutsche Bank, 18
developed world
  economic inequality in, 176
  economic model in, 66, 144,
    176, 178, 181, 182, 211–12
developing world
  business model in, 131–5, 193,
    201, 212
  economic growth of, 176–7, 183,
    185, 212, 257–8
  infrastructure in, 177, 236
  System D growth in, 18, 27
  water shortage in, 134
  wealth gap in, 176–8, 182, 257
  see also Africa; Asia; Latin
    America; *specific countries*
Devil's Dictionary, The (Bierce),
    87–8
Diamond Bank, 142
Dias, Sonia Maria, 227
Diggers, 173
Digital Millennium Copyright Act,
    153
dollar, as global currency, 78–9
Domestic Workers' Bill of Rights,
    234–5
Donizetti, Gaetano, 231
Downy, 134–5
Drake, Francis, 87, 106
drugs
  discount, 114–15
  illegal, 247
DVDs, pirated, 5–7, 12–14, 15,
    122

eBay, 150
Ebeyenoku, John, 213, 216
economic development, 19, 28
  as a human right, 237
  redefinition of, 184–5
economics
  Aristotle's definition of, 98
  efficiency in, 171, 172
  80/20 conundrum in, 96
  modern definition of, 19
  wealth gap in, 173–8, 182, 257
  see also business; free market
    system
Economic Times, 237
economists, System D's assessment
    by, 16, 19–20, 66, 130, 181,
    183, 201, 211, 237
education, 196, 239, 240
"Eighteenth Brumaire of Louis
    Bonaparte, The" (Marx), 183
Eleazars, Ugochukwu, 63
electricity, 67, 69, 214–15
electronics industry
  gray-market, 153
  Nigerian trade in, 54–61, 62–3
  smuggling in, 124, 203–4, 206,
    207, 246
  see also computer industry;
    mobile phone industry
Eleshin, Omotola, 49–50, 141
Emirates, 71
employment
  business tax breaks and, 192
  System D's provision of, 26, 172,
    178, 179, 236–7, 257
  21st century, 19
Encore Technical Sales, 203
Encyclopedia Britannica, 105
entrepreneurialism, 18, 26, 28,
    257
environmental issues, 32, 43, 47,
    215, 240–2
Enzensberger, Hans Magnus, 112

Ethiopian Airlines, 71
Europe
  literacy growth in, 101
  Nigerian trade with, 65
  post–World War II economic
    development in, 211–12
  16th-century economic
    transition in, 157, 158–9
  smuggling into, 115
  System D in, 19, 37, 161–3
  2008/2009 financial crisis effects
    in, 18–19
  see also specific cities and countries
EVGA, 203
e-waste, 241–2
exchange rate
  importance to System D trade,
    78–9, 220
Eze, Sunday, 58
Ezeagu, Charles, 23
Ezeifeoma, James, 71, 72, 141,
    172–3, 179, 255

Fable of the Bees, The (Mandeville),
    97, 100
Fanon, Frantz, 183
fashion industry, 79–80, 82–3
  labor issues in, 141, 242–3
  piracy in, 93, 110–12, 140–1
Fashola, Babatunde, 190, 195, 196,
    199, 200, 201, 202
Feiyang, 93–5
Festac Town, Lagos, Nigeria, 42,
    43, 45
Festac United Okada Riders, 46
feudalism, 158
financial crisis of 2008/2009
  in China, 96, 97
  System D resilience to, 18–19
  in United States, 148, 152
Financial Mail, 237
flea market, 150, 256
Fontaine, Laurence, 115

food industry
  formalization in, 147, 148–9,
    159, 167, 229
  street peddling in, 6, 11, 13, 39,
    65, 159–61, 166–8, 229
  System D producers in, 146–9,
    166–8
formal businesses,
  relationship with informal firms,
    12–13, 130–4, 140–1
formalization
  bureaucracy in, 149, 159, 167,
    210
  in computer industry, 204, 206–9
  costs and benefits of, 207–8, 209,
    211, 212
  degrees of, 233–4, 235
  effects of, 210–11
  in food industry, 147, 148–9,
    159, 167, 229
  obstacles to, 209, 210
419 Advance Fee Fraud, 59, 188
Fox, Paul, 130
Foz do Iguaçu, Brazil, 117, 119,
    120, 122, 245
France, System D in, 163
"Fraternity of Vagabonds, The"
    (Awdeley), 157
free market system, 22–3, 175, 181,
    182, 220, 256

Gafunk Nigeria Limited, 61
Gala sausage roll, 140
Galatzer, Natalie, 147
Galeria Pagé (Ciudad del Este),
    245–7
Galeria Pagé (São Paulo), 11, 12,
    200
garage sales, 150
garbage recycling,
  in Brazil, 225–7
  in China, 169–70
  in Nigeria, 29, 38–41

gasoline, smuggling of, 115
Gates, Bill, 109, 176
*General Theory of Employment,
    Interest and Money, The*
    (Keynes), 175
generators, 67
George II, King of England, 174
Germany, System D in, 163
Gesell, Silvio, 175
Glissant, Edouard, 178
globalization, 69–70, 256
  peddlers as agents of, 70–1
  see also System D, global trade in
Gomorrah (Saviano), 110
Gonçalves, Reginaldo, 12
Goodluck, Akinwale, 136, 137,
    138, 139
Gould, Jay, 176
government
  economic regulation by, 22
  privatization in, 26
  System D interaction with, 46,
    48, 49, 50, 55, 75–6, 77–8,
    93–5, 114, 129, 201–2, 207,
    217, 218, 219, 220, 221, 225,
    227, 228, 232–8, 240–2, 251–2
  use of pirated software in, 108
Gramsci, Antonio, 22
Granta, 105
gray market, 20
Great Britain
  historical conflict resolution in,
    222–3
  historical wealth gap in, 173–4
  System D criticism in, 163–4
  see also London, England
Great Transformation, The
    (Polanyi), 22–3
Greece, ancient, conflict resolution
    in, 222
Grimmelshausen, Hans Jakob
    Christoffel von, 104–5
growth, 18, 25, 27, 184–5, 193–4

Grumbling Hive, The (Mandeville), 97, 100
Guangzhou, China, 23
  African traders in, 68, 69, 72–4, 75–9, 83, 84, 86–7, 88, 252–5
  business regulations in, 80, 82
  international population in, 72
  policing of, 89, 170, 253, 254
  recycling in, 169–71
  smuggled computers in, 127
Guangzhou Dashatou Second Hand Trade Center, 86, 88–91
Guarda Municipal, 6, 11
guarda-roupas, 120–1
Guattari, Félix, 210
Gudeman, Stephen, 184–5
gun running, 20
Guys and Dolls, 165
Gypsies, 163

Hammoud family, 244, 247
Hancock, John, 249
Harare, Zimbabwe, 220
Harlem, N.Y.
  street peddling in, 161
  System D income in, 154
harmattan, 40
Harmon, Thomas, 157–8
Hart, Keith, 20, 25, 26, 135, 256
Harter, Mandy, 149
Hausa tribe, 39
hawkers, 9–10, 25, 52, 190
health insurance, lack of in System D businesses, 194–5
herbal medicines, 231–3
Hesler, Jeffrey W., 117, 247–8
Hill, Archibald A., 160
Himalayan News Service, 237
Homeland Security Department, U.S., 245, 246
Hong Kong
  smuggling from, 126–7
  smuggling into, 125–6

household work, 27, 234–5
Housing Works, 153
Houston, Tex., System D income in, 154
Hürriyet, 20

Ibekwe, David, 74–7, 78, 79, 84, 92, 93, 179, 189, 252
IBM, 127
Ibn Khaldun, 99
ICMS, 122–3
Icompy, 24, 203, 204
Igbo tribe, 74–5, 173, 201
Ike, Uche, 42
Ikedi, Vitalis Okwudili, 252–5
Ikeja Computer Village, 58–61
  products sold at, 60
  relocation of, 195
  toxic dumping in, 241
  value of, 61
income patching, 152, 166
Independent (magazine), 160
Independent (U.K.), 163
India
  business tax breaks in, 192, 193
  child labor in, 241
  cooperative development in, 228
  pre–Revolutionary War trade with, 250
  recycling industry in, 227
  System D recognition in, 237
  toxic dumping in, 241–2
Indian reservations, smuggling from, 128
Inditex, 140–1, 242–3
inequality, 173–7, 178, 181
informal economy
  coinage of term, 20
  problems with definition, 20–1, 25
  street attitude toward phrase, 21–4
Informal Economy, The (Portes), 179

infrastructure, 26, 219
 see also water system, electricity
Ingram Micro, 203
innovation, 192–4
Intcomex, 203
International AntiCounterfeiting
 Coalition, 96–7
International Market Association,
 58
International Textile, Garment and
 Leather Workers' Federation,
 242
Internet
 piracy on, 109
 smuggling on, 127–8
invisible hand, 174
Ireland, System D in, 162–3
Irish Independent, 162
Italy
 Renaissance medicine in, 231–2
 System D in, 163

Jacobs, Jane, 149, 219
Jandira, 6–7, 11, 14, 15
Jefferson, Thomas, 250
Jeremiah, Michael, 95
Jinifa Allied Limited, 71, 72, 172
Johnnie Walker, 226
Jomana Import Export, 246
Jones, Kate, 165–8
Jonson, Ben, 223
Jua Kali, 228–9

Kantor, Brian, 237
Kassab, Gilberto, 244
Kennedy, Joseph, 128
Kenya, System D in, 234, 236
Keynes, John Maynard, 175–6
Khatiwada, Yubaraj, 238
Kick Against Indiscipline (KAI),
 190, 195, 196
Kimball, Curtis, 147
Kiva, 41

Klamer, Arjo, 19
Kunrunmi, Fatai, 40
Kuznets, Simon, 176–8, 182

La Cocina, 148, 229
Ladipo Market, 62–4
 toxic dumping in, 241
Lagos, Nigeria, 21–2, 25, 29–34,
 37–66, 186–7
 banking in, 142–3
 bribery in, 31, 46, 49, 50, 56,
 76, 218
 child labor in, 239–40
 commerce in, 32–3, 34, 38, 45,
 52–5, 187
 crime in, 32
 cyber cafés in, 59
 economic production of, 34
 environmental problems in, 43,
 47, 215, 241
 extortion in, 217, 218, 219
 garbage scavenging in, 29, 30,
 38–41
 green spaces in, 196
 health care in, 229
 herbal medicine merchants in,
 231
 import duties in, 76
 infrastructure in, 31, 32, 42, 44,
 58, 213–15, 216
 neighborhood conditions in, 30
 police in, 53–4, 58, 190, 195
 population of, 31
 poverty in, 33
 public transportation in, 44–52,
 53–4
 recycling in, 213, 215–16
 System D crackdown in, 190–1,
 195–6, 198–9
 technology in, 58–9, 60, 215
 traffic in, 31–2, 46–7, 52
 water in, 42–4
 see also Alaba International

Market; Auto Spare Parts and Machinery Dealers Association (ASPAMDA); Ikeja Computer Village; Ladipo Market; Oshodi
Lagos Waste Management Authority (LAWMA), 40
Latin America
retailing in, 131
2008/2009 financial crisis in, 19
"Law of Freedom in a Platform, The" (Winstanley), 173
layaway plans, 151
Lebanon, South American immigrants from, 244–5, 246, 247
L'Elisir d'Amore (Donizetti), 231
lemonade stands, 150
Lemon Frauds, 159–60
Lenovo, 127
Leo IV, Pope, 98
Library of Congress, 153
licenses
cost of, in China, 80
libertarian view of, 184
time required to get, 210
vendors without, 5–8
Liebling, A. J., 165
Lima, Peru, squatter communities in, 205, 206
liquor
counterfeit, 226
smuggling of, 128
local control, 180, 184–5, 221, 257–8
London, England, street economy in, 24, 35–7, 101, 156, 158
Los Angeles, Calif., System D income in, 154
Los Angeles Economy Project, 154
Luanda, Angola, System D crackdown in, 197
Luden's, 231

lumpenproletariat, 183
Luther, Martin, 156, 157

machine industry, 64, 69
Mafia, 110, 184, 243
Maker Faire Africa, 229
Ma Laboratories, 203
Man, Economy, and State (Rothbard), 172
Mandeville, Bernard, 97–8, 99–100, 175
Márcio, 10, 11, 13, 14, 15
Martin, Mariano, 131, 132, 134, 135
Marx, Karl, 183
Matilde, 150–1
Maxwell Street Market, 154–6
Mayhew, Henry, 24–5, 36, 37
Meagher, Kate, 219
megacity, 22, 196
melamine, 250
mercantilism, 158
Mercosur treaty, 206, 208
Mexico
U.S. immigrants from, 150, 151, 166, 167–8
U.S. smuggling from, 114–15
water shortage in, 134
Miami, Fla., System D income in, 153–4
Miami Herald, 247
microcredit, 41
Microsoft, 61, 109
Middle East, street peddling in, 14
milk of magnesia, 231
minimum wage, 10, 39, 43, 46
Miranda, Emily, 145–6
Mission Minis, 146–7
mobile phone industry
airtime selling in, 135–9
Chinese retailing in, 126
in developing world, 177
illegal dumping in, 240–1

mobile phone industry *(cont.)*
  in Nigeria, 60, 64, 136–9, 215
  piracy in, 88, 89–92
  street sales in, 60, 64
  unlocking in, 60, 153
"Modern Prince, The" (Gramsci),
  22
molue, see bus system, Lagos
Monalisa, 244, 247
money laundering, 245, 247
Montoya, Martín, 198
moonlighting, 19, 152
Morales, Alfonso, 154–6, 235
Morales, Evo, 234
Morocco, retailing in, 133–4
motorcycle taxis, 44–7, 121, 129,
  201–2
  see also okada
Movimento Nacional dos
  Catadores de Materiais
  Recicláveis (MNCR), 227
MTN, 136–9, 213
Musa, Yusuf, 44, 45–6, 47
music industry, piracy in, 5, 104–5,
  109–10, 122
Mwangi, David, 83
Mystery of Capital, The (de Soto),
  205

Nairobi, Kenya, System D
  crackdown in, 197–8
National Agency for Food and
  Drug Administration and
  Control (NAFDAC), 232,
  233
National Union of Road Transport
  Workers (NURTW), 48, 49
Nepal, System D in, 237–8
New York, N.Y.
  business tax breaks in, 192
  food carts in, 159–61, 167, 168,
  229
  post-Depression, 164–5

New Yorker, 165
New York state, workers' rights in,
  234–5
New York Times, 96
New York Times Magazine, 111
Nietzsche, Friedrich, 87, 181
Nigeria
  American used car imports in,
  84–5
  apprenticeship system in, 74–5,
  173
  Chinese merchants in, 84
  Chinese trade with, 63, 64,
  67–70, 71, 72, 73, 75–9, 86–7,
  88, 95, 188–9
  computer market in, 58–61
  corporate retailing in, 136–40
  electricity supply in, 63, 67,
  213–15
  e-mail scams in, 59
  European trade with, 65
  film industry in, 57
  GDP of, 34
  government in, 31, 47, 48, 191,
  192, 215, 216, 219, 232–3
  individual earnings in, 39, 43,
  50, 138
  mobile phone industry in, 60,
  64, 136–9, 215
  pirated merchandise in, 91–2
  population of, 136
  regulation in, 232–3
  smuggling into, 33, 85, 92, 188
  toxic dumping in, 241
  see also specific cities
Nigeria Corporate Affairs
  Commission, 75
Night Club Era, The (Walker), 164
Nike, 240
Nnadi, Dera, 76
Nollywood, 57
Nwaochei, Chris, 186–90
Nwankwo, Wilfred, 222

Index

Obasanjo, Olusegun, 31
Obi, David, 67–70, 72, 73, 214,
255
Oboro, John, 61
Ojota Mechanic Village, 213,
215–16
okada, 44–7, 76, 201–2, 218
Okafor, Chief Arthur, 86–7, 88,
89, 193
Okonkwo, Israel C., 191, 192, 216
Olusosun, Lagos, Nigeria, 29,
39, 40
Onyeyirim, Prince Chidi, 54
Onyibo, Remi, 58
Organisation for Economic
Co-operation and
Development (OECD), 18,
19, 179
organ trafficking, 20
organized crime
accusations of System D's
connections to, 21, 110, 243
excluded from System D
statistics, 27
state as an entity of, 184
Oshodi
destruction of, 195
policing of, 53–4
products sold at, 53
Other Path, The (de Soto), 204–5
outsourcing, 171
Owonifari Electronics Market, 54–5

Paraguay
bribery in, 114, 207
business tax breaks in, 207–8
economic activity in, 114, 118,
209
Lebanese population in, 244,
245
population of, 117
smuggling from, 9, 26, 113–14,
116–24, 204, 206, 207, 209

System D's importance to, 25–6
see also Ciudad del Este,
Paraguay
Paraguayan American Chamber of
Commerce, 248
Paraguay Vende, 206, 209
Pareto, Vilfredo, 96
Paris, France, street economy in,
156
parks and green space, 196
patent medicines, 231
Paulo Roberto, 9–10, 13, 14, 20
Payless, 189
PC Tronic, 113–14
peddlers
as early globalizers, 70–1
in London, 157–8
in New York, 159–61
in U.S. Revolutionary War, 249
morality of, 156–8, 250
war profiteering of, 115–16,
249–50
Pedro I, Emperor of Brazil, 14
Pemex, 115
Penner, Reinaldo, 206, 207, 208,
209, 247
Pepto-Bismol, 231
Peru
book piracy in, 105–6
formalization of firms and
squatter communities in, 205–6
Peters, Segun "Satin," 39
PharmAccess Foundation, 229
pharmaceutical industry, 114–15
see also herbal medicines
Philippines, System D in, 233
Photoshop, 107
Piepowder, 222–3
piracy, 86–112, 218–19
benefits of, 110–11, 177
child labor and, 240
in American business, 108–9
in Brazil, 4–6, 122

piracy *(cont.)*
  in China, 86, 88–91, 92–7, 106,
    109, 111
  costs of, 107–8, 109–10
  of DVDs, 5–7, 12–14, 15, 122
  fashion, 93, 110–12
  history of, 87–8, 97–105, 106
  impact on companies whose
    goods are copied, 111
  impact on System D profit
    margins, 95–96
  literary, 97, 101–6, 109
  mobile phone, 88, 89–92
  music, 5, 104–5, 109–10, 122
  online, 109
  philosophical view of, 87–8
  policing of, 94, 95
  profitability of, 5, 91, 93, 94, 95,
    105, 106, 200
  quality variation in, 92
  software, 107–9
  use of force in, 218
Polanyi, Karl, 22–3
politicians, System D criticism by,
    16, 130, 163, 201
Pollin, Robert, 236
Poor Laws, 174
Portes, Alejandro, 179–80, 193,
    211
Positivo, 204
poverty, prejudice against, 165
press, System D criticism in, 20–1,
    159–60, 162
Procter & Gamble, 130–5, 193,
    231
Prohibition, 128
Proudhon, Pierre-Joseph, 174–5,
    185
Provincial Congress of
    Massachusetts, 249–50
public services, System D's
    provision of, 26, 42–52, 169,
    213–15

publishing industry
  illegal sales in, 153
  piracy in, 97, 101–6, 109
Puma, 93
Pure Water, 42–4, 232, 233, 239
pushcarts
  as an economic entrypoint, 172
  in New York, 159–61

Quark, 107

Radiohead, 109
Ramirez, Juan V., 113–14, 118,
    194, 207
Raustiala, Kal, 110
recycling industry, 7, 169–71, 213,
    215–16, 225–8
  cartels in, 226–7
  see also scavengers
Reuters, 162
Revolutionary War, 191, 249
Rimbaud, Arthur, 70–1
Rockefeller, John D., 176
Rogers, Will, 128
Rome, ancient
  conflict resolution in, 222
  street markets in, 35
Roque Santeiro, 197
Rothbard, Murray, 172, 183–4,
    220
Rua 25 de Março
  Chinese merchants at, 7–8
  daily life at, 3–16
  development plans for, 199–200
  licensed vendors at, 8, 15
  pirate DVD market at, 5–7,
    12–14, 15
  policing of, 6, 11, 13
  products sold at, 3–4, 5, 7–8, 9,
    10, 11, 13–14
  profitability of, 5, 8, 10, 12, 15
  rules at, 14–15
  sanitation at, 9

smuggling into, 120, 122, 123
unlicensed vendors at, 9–10, 11,
    12, 14
Runyon, Damon, 164–5

Saboru, Andrew, 29, 30, 38, 40–1,
    141, 212
sacoleiros, 119, 120, 121, 122, 123
Safadi, Khaled T., 246
Saltzberg, Joanne, 165, 168
San Francisco, Calif., food industry
    in, 146–9, 229
San Salvador, El Salvador, System
    D crackdown in, 198
Sanwo-Olu, Jide, 199
Sanyuanli, 72, 73, 92, 258
São Paulo, Brazil
    recycling in, 7, 225–7
    smuggling into, 119–20, 122,
        123, 124
    street peddling in, 14
    see also Rua 25 de Março
Sarkozy, Nicolas, 163
Saro-Wiwa, Ken, 21
Saviano, Roberto, 110
scavengers, 29, 30, 38–41, 215
    profitability of, 38–9, 226–7,
        228, 241
    see also recycling industry
Scavenger's Association, 40
Schneider, Friedrich, 26, 27, 154
Schumpeter, Joseph, 23, 116
Schwartz, Sigmund, 160–1
Seagram's, 128
Sears, Dick, 149
Sears, Roebuck & Co., 149
Self Employed Women's
    Association (SEWA), 228
Sengupta, Arjun, 237
Sepeda, Genoveva, 165–8
September 11, 2001 terrorist
    attacks, 244, 245
Shakespeare, William, 101–4

shan zhai, 90
Sheetrock, 250
Shenzhen, China, smuggling from,
    125–6
shoes, 188–9
Shopping Mundo Oriental, 12
Siemens, 251
size of businesses, 19, 193–4
Slim, T-Bone, 185
Slot Systems Limited, 60
smartphones, 126, 153
Smith, Adam, 19, 84, 100, 173–4,
    250
smuggling, 9, 26, 33, 73, 85, 92,
    113–29, 188–9, 246, 251
    computer, 113–14, 124, 127–8,
        203–4, 206, 207, 209
    conditions leading to, 128
    history of, 115–16, 128
    persistence of, 129
    potential danger of, 251
    profitability of, 114, 118, 123–4,
        188–9, 204
    see also Ciudad del Este,
        Paraguay
Social Compact, 153
South Africa, System D in, 135,
    236–7
Southern Metropolis Daily, 72
Soviet Union, 230
Soyo, 203
Sozaboy (Saro-Wiwa), 21
Spain, System D in, 162
Sprigman, Christopher, 110
squatter communities, 64
    formalization of, 205, 206
    System D's reach into, 26
Stalin, Joseph, 230
Standard, 197, 220
Stanley, Frederick T., 149
Stanley Works, 149
State Department, U.S., 249
Stiglitz, Joseph, 24, 133

Index

Strand bookstore, 153
street markets, 3–16, 20, 178
  conflict resolution in, 223–5
  history of, 14, 24, 35–7, 101,
    156–61, 223
  see also Alaba International
    Market; Ikeja Computer
    Village; Ladipo Market;
    Maxwell Street Market;
    Oshodi; Rua 25 de Março;
    umbrella stands
street peddling
  criticism of, 156–61, 190,
    249–50
  in food industry, 6, 11, 13, 39,
    65, 159–61, 166–8
  hardware for, 12, 13
  in India, 193
  Nigerian crackdown on, 195
  rewards of, 6–7, 172
  in United States, 159–61
  worker exploitation in, 160–1
Street Vendor Project, 229
Stroessner, Alfredo, 117
swap meets, 150, 151
Swissinfo, 162
Switzerland, System D in, 162, 163
System D
  advancement in, 38–9
  American tradition in, 149–50
  banks' relations with, 41, 141–4,
    206, 236, 237–8
  benefits of, 25–6, 163, 172, 178,
    179, 180, 181–3
  business interaction with, 9,
    12–13, 16, 26–7, 28, 77, 94,
    130–44, 152–3, 208–9, 242–3
  business investment in, 139, 140,
    141–4
  business model in, 143, 169–85,
    193, 212
  cash basis of, 12, 78, 89, 141,
    243, 248

children in, 20, 150, 239–40, 241
class-based bias against, 164–8
crime and, 20, 27, 217, 218, 219,
    239, 243, 247, 248
criticism of, 16, 19, 20–1, 130–1,
    161–3, 179–80, 183, 190–1,
    193, 194–5, 201
definition of, 17–18, 25, 26
distribution chains in, 133–4,
    137, 140
formalization of, 147, 148–9,
    159, 167, 203–12, 233–4
global exchange rates' effect on,
    78–9
global trade in, 9, 16, 18, 28,
    63, 64, 65, 67–85, 86–7, 88,
    89–97, 188–9, 220, 252–6; see
    also smuggling
government crackdowns on,
    129, 190–1, 195–8, 200–2
government interaction with,
    46, 48, 49, 50, 55, 75–6, 77–8,
    93–5, 114, 129, 201–2, 207,
    217, 218, 219, 220, 221, 225,
    227, 228, 232–8, 251–2
government investment in,
    236–7
government regulation of,
    232–5, 240–2
growth in, 40–1, 60–1, 63, 65–6,
    75, 172–3, 179, 184, 193–4,
    198, 212, 213–58
ideological neutrality of, 183–5
immigrants in, 150, 151, 163–4,
    166, 167–8
innovation and risk taking in,
    193–4, 255
internal view of, 21, 22, 23–4
labor issues in, 83, 130, 141, 152,
    161, 194–5, 228, 229, 233,
    234–5, 242–3
monetary value of, 16, 26, 27–8,
    58, 135, 153–4, 162, 243

288

organization in, 46, 49, 55, 58,
170, 184, 198, 213, 216–18,
219, 220–1, 223, 224–30, 234,
242, 257
political involvement of, 28, 228,
230
poor workmanship in, 83, 84
postcolonial emergence of,
178–9
profitability of, 5, 8, 10, 12, 15,
16, 33, 38–9, 42, 43, 45, 46,
49–50, 65, 68–9, 77, 83, 91,
93, 94, 95, 105, 106, 114, 118,
123–4, 135, 138, 151, 155–6,
166, 167, 170, 188–9, 200,
204, 226–7, 228, 239, 241
public services provided by, 26,
42–52, 169, 196
recognition of, 182–3, 240,
255–6
size of, 16, 18, 19, 27, 182, 233,
234, 236–7
tax evasion in, 10, 12, 78, 80–1,
82, 94, 122–3, 150, 191, 192,
235
tax revenue lost to, 162, 163, 235
2008/2009 financial crisis
resilience of, 18–19
women in, 228
see also Ciudad del Este,
Paraguay; Guangzhou,
China; Lagos, Nigeria; street
markets; *specific industries*

taxation
relationship to smuggling,
122–3
social contract implicit in, 80–1,
191–2
tax breaks for developers similar
to System D tax avoidance,
192–3
Tech Data Worldwide, 203

technology
Chinese retailing of, 126
global impact of, 176, 177
System D in spread of, 26,
58–60, 61, 177–8, 215
see also electronics industry
Tehelka, 241
Tein, Michael, 246–7
Temple, Peacemaker, 64
terrorism, accusations of funding
through System D, 243–9
Thebes, 98
Theory of Moral Sentiments, The
(Smith), 86, 173–4
ThinkPad, 127
3+1 Group on Tri-Border Area
Security, 245
Tijuana, Mexico, discount drug
market in, 114–15
Tinubu, Bola, 199
Tokyo, Japan, fish market in, 224
Tonel Franklyn Limited, 63
Tonson, Jacob, 102–3
trade
Aristotle's view on, 98
in Muslim thought, 99
transportation industry, 44–52,
53–4, 76, 201–2, 218
Tsukiji market, 224

UAC of Nigeria, 139–40
Uche, Emanuel, 64
umbrella stands, 136, 137–9
Unger, Roberto Mangabeira,
180–1, 182, 257
Unilever, 135
United Citizen Peddlers'
Association, 160
United Independent Vendors
Movement, 198
United Kingdom, *see* Great Britain
United Nations' Inter Press
Service, 198

United Nations' World Institute
for Development Economics
Research, 178
United States
big-box retailing in, 132
Chinese trade with, 80
GDP of, 28
low-income consumers in, 135
Nigerian used car imports from,
84–5
post–World War II economic
development in, 211–12
sales tax avoidance in, 150
small business in, 24, 131
smuggling in, 114–15, 116, 128
software piracy in, 107
street peddling in, 159–61,
249–50
System D in, 145–56, 165–8
terrorism allegations by, 244–9
2008/2009 financial crisis in,
148, 152
undeclared income figures for,
153–4
workforce in, 152
World War II profiteering in,
116
Univinco, 4, 199–200
urbanization, 30–1
Urias, Claudia, 4, 15, 184

Van Heusen, 149
Vectro, 95
Vicks VapoRub, 231
Vietnam, 84
visas, 68, 252–6

Walker, Robert, 102–3
Walker, Stanley, 164

Walmart, 132, 193, 194–5
war, smuggling during, 115–16
Ward, Ned, 97
Washington, D.C., System D
income in, 154
watches, counterfeit, 111
water system, Lagos
government monitoring of, 232
lack of municipal supply, 42–3
wealth gap, 173–8, 182, 257
Wealth of Nations, The (Smith), 3,
17, 19, 29, 67, 100, 113, 130,
145, 169, 174, 186, 203, 213
Weber, Max, 32
Wei, Alex, 24, 194, 203, 204, 207,
208
Wen, 82–3
*Whimzies: or, a New Cast of
Characters* (Braithwaite), 158
Whole Foods, 147
wholesalers, 133
Wholesome Bakery, 149
Windows, 109
Winstanley, Gerrard, 173
women, 228
Women in Informal Employment:
Globalizing and Organizing
(WIEGO), 211, 229
World Bank, 178
World War II, profiteering in, 116

XYG (Xinyi Glass), 63

Zara, 140–1
see also Inditex
Zeltner, Louis, 161
Zhang, Ethan, 23–4, 79–83, 95–6
Zigas, Caleb, 148, 149
Zulehner, Carl, 104

ROBERT NEUWIRTH is the author of *Shadow Cities: A Billion Squatters, a New Urban World*. He has worked as a business reporter and an investigative reporter, and has covered cops, courts, and political campaigns. His articles have appeared in a variety of publications, including *The New York Times*, *The Washington Post*, *Scientific American*, *Dwell*, *Fortune*, *Forbes*, *The Nation*, and *Wired*. Neuwirth has also taught in the college program at Rikers Island, New York City's jail, and at Columbia University's School of Journalism. His work has been supported by the Fund for Investigative Journalism, the John D. and Catherine T. MacArthur Foundation, and the Nation Institute. He lives in Brooklyn.

A NOTE ON THE TYPE

This book was set in Janson, a typeface long thought to have been made by the Dutchman Anton Janson, who was a practicing typefounder in Leipzig during the years 1668–1687. However, it has been conclusively demonstrated that these types are actually the work of Nicholas Kis (1650–1702), a Hungarian, who most probably learned his trade from the master Dutch typefounder Dirk Voskens. The type is an excellent example of the influential and sturdy Dutch types that prevailed in England up to the time William Caslon (1692–1766) developed his own incomparable designs from them.

Composed by Scribe, Philadelphia, Pennsylvania
Printed and bound by RR Donnelley, Harrisonburg, Virginia
Designed by Virginia Tan